M000033613

Rajni Bakshi was educated at Indraprastha College, Delhi, George Washington University, Washington DC and the University of Rajasthan, Jaipur. For the last eighteen years she has been writing for a wide variety of English and Hindi newspapers and magazines. She is the author of *The Long Haul*, about the Mumbai textile workers' strike of 1982-83. Rajni has also been involved in the struggle for and debates about evolving a more creative model of development. She lives in Mumbai.

# BAPU KUTI

## Journeys in Rediscovery of Gandhi

*Rajni Bakshi*

PENGUIN BOOKS

Penguin Books India (P) Ltd., 11 Community Centre, Panchsheel Park, New Delhi 110 017, India
Penguin Books Ltd., 27 Wrights Lane, London W8 5TZ, UK
Penguin Books USA Inc., 375 Hudson Street, New York, NY 10014, USA
Penguin Books Australia Ltd., Ringwood, Victoria, Australia
Penguin Books Canada Ltd., 10 Alcorn Avenue, Suite 300, Toronto, Ontario M4V 3B2, Canada
Penguin Books (NZ) Ltd., 182-190 Wairau Road, Auckland 10, New Zealand

First published by Penguin Books India (P) Ltd. 1998

10 9 8 7 6 5 4 3 2

Motif of the Kuti reproduced from *A Hut: Revolution and After* by Vinoo Kaley.

Typeset in Palatino by Digital Technologies and Printing Solutions, New Delhi

Printed at Chaman Enterprises, Delhi.

*In Memory of*
*Bir*
*and*
*Vinoo*

# Contents

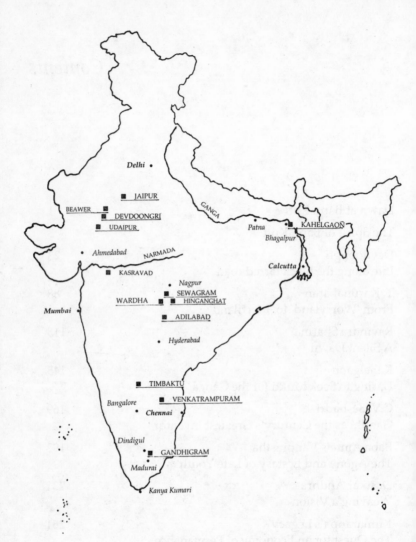

*The international boundaries shown on this map purport to be neither correct nor authentic - Publisher*

## Dawn at Bapu Kuti

The cadence of prayers at *brahma-murat* slowly fades into the darkness around Bapu Kuti. There is the sound of gravel crunching underfoot, as those who gathered for prayers on the porch of the Kuti return to their rooms. A deep, pervasive stillness remains. It will be a while before the first sun rays peep over the horizon.

The silence slowly makes way for the birds as they flutter awake in the grand trees around the Kuti. Soon the squirrels are also up to begin their day-long scurrying in and out of Mahatma Gandhi's home. The sun rises hestitantly, glimmering shyly behind the trees before glowing as a cool orange orb filling the porch with a gentle light. Just about then Haribhau arrives to unlock the Kuti and sweep it clean for another day of visitors and pilgrims.

This familiar sequence of dawn at Bapu Kuti always fills me with an ineffable joy. The silence welcomes anyone who makes their way to Bapu Kuti, to spend time on its packed clay floor, perhaps leaning against one of the black wooden poles that hold up the bamboo roof.

It was at one such dawn that the idea of bringing together these stories, first came to me.

# The Spirit of Bapu Kuti

*Long after Mahatma Gandhi had left his Kuti forever, it was Haribhau's job to arrive there every morning at the crack of dawn. As he meticulously swept the Kuti and its surrounding yard with a flat straw broom, memories and images played bittersweet tricks on him. Sometimes he would see Bapu strolling with his arm leaning on Mahadevbhai's shoulder.*

*There had been a time when the Kuti and its surrounding homes bustled with activity as important people came to see Bapu. Hari could not follow their discussions, but at the age of fifteen he knew that these meetings helped the struggle for swaraj, self-rule. It was Hari's duty to cycle daily to Wardha station with Bapu's outgoing mail and this was always a sizable wad of letters. Hari was also responsible for preparing Bapu's bath water which had to be just right, not too hot and not too cold. Hari accomplished this vital chore with some help from a thermometer.*

*Forty years later, as he swept clean the small enclosure in the Kuti where Bapu had his bath, these memories often came back to him. Few people were interested in Hari's recollections, so he quietly went about his work. On most days he completed his morning chores and then returned to his home in Sewagram, the village lying just outside the boundary of the Ashram. But the Kuti was never alone for long. Tourists and pilgrims filed through it all* day. *Some passed through it quickly for they found little to see, just the usual charkha, walking stick and a narrow mattress covered in crisp white khadi. Others entered with a sense of reverence and stayed a while, as if trying to listen to the kuti.*

*Perhaps Hari noticed that as time went by there were more and more such 'listeners'. They came from far corners of India and the world. These were the ones who paused to enjoy the free flow of light and air through the Kuti. They stared at the 'Aum' on the clay wall below which Bapu sat at work. Most of them were not bowing in unquestioning reverence to the man whom Hari had lovingly served. That man, M.K. Gandhi, was born on October 1869 and his richly varied, multi-faceted life was ended by an assassin's bullets on 30 January 1948.*

*The historical Gandhi, like all mortals, was a limited being. Those who flock to Bapu Kuti at the twilight of a century, and the dawn of a new millennium, are in affectionate awe of the civilizational Gandhi. This Gandhi, free from the bondage of time and space, lingers in the aakar—the form and spirit of the Kuti.*

*What is the civilizational Gandhi?*

*Let us search for answers through the Kuti and what it seems to say to successive generations. But first, let us step back in time to watch the mud, bamboo and wood come together, before we journey with the spirit of Bapu Kuti.*

\*

## Miraben's labour of love

Madeleine Slade was born into an aristocratic British family on a cold November day in 1892. Ensconced in lace, frills and strict discipline, she was just like any other well-bred baby. But a good soothsayer could have told the family that for most of her adult life Madeleine would be known as 'Miraben'. She was destined to go unimaginably far from the silk and fripperies of a débutante. For Madeleine's future was linked to an Indian who was then an obscure attorney-at-law, freshly enrolled at the High Court in London.

In 1893 this man, M.K. Gandhi, sailed from Mumbai to South Africa to 'try his luck' as an attorney there and instead became the 'Mahatma'. Of course, at that stage of infancy, there was no way of knowing how Madeleine would make history with this man or that his life and ideas would become the second love of her life.

Madeleine grew up to be a restless soul seeking higher truths. She had an innate dislike for the advancing machine age. The teenage Madeleine watched with dismay as noisy, dangerous-looking automobiles replaced horse carriages on the streets of London. The social whirl of being an admiral's daughter held no attraction for this tall, solemn young woman. Madeleine adamantly refused to accompany her parents to the Emperor's Durbar at Delhi in 1911. She was happiest in the peaceful surroundings of her grandfather's country estate.

At the age of fifteen, Madeleine fell irrevocably in love with the music of Ludwig von Beethoven. She found 'something far beyond the music as such: I was contacting the spirit speaking through sound, the spirit of Beethoven. Yes, I had found *him*.'

So she went in search of Romain Rolland, the French philosopher and writer, who had written a loving account of Beethoven's life and work. But when she met Rolland he was more keen to talk about his latest book *Mahatma Gandhi*. Madeleine had never heard the name. But Rolland said enough to intrigue her.

Madeleine bought a copy as soon as Rolland's slim book on Gandhi was released and read it through that very day.

Life was never the same again. Her quest for meaning and purpose had found its destination. Later in her autobiography, *The Spirit's Pilgrimage*, this was all Madeleine could say about that great leap in her life:

> Now I knew what that 'something' was, the approach of which I had been feeling. I was to go to Mahatma Gandhi, who served the cause of oppressed India through fearless truth and non-violence, a cause which, though focused in India, was for the whole humanity. I did not weigh the pros and cons or try to reason *why* this was the outcome of my prayers. The call was absolute, and that was all that mattered.

There followed a year of 'severe training' which included learning to spin, sleeping on the floor and gradually turning into a vegetarian. Then she wrote to Gandhi, at Sabarmati near Ahmedabad, requesting his permission to join the ashram community. The answer was a welcoming 'yes'.

Thus, in 1925, at the age of thirty-three, Madeleine Slade sailed to India, her adopted home, and found in Gandhi her spiritual father. He called her 'Miraben' and indeed her devotion to 'Bapu' was not unlike Mirabai's bhakti for her beloved Giridhar Gopal. The bond which grew between them was unique and beyond the comprehension of most people. Years later Gandhiji's affectionate biographer Louis Fischer wrote: 'Her bond with him was one of the remarkable platonic associations of our age. He often said to her, "When this body is no more there will not be separation, but I shall be nearer to you. The body is a hindrance".'

Miraben immersed her entire being in striving to be a

good satyagrahi. This demanded a tough personal discipline to cultivate fearlessness. It also meant unflinching hard work for the improvement of conditions in Indian villages. Six years later, in 1931, when she travelled with Gandhi to the Round Table Conference in London, Miraben bore little resemblance to Miss Slade. The woman who appeared beside Gandhi in several newspaper photographs was wrapped in a white khadi saree and a simple woollen shawl. Her head was decorously covered by the *pallu* of her saree.

The photo which went down in history, showed her beaming joyously and standing with Gandhi and a large group of cheering women workers at a Lancashire mill. Gandhi had gone there to explain why Indians must reject British cloth, even though it caused unemployment in Lancashire. Gandhi convinced many Lancashire workers that India's struggle for swaraj through swadeshi served the larger good of humanity. It was not a matter of narrow national interest.

Back home in India, Miraben returned to her duties as a faithful village worker. The Sabarmati Ashram was no longer Gandhi's headquarters. The Sabarmati community had been disbanded in 1930 when Gandhi marched to Dandi and challenged the British Empire by lifting a pinch of salt from the beach. He had then vowed that he would not return to Sabarmati unless he attained *purna swaraj*, complete freedom from the British. Now Gandhi sought a new headquarters, preferably somewhere in central India.

This search culminated at Wardha, a small market town at the heart of the central Indian plains. The settlement stood at the edge of the dwindling Dandakarnya forest. Jamnalal Bajaj, one of Gandhi's closest devotees, owned vast tracts of land in the area. Thus, in 1933, Wardha became Gandhi's base for the rest of his life. Here, Maganlal Gandhi, Bapu's nephew, set up a vigorous centre for research and action on village industries. After the untimely death of Maganlal, that neighbourhood came to be called Maganwadi. The centre which he started still stands by the name of Magan sanghralaya.

Following Gandhi's instructions Miraben set out to live and work in a 'typical' village. She settled at a village called Segaon, about five miles east of Wardha. Bajaj owned a large fruit orchard nearby. At first Miraben lived in a tiny thatched hut. But when, in 1936, Gandhi decided to move there himself, Miraben and two fellow-workers picked a one-acre plot on the Bajaj lands and began work on a house for Bapu and 'Ba'—as Kasturba Gandhi was fondly called. They used only local, renewable materials and constructed a rectangular single room structure of wood, bamboo and mud. This was true swadeshi, procuring the essentials of life from the immediate vicinity. Gandhi was firm that all materials used in the construction of houses should be procured from within a five mile radius.

Gandhi had dreamed of living there in peace with just Ba and a few fellow-workers. But soon Sewagram, as Segaon was renamed, became a bustling community instead of the hermitage Gandhi expected it to be. 'Such has been my fate,' he wrote to Miraben, 'I must find my hermitage from within.'

Eventually, a cowshed was added and Miraben was allowed to design and build a small cottage for herself. It had a main room and a smaller side room where Miraben taught carding and spinning to the villagers from Sewagram. Soon after this kuti was ready, Gandhi suffered a severe attack of malaria which left him very weak. Gandhi and Kasturba's home was so crowded now that he could not get enough rest there. Could Bapu be shifted to her cottage? the doctor asked

8

Miraben. She needed no persuading. And so Gandhi settled in the small carding room and slowly recovered his strength.

As soon as Gandhi left on a tour, Miraben sought Bajaj's permission and began to make alterations. She was determined that the little kuti should now be *Bapu's* home. The structure was expanded to include a bathroom and massage room. Two small alcoves were added on both sides of the main room. Miraben was manifesting her image of what Gandhi's dream home would be—simple, utilitarian and aesthetically pleasing. It used materials that would be accessible and affordable for even the most humble peasant.

On his return Gandhi scolded Miraben and the fellow-workers for all the fuss with the alterations. Yet the neat little structure did satisfy both his needs and his principles. So he accepted Miraben's labour of love. This was where Louis Fischer, like numerous other international journalists, met Gandhi and made him famous as the saint-politician whose unique revolution was housed in a mud hut. In May 1942, after spending a week with Gandhi at Sewagram, Fischer wrote:

> There he sat, four-fifths naked, on the earth in a mud hut in a tiny Indian village without electricity, radio, running water, or telephone. It was a situation least conducive to awe, pontification, or legend. He was in every sense down-to-earth. He knew that life consists of the details of life.

Eventually the Sewagram settlement became more and more crowded and other structures were added. A young economist disciple of Gandhi, J.C. Kumarappa, later described this colony as 'the de facto captial of India since service of the country is the function of a capital city.'

On the evening of 30 January 1948, Nathuram Godse's bullets ended the historical Gandhi's stay on earth. The ashes of this mortal self were scattered in rivers and fields all over India. And, instantly, the Bapu Kuti was frozen in time.

The home that Miraben built became a place of pilgrimage. Well into the twilight of the twentieth century its doors remain open to all, from every corner of the world, every day of every year from sunrise to sundown.

## The civilizational Gandhi

Freed from the hindrance of the body, the presence of the civilizational Gandhi spread, quietly nebulous, across time and space. Just what is this 'presence'?

The Gandhi who fell to bullets at Birla House, in New Delhi, had categorically told his followers that there could be no such thing as 'Gandhism'. He did not want to leave behind any sect, for, he said: 'I do not claim to have originated any new principle or doctrine. I have simply tried, in my own way, to apply the eternal truths to our daily life and problems.'

The historical Gandhi was a finite being complete with common frailties and unique strengths. His role as a father and husband are open to criticism. His various political actions—during negotiations with the British or on the formation of Pakistan—can be questioned, dissected, even condemned. This Gandhi is now only of academic historical interest.

What lingers as the spirit of Bapu Kuti are Gandhi's dreams and aspirations for a great evolutionary leap in human civilization. And Gandhi took pains to stress that he had no unique claim on these hopes.

The vision of a society with plenitude and justice for all had once been known as Rama Rajya. Gautam Buddha had urged Right Livelihood as an essential prerequisite for the evolution of the individual and well-being of all. In the nineteenth century the American poet, Henry D. Thoreau, went to jail to protest 'free' America's hypocrisy in tolerating slavery. The British essayist, John Ruskin, preached the dignity of manual labour, urged the simple life and condemned the debilitating complexities of the modern economic system. In Russia, Count Leo Tolstoy abandoned an aristocratic lifestyle and chose a way of life that extolled manual labour, mimimum needs and non-violence.

All these were powerful influences in the flowering of the young M.K. Gandhi. These voices gave a direction to Gandhi's innate yearning for a more just society. In turn, this gave him a special insight into the flaws of 'modern' industrial civilization and its inherent violence. Thus, when he went to the great Paris Exhibition of 1890, he was not impressed by most of the fancy modern goods and inventions displayed there. He agreed with Leo Tolstoy that the Eiffel Tower was a monument to man's folly. The Tower, Gandhi observed, 'was a good demonstration of the fact that we are all children attracted by trinkets.'

Gandhi turned his back on such trinkets and launched on a search for ways of living a wholesome life. This journey led him to several prescriptions for curing the malaise of human civilization. The rudiments of his vision had taken shape by 1908, when Gandhi was forty years old.

That year, Gandhi spent a month having extensive discussions with 'every known Indian anarchist in London'. Their bravery impressed Gandhi, but not their ideas. He was sure that violence was 'no remedy for India's ills, and that her civilization required the use of a different and higher weapon for self-protection.' As he sailed back to South Africa, Gandhi spent the long quiet days of the voyage writing down his ideas on what this 'higher weapon' could be. He used the ancient mode of dialogue to pose a challenge and then articulate the counter-point.

The result was a small booklet called *Hind Swaraj or Indian Home Rule.* The booklet is, in Gandhi's own words, 'a severe condemnation of "modern civilization".' India, Gandhi argued, is being crushed not by the English but by modern civilization. True civilization 'is that mode of conduct which points out to man the path of duty. Performance of duty and observance of morality are convertible terms. To observe morality is to attain mastery over our mind and our passions. So doing, we know ourselves.' Instead, the modern civilization rested on the principle of 'might is right'—thus, colonialism and the annihilation of entire tribes in the Americas.

Gandhi anticipated and answered the criticism that he was anti-machinery. On the contrary he deeply appreciated any machine which eliminated drudgery and enhanced human creativity. Machines, he argued, become a problem when they encroach upon a person's individuality and 'cripple the limbs of man'. For Gandhi a machine, like the human body, was useful only to the extent that it subserves the growth of the soul. Nothing is more detrimental to such growth than the loss of livelihood and lack of adequate nutrition.

So Gandhi challenged all modes of production and economic organization which enslave people in deadening mechanical jobs and also leave millions without the means of earning an adequate livelihood. These concerns were shared by another creative giant, Charlie Chaplin, who had an intense brain-storming session with Gandhi at London in 1931. Chaplin's subsequent masterpiece film *Modern Times* captured both the absurdity and horrors of a society where man becomes dependent on machines.

Gopal Krishna Gokhale, Gandhi's mentor, dismissed *Hind Swaraj* as 'crude and hastily conceived'. When Gandhi returned to live in India in 1915, Gokhale urged him to spend a year travelling, observing and learning. Gokhale was sure that this would lead Gandhi to change the views expressed in *Hind Swaraj*. But Gandhi's India experiences had just the opposite effect.

By then, the mindless industrialization and trade rivalries of the western world had already culminated in the brutal violence of the First World War. Later, the Second World War and the atom bombs over Hiroshima and Nagasaki further vindicated Gandhi's critique of modern western civilization. Thus, *Hind Swaraj* was actually 'Vishwa' Swaraj, its concern was all of humanity, not just India.

In 1947, on the eve of Independence, forty years after writing *Hind Swaraj*, Gandhi wrote to Jawaharlal Nehru:

> I believe that if India is to attain true freedom and through India the world as well, then sooner or later we will have to live in villages—in huts, not in palaces. A few billion people can never live happily and peaceably in cities.

## A later generation 'discovers' the Kuti

Forty years after that midnight tryst with destiny, in 1987, some of India's most reputed architects were gathered at the Bapu Kuti. All three men were seeing the Kuti for the first time. One just stared at it and despaired at the follies in his own design of buildings. Another turned poet and saw love manifest in the mud structure. The aesthetic and functional beauty of every little detail held them in awe.

The Kuti had the same effect on the small group of young scientists who had invited the architects to Sewagram Ashram. The Kuti was like an oasis for these young people, a place to nurture their ideas and strivings. For almost ten years this group, called the Academy of Young Scientists, had scoured the country for clues on forms of strong and comfortable housing that even the poorest Indians could afford. Along the way they 'discovered' the Bapu Kuti as a living manifestation of all the lessons they learnt in the field. They realized that just as handspun cotton had symbolized self-reliance in cloth, mud symbolized self-reliance in housing.

The half-a-century-old Kuti makes nonsense of the common belief that mud houses are *kuchcha*, temporary. Its periodic maintenance uses locally available biomass resources. This involves a small fraction of what it costs to maintain most modern cement structures. The Kuti is naturally cool in summer and in winter it is warmer than a cement structure.

So the Academy of Young Scientists set about examining the Kuti in closer detail. At first this was a technical study, for they wished to replicate the Kuti at an international conference on mud architecture, being held in Trivandrum at the end of 1987.

This detailed structural documentation became a booklet titled *A Study in Sepia: Man of the People Conceives Architecture for the People*, also called *Mrudgandha*. But spending time with the Kuti opened the door to unexpected possibilities. The young scientists found themselves face to face with a whole worldview.

Formal history, they found, had done Gandhi an

injustice. It lauded him for choosing to live in *poverty*. This entirely missed the essence of Gandhi's striving. For one, Gandhi's lifestyle decisions were small manifestations of a deep inner journey. They were not strategic moves aimed at any external audience. He liked the mud house because, for him, it was synonymous with indigenous creativity, *not* poverty and squalor. The Kuti's comfort and ambience are living proof of this.

The Kuti now seemed to 'speak' to the young scientists. This was not the voice of the saintly 'father of the nation' whose statues are buried under flower garlands in every city of India. This was the vibrant spirit of a forty-year-old M.K. Gandhi, who wrote down his credo in *Hind Swaraj*.

By 1987, most of what Gandhi had warned against was already a reality. Millions of Indians are caught in tension-packed lives in crowded, filthy cities. Most Indian villages have receded still further from the dream of creative self-sufficiency. Farmers have become completely dependent on chemical fertilizers and pesticides which are destroying the soil and poisoning the food chain. Yet, even when thousands were killed by the gas leak at Union Carbide's pesticide plant at Bhopal, in 1984, some policy-makers saw this tragedy as the 'price of progress'.

The emergence of a rural rich did not improve the lives of the majority. Instead, as natural resources dwindled, even drinking water became scarce in many villages. This threatened the survival of those who had once managed a subsistence living off the land. Gainful employment per capita per year was down from about 250 days in 1937 to 160 days in 1987.

The young scientists had rejected a routine life of laboratory research in the quest for solutions that could take India out of this stalemate. This group was part of a loosely knit fraternity of post-midnight's children who squarely faced the many dead ends that Independent India had reached.

By 1980 it was clear that the political parties and the national elections were failing to address the five basics—*roti, kapda, makan, swastha, shikhsa;* ie. food, clothing, shelter, health and education. The Naxalite dream of a class revolution had failed. The Sarvodaya leader Jayaprakash Narayan's bid for a student-led *Sampoorn Kranti,* or Total Revolution, had also petered out by the mid-70s.

So where do we go from here? This question fuelled a burning urge to action for a wide variety of people, many of them professionals trained in the disciplines of modern science.

With some poetic licence one of the young scientists, Vinoo Kaley, captured the dilemmas and agony of this question in a dialogue between various policy makers and the spirit of the 'Kuti'. The dialogue was published in a booklet called *A Hut: Revolution and After* or *Krantigandha.* Why, asks the Kuti, does 'industry' necessarily mean a big cement plant? Why is the same importance not given to a small lime-kiln, a loin loom, a local oil-seed crusher or a bullock cart-making workshop? Why do paper mills get bamboo at sixty paise per tone while the artisan pays fifteen rupees per bamboo? The answers appear to lie in marrying Gandhi's worldview with the demands of the present. But how?

*A Study in Sepia* and *A Hut: Revolution and After* were the swan song and lasting remembrance of the Academy of Young Scientists. When I first stayed at Sewagram, in 1987 the group was about to disperse. The quest of its individuals continued and their endeavours flowed into the larger fraternity.

Not everyone in this fraternity feels as close to Bapu Kuti, as the loving authors of *A Hut: Revolution and After*. But over the years, and several visits to Sewagram later, I realized that something like a '*spirit*' of Bapu Kuti is a *sutradhar*. It links seemingly unrelated and diverse efforts.

## Journeys to Sewagram and the future

Two radically different writers were responsible for first setting me in the direction of Sewagram. Some time in the early-80s Claude Alvares wrote a small newspaper article describing a visit to Sewagram. I recall nothing of what the article said. But its description of the Ashram grounds and Bapu Kuti somehow left me with a hankering to go there *soon*. The other was Louis Fischer, the American author of *The Life of Mahatma Gandhi* which was first published in 1950.

Fischer's book came my way in 1984. I read it soon after leaving a job as the *Telegraph's* Mumbai correspondent. I had quit in the hope of going to work with a group in the villages of Madhya Pradesh. Fischer's classic broke through the haze of my youthful confusion, evoking a multitude of questions and longings. The book was packed with endearing moments and, for me, the most important images related again to that ashram some where near Wardha.

So, a compelling, inexplicable pull took me to Sewagram that first time, in October 1986.

A terrible turmoil of doubts and dilemmas, at that stage of life, made any subtle 'listening' difficult. Yet, even then, the Ashram *parisar* immediately struck me as a *living* place. This meant *being* there, more than just optic *seeing*. So a one-day tourist visit was as good as not going there.

I returned to spend a week there in early 1987. Then, I somehow also found myself at Maganwadi, though I had no clue about its historic significance. There I met Vibha and

Anand who were part of the Academy of Young Scientists. Vibha was working at the Centre of Science for Villages with a special interest in technology to suit the needs of rural women. Anand, a toxicologist, was recovering from exposure to toxic gas at the Union Carbide plant at Bhopal. He was part of a team of scientists, sent by the Central government, to monitor the dismantling of the unit from which a leak of poisonous gas killed over 3000 people in December 1984.

Vibha and Anand seemed to understand that compelling pull to Sewagram more than I could articulate even to myself. They shared in my joy and wonder of learning to spin and acquiring a little *kitab charkha*. And I got a fleeting glimpse of their exploration with Bapu Kuti.

On the way back from Sewagram, on the train to Mumbai, I read *Hind Swaraj* for the first time. At that point, like many others, I was puzzled by the radical prescriptions of this little booklet. Its spirit took a while to sink in. Later, over the years, writing about various kinds of movements and campaign, I realized that most of their demands have been anticipated in *Hind Swaraj*. All over India people are struggling for community control over their natural resource base—*jal, jungle, zameen*; i.e. water, forests, land. The protests are directed against a model of 'development' which centralizes decision-making and favours an urban oriented industrialization at the cost of rural communities.

In the summer of 1990 such a protest brought hundreds of adivasis and farmers from along the banks of the Narmada to squat on one of the grand avenues in New Delhi, near the Prime Minister's residence. This was a dharna by the Narmada Bachao Andolan, led by Baba Amte and Medha Patkar and actively supported by scores of middle-class professionals. A few yards from the dharna site was Tees January Marg. At some point during the dharna Rakesh Diwan, an activist from Madhya Pradesh, and I went down that road looking for a public phone. This took us to the doorstep of Birla House, where forty-two years earlier Gandhi had been shot dead.

Suddenly the dharna around the corner seemed all the more poignant. Four decades after Independence, those protesters were fighting for a part of the true swaraj that Gandhi had worked for. Why, they asked, are we never involved or even consulted about projects and policies that affect us? Should we not have some say in deciding whether a mega-dam on the river Narmada is truly in the 'national interest'?

It struck me that Gandhi is rarely mentioned at such gatherings. I wondered aloud why this is so. How many activists here would 'own' Gandhi, that is, see themselves as travellers of that *path*. Not many, said Rakesh Diwan. Why? I persisted. Because, Rakesh sighed, *claiming* to tread Gandhi's path makes you 'work' on the *self*, it makes a person measure oneself by a tough yardstick, and many people don't want to do that!

Over the years such ponderings were balanced off by interaction with elders who have spent a lifetime striving to live by that yardstick. There is Jyotibhai Desai, a master teacher-trainer, who devoted his working life to the practice of Nai Talim. In the same half a century, the world has gone further away from the society envisioned by Nai Talim. But Jyotibhai's infectious joy and unflappable calm makes any kind of fretting seem ridiculous.

Why do you worry so? Jyotibhai asks his younger friends with that ever-present smile. The great flood, he assures, is already receding though few can as yet *see* this.

In November 1992, I found that Thakurdas Bang held

the same view. The veteran leader of the Sarvodaya movement had just won the Jamnalal Bajaj Award and I was at his home in Gowpuri, Wardha, to interview him for the *Illustrated Weekly*. I began by asking him how it felt to be working for ideas that seemed to be losing ground all the time. On the contrary, he said confidently, the ideas we call 'Gandhian' were much more marginal fifty years ago. The nature of global industrialization and the environmental crisis have now brought more and more people to the same conclusions.

Earlier in 1992, the United Nations Earth Summit at Rio de Janeiro had put the seal of 'official' recognition on the term 'sustainable development'. This event was preceded by almost two decades of work, by a wide variety of activists all over the world. This work has established that the earth cannot indefinitely sustain the prevailing notions and modes of 'development' and 'progress'.

Recognition of the human cost of this progress is just inching its way into the international mainstream. In August 1995, the *Time* magazine carried a cover story called 'Twentieth Century Blues' which quoted the work of evolutionary psychologists to show that the edifice of modern life is fundamentally unsuited to the basic psychological needs of human beings. In some industrial countries the rate of depression is doubling every ten years. The author of the article hesitantly suggested that 'plainly, more gross domestic product isn't the answer to our deepest needs'.

This realization now preoccupies a wide range of academics, scientists and activist groups in the West. One such group, based in San Francisco, calls itself 'Redefining Progress' and is campaigning to replace the concept of gross

national product (GNP) with that of genuine progresss
indicators (GPI).

This battle of ideas seems too distant and abstract to
most people. Yet this epochal struggle underlies the day to
day challenges of countless millions. Devdoongri in
Rajasthan, or Kasravad by the Narmada or Adilabad in
north Andhra are tiny dots on the large canvas of a work in
progress. The stories that follow attempt to relate a small
part of this reality.

*

*Bapu Kuti is both a metaphorical and literal* sutradhar *for these
stories. For the legacy of the civilizational Gandhi is unwittingly
enriching diverse saplings, all over the world. These strivings do
not bear Gandhi's name. And perhaps this, for Bapu, would have
been the best of all tributes.*

*In India, Sewagram Ashram has become the unofficial centre
of the striving for alternatives. Located virtually at the centre of
India, it is almost equidistant for people coming together from
different parts of the country. Over the years, the Ashram has
added both accommodation and services that can cater to
gatherings of hundreds of people.*

*Most of those who gather here are not clad in self-spun khadi,
the formal uniform of Bapu's avowed disciples. Many are not
seeking the Kuti, or Bapu, but manage to stumble upon them as
they attend a camp or meeting at Sewagram Ashram. Leafing
through books, by and on Gandhi, at the Ashram's bookstall, some
pick up the unabridged* My Experiments with Truth, *for they
have just never got around to reading it from cover to cover. Others
pick up* Hind Swaraj *or his disciple J.C. Kumarappa's* Economy
of Permanence. *Leafing through the books, pondering over the*

different facets of Bapu Kuti, many find themselves as fellow-travellers with Gandhi.

For most of them the spirit of Bapu Kuti is not easily definable. Yet it seems to encompass the core of their strivings. For a closer look we need to free ourselves from the constraints of chronological time and geography. So imagine for a moment that the Bapu Kuti is a revolving time door. Let us step through . . .

# Devdoongri
## Life along the black tarred road

*At the northern end of the Aravalli range, on a low hill that stands apart, is a tiny temple made of rough stones and clay tiles. The gram deva, village deity, who resides within, stands as a sentinel along a busy pathway that may be ancient. Perhaps this is the route which Sri Krishna took as he frequently travelled from Dwarka to Hastinapur and the ill-fated Kurukshetra. Or, is it a coincidence that the nearest township is called Bhim? Local memory is fuzzy and somewhat indifferent to such curiosity. That old route is now a major national highway which links New Delhi with the commercial centres of Ahmedabad and Mumbai.*

*In the shadow of that low hill with its tiny temple, the* dev doonger, *lies the hamlet of Devdoongri. On its eastern edge, just below the slopes of a barren hill, lives an unusual family. Their mud-and-stone home welcomes a wide assortment of guests. Squatting on the packed mud floor of the kitchen a next-door neighbour could be sharing a meal with a senior bureaucrat from the state capital, a journalist from Mumbai or a marginal farmer from an adjoining district.*

*Over the years I have often shared the strivings and laughter of this household. Sometimes, amid mundane domestic chores like sweeping the floor or feeding the goat, this home would remind me of the Bapu Kuti. But the likeness was difficult to voice. Any comparison with the Kuti or its history-making occupant, would be embarassing for my hosts. They were trying to live and work in simple ways that came naturally to them.*

\*

## A new family at Devdoongri

The black tarred national highway runs within inches of Mot Singh's well, which lies on the outer edge of Devdoongri. As his life faded to a close, Mot Singh spent long hours at that well, watering the vegetables on his tiny patch of land. Often, he was there in the pre-dawn dark, ready for a day's work, suppressing his cough by smoking yet another *beedi*. Even at that hour the silence was regularly broken by the roar of zooming trucks or buses.

That road is a corridor that links fragments of the modern industrial world across vast stretches of hinterland. Mot Singh, standing outside it, no longer looked in longingly nor did he try to breach the invisible barriers of this corridor.

He had done that as a young man. Like millions of others, Mot Singh once ventured down that road to cities where he sold his labour for a wage and lived in filth and stench. Having exhausted his youthful energy there, he returned to his stone-and-mud home at Devdoongri. Now the mornings saw him in his field by the well where, in some years, vegetables grew well enough for him to earn a small livelihood by selling them in nearby Bhim.

The afternoons found Mot Singh on the rough wooden bench of the tea shop at 'Chalis Meel', a junction on the highway which gets its name from the road marker which tells travellers that they are forty kilometres from the city of Beawer. The weathered wooden shack of the tea shop was a short, half a kilometre, walk down the highway from Mot Singh's well. The tiny cups of over-boiled tea were an excuse for gathering and speculating about affairs of other people, near and far. Mot Singh's humour and fertile imagination were the life of these gatherings at Chalis Meel.

In his life of fifty-odd years, Mot Singh had seen many bad, dry years. Over the centuries his ancestors had learnt to live with long droughts. They accepted that for every hundred years there are only twenty years of good rain followed by *zamana*—a good harvest. But now, as Mot Singh neared his end, there came an eight-year stretch of such poor rain that people and cattle alike grew desperate. This unbearable *sookha* brought to mind tales of other harsh times. Virtually every able-bodied man set out down that tarred road. Those who stayed behind lived in wait of the money these migrating men might send. And they hoped that the government, which built and sometimes even repaired that road, would do something. But the government's promises are like a mirage, always receding and then vanishing.

Mot Singh began to feel like the children in the folk tale which spoke about a terrible time when starvation stalked every poor home. Having exhausted the last morsel of grain, a mother set out in search of food. Before leaving, she tied a pot high up near the ceiling, and told the children that it contained *khichadi* which she would feed them on return. For several days the children survived by gazing hopefully at that pot and waiting faithfully for their mother. Eventually the mother returned—empty-handed. The children died when they realized that the pot too was empty.

The pot in Mot Singh's house was not yet empty but it was never adequately filled either. In the old days it was said that only three creatures were sure to survive even the worst famine: the brahmins, sheep and camels. In modern times,

Mot Singh found that two additional creatures were guaranteed survival: the *sarkar*, government, and the sarpanch, village head. He mused over these stories with a wry smile. The story-telling was punctuated with chuckles that often dissolved into a racking cough that shook his frail frame—his greying moustache quivering on the dark wrinkled face. Then Mot Singh would reach into his kurta for another *beedi* as, he insisted, it was the only sure way to control every bout of coughing. Starvation no longer boldly *stalked* the land but crept up slowly under different guises.

It was some time in the seventh year of that long famine that one day Mot Singh noticed some strangers, two men and a woman, carrying out repairs on his neighbour Jait Singh's empty house. The two-roomed stone-and-mud structure had been crumbling over the years since Jait Singh lived in a hut at his fields. The tea-shop gossip was soon rife with conjectures about the strangers.

It turned out that one of the men was Shanker Singh, a cousin of Jait Singh's wife who came from a village about twenty-five kilometres eastwards down the road. This Shanker dressed in jeans and shirt like city folk. But so did Mot Singh's son who was working in Baroda and spent far too much time arranging his hair to look like Amitabh Bachchan. It was the other young man and the *bhenji* who were harder to figure out. The young man called Nikhil was, like Shanker, slender and of medium height. But his lighter skin and features clearly marked him out as a *pardesi*. They said he had come from Delhi but he didn't quite walk or talk like big city people.

The delicately built, fiercely energetic *bhenji* was the greatest mystery in this small group. She conversed easily in the local dialect and seemed familiar with village ways. She wore simple cotton sarees and at first seemed like a school teacher or doctor. But her carriage spoke of an unusual purposiveness and confidence. Once upon a time, murmured the tea-shop gossips, she was a collector somewhere. This made no sense at all. Collectors, both present and former, roamed about in jeeps and cars not in the local bone-rattling buses and certainly never went about on foot. And what did she plan to do in Devdoongri, an obscure cluster of stone-and-mud homes no different from thousands of villages along that trunk road?

Before the mystery deepened any further, Mot Singh sauntered across the small field beside his house, past the grand neem tree, to where the three were building an additional room to Jait Singh's house. Several children were already there avidly observing the strangers. Standing slightly apart from the cluster of giggly children was Narayan, a tall, gangly teenager. Narayan followed his uncle Mot Singh into the compound and stood aside, shy and quiet, listening intently.

The strangers were busy constructing a narrow room, laid at right angles to the existing structure. This, they told Mot Singh, would serve as a kitchen and an extra living space. Like the rest of the house this room had walls made of thin flat stones picked up from the nearby foothills. The stones were piled up and held together with a mixture of gravel and mud. The walls were then given a protective covering of mud, topped off by a final layer of fine clay mixed with cow-dung and hay.

These procedures were familiar to Mot Singh. What stood out were the saplings of bamboo and gulmohar which these outsiders had planted along the eastern wall of their compound. That first visit was the beginning of a friendship that endured past Mot Singh's death and shaped Narayan's life. But Mot Singh lived long enough to see the bamboo and gulmohar become tall and sway gracefully in the breeze. In full bloom the flaming gulmohar became a sign-post, visible from the road, helpful to the many who flocked to Devdoongri. The story of their coming takes us much further back in time.

## Aruna: from IAS officer to village worker

The year was 1969. The President of India was on a state visit of Vellore. His wife wanted to buy sarees while her husband went about his official duties. The youngest, and perhaps the only woman IAS officer available, Aruna Roy, was assigned to assist Mrs V.V. Giri. Resplendent in her rich silks and en route to buying several more, Mrs Giri was surprised to see Aruna clad in a crisp, simple handloom cotton saree.

'Why are you dressed like that? Are you a Gandhian?' Mrs Giri asked Aruna, almost rhetorically. Wary of any label, Aruna smiled and said that she just preferred wearing handloom cottons.

Labels would continue to follow Aruna. But she could not know this then, on her first posting as an IAS probationer. It was a little later that she was called the 'rebel' IAS officer, waging a struggle against the colonial ethos of the service. Still later she was the IAS 'drop-out' who became a 'social worker'. Some bureaucrats would call her a 'Marxist' but to Marxists she seemed like a 'reformist'. Later, the mere combination of her Bengali surname 'Roy' and her championing of land rights around Devdoongri earned her the label 'Naxalite' from the district police officials. And so it went on. But none of the labels even fractionally conveyed the truth of her search. For all labels relied only on appearances.

Aruna traversed a long, twenty-year journey between that first IAS posting at the age of twenty-one, and the arrival

28

at Jait Singh's ramshackle house in Devdoongri. She had joined the IAS with the feeling that it was one way of working for social justice. In the late-60s there were still young people who saw the IAS as the chosen elite that would set the country on its feet.

Within the first few weeks of her district training, Aruna was rattled to find this lofty ideal dissolving into an illusion. The novice officer felt baffled by the complexity of wheels within wheels which moved various competing vested interests. It was a few years before she became absolutely certain that the IAS was not there to implement either the letter or the spirit of the Constitution. It simply served the interests of the resident power elite. Some good work in 'soft' areas like literacy, family planning and health, could not compensate for the genetic flaws. To challenge the power structure from within was to put oneself at peril and, even then, the chances of success were slim.

So, seven years after her first posting, Aruna quit the IAS. Thus began the search for a life not defined by postings but by Aruna herself and the people she chose to work with. It was a farewell to more than a job and its comforts. She saw herself saying goodbye to middle-class inhibitions, to timidity and the middle-class habit of withdrawing as soon as there is social conflict and the threat of public criticism.

For the next decade Aruna became an integral part of life at the Social Work Research Centre in the village of Tilonia, a small railway station between Jaipur and Ajmer. The 'Centre', as it is known for miles around, was set up by Bunker Roy in 1972 at a time when the term NGO, non-governmental organization, was not common currency. Aruna and Bunker had met when she was a student at Indraprastha College and he was at St. Stephen's College in

Delhi. They were married in 1970, shortly after Aruna joined the IAS.

By the mid-80s, Bunker was a widely recognized authority on non-governmental initiatives for rural development and an advisor to the Planning Commission. Meanwhile, Aruna had realized some of her original objectives. She had been able to actually work *with* people at the lowest end of the economic ladder, rather than merely 'dealing' with them as statistics on a file. This had fine-tuned her understanding of social and economic realities. But eventually the inadequacies of her own work at the Centre stared her in the face.

The SWRC had enhanced the quality of life for many people around Tilonia. It had opened new opportunities for some and within ten years most of its staff was local, not upper-middle class people from the cities. Yet it was a sort of parallel bureaucracy, supplementing the government's machinery, sometimes by assisting, and at other times challenging, its functions. This wasn't necessarily empowering people at large.

The walls of the SWRC campus enclosed a 'created', and somewhat privileged, community however simple and frugal its lifestyle. By then Aruna was convinced that even the most well-meaning rural development 'programmes' could not alter the pervasive inequities and injustices she had seen all over India. Clearly, a voluntary agency, geared for setting up of an alternative local structure for development, is not equipped to organize the people for struggles. People who work there may learn and grow but this did not generate a momentum for confrontational politics and sustained protest. All around her Aruna saw development programmes failing because they did not take the politics of the ground reality into account. An effort for deep-rooted social change would have to derive its strength from the people it intended to benefit.

So there arose in Aruna a longing to live and work in a village community. Perhaps there the people's own initiative would be the engine for change. But where to begin? She started by quitting her formal position at SWRC, in 1983, and launched on yet another search. For the next four years Aruna groped for ways to realize her dream. The fulfilment of that vision awaited a confluence with fellow-travellers then unknown and that mysterious and elusive juncture of time.

## Shanker: self-discovery of hidden talents

Shanker Singh had once travelled down the black tarred road much like Mot Singh. Shanker's widowed mother cultivated a small patch of land at Lotiana, their village along the same national highway about twenty-five kilometres from Devdoongri. In 1970, while Shanker was still in his teens, his mother arranged her only son's marriage. Their land had barely sustained mother and son. How was Shanker going to feed his bride Anshi and the children who would inevitably follow? So, leaving Anshi with her parents, he set out on the road that merged into the anonymity of Ahmedabad and Baroda.

Shanker was not, however, destined for anonymity. The cart from which he sold hot *pakoras*, outside Baroda station, could not hold him long. The *namkeen* factory, where he spent hours frying tonnes of *sev* or mixing ingredients, also soon saw him on his way.

To where? Even Shanker wasn't sure but countless questions and possibilities stirred within him. On one of the many trips up and down to Lotiana, his home village, Shanker found himself at a poultry farm on the outskirts of

Ajmer. The job of feeding the chicks, cleaning their coops and occasionally catering to the whims of the owner, left him with enough time to study for a college degree by correspondence. All through, Shanker was watching, listening and learning about the ways of the world and coming to his own conclusions. Meanwhile, Shanker's real talent remained untapped.

Then, by a quirk of fate Shanker found himself at SWRC Tilonia, where a motley group of young men from surrounding villages were putting together a most unusual drama troupe. Here, at last, Shanker was in his element. His warm, incisive wit and humorous way of perceiving reality created a world of wonders. Suddenly, Shanker found himself the fulcrum of what came to be known as the SWRC Communication Team. Through a combination of song, dance, drama and innovative glove puppets, which anyone can easily use, this team explained the finer points of education, health , environment and politics to audiences, making them thoughtful even as they rolled with laughter. Before long, the Communication Team was enthralling gatherings not only in villages of Rajasthan but in Delhi and at the Festival of Fools in Oslo, en route to London.

Finally, after eleven years of marriage and the birth of two daughters, Shanker could provide a home for Anshi. Once the family settled into the comfort and security of the SWRC it also grew. Kammo and Neelu soon had a brother whom Shanker and Anshi named Vikas. Life could have comfortably drifted along on this track indefinitely if only that nagging restlessness would stop haunting Shanker.

The Communication Team's work was good but this wasn't enough. It could only hint at answers. It could not, in itself, solve the problems of thousands of young men like Shanker who had few options at either end of the black tarred road. There are few means to earn a livelihood in the village and only a life of squalor and drudgery as labourers in urban industrial centres. Shanker knew that his burning desire to solve this problem was not enough. But perhaps living and working among the people may open ways that were not yet apparent. Besides, Anshi longed to return to their own social world.

That didn't necessarily mean Lotiana. There his participation in the *natak mandali* was frowned upon; after all he was not of the *nat* caste. 'Those who are born into the performing castes must perform, and those who aren't must not,' Shanker was told. Even his mother strongly disapproved. Like millions of other young men, Shanker found himself caught between the half-tumbled edifice of caste and the uncertain culture of modernity.

People who had once earned a good livelihood as artisans, working creatively, with some control over production, were now merely cogs in the wheel of mechanised production. Shanker found that the terms 'Harijan' or 'scheduled caste' were no longer confined to the traditional caste groups which handled human waste or dead cattle, but effectively also included the unskilled labourers or workers who keep their bodies and souls together only on terms set by the city. But after years of struggle and drudgery, Shanker had found that he did have a special skill, an inborn ability to communicate ideas and feelings to large gatherings of people. So he defiantly persevered as an actor and performer, and this commitment to communication became his own struggle against all forms of social oppression.

Clearly he couldn't settle in Lotiana. The caste and clan associations there would be inhibiting. Then, on a visit to see his mother, Shanker met his cousin sister's husband, Jait

Singh. They got talking and Jait Singh mentioned his empty house at Devdoongri, in the shadow of a low hill with a tiny temple. It beckoned like a homing beacon.

## Devi Lal: hunger versus squalor

Devi Lal's house lay across the fields to the east of Jait Singh's house, a small distance from the main cluster of houses in Devdoongri. For centuries, the outer fringe of the village had been the assigned place for Devi Lal's ancestors. Except that now Devi Lal could go to school and sit next to Mot Singh's children and his nephew Narayan, who were higher in the caste ladder. But there was no chance of any of them sitting in the same classroom as the children of the local one-time Raja, not that Devi Lal wanted to go to an elite English-medium school. His dream was to earn a livelihood in the village which would provide him two square meals and other essentials of life.

When the new stirrings of activity began at Jait Singh's house, Devi Lal was quickly over to meet the new people. Soon the soft-spoken, lanky youth was a regular visitor, helping out with fixing the house and chatting, getting to know the new neighbours. The newcomers were astonished that Devi Lal had not only passed the eleventh class board examination but had also qualified for a government scholarship. Before long Devi Lal was sharing with these new friends some of the questions and dreams which he would write about in his diary:

> For eight years we have been in the grip of famine. We do not have adequate food, clothes, homes or education. So, men go to find work in Gujarat and Bombay. But there a man falls into the grip of contractors and capitalists. He still doesn't get

enough to eat proper, regular meals or have an adequate home. Soon, he falls ill and cannot work. The contractor does not give him money for the treatment. Sometimes the other workers have to put together just enough money to send him home. But many such men soon die. The wife has to sell what little land she has to somehow feed the children. Later, his sons go through the same cycle. Why doesn't the government develop the villages so people don't have to go to the cities in search of work? If that happened, then maybe so many of us wouldn't have tuberculosis and jaundice and malaria.

Devi Lal's father, and possibly even grandfather, had lived with this reality. It was now difficult to imagine that once there may have been a time when things were different. Any trace of the traditional industries had been destroyed long before Devi Lal was born. The weavers, leather or metal workers, potters and other producers who occupied the centrestage of the village, were entirely marginalized by the rise of modern industry. Yet the skills were not entirely wiped out. Some of the best skilled workmen at construction sites all over India are from Rajasthan, and many of them, who come to the metropolises, may make a handsome wage. Nevertheless, they live in fetid urban slums.

In the village Devi Lal could live with relative dignity but would always be battling hunger. A job in the city would bring better food but a degraded existence. 'Development,' Devi Lal would say in his soft simple way, 'should mean productive work in the village that would take the sting out of the cyclical drought.' With genuine puzzlement, Devi Lal asked Aruna and the others, 'How can the government run famine relief works for two months and then forget about us for the next ten months?'

Often, Narayan would also join these discussions. Together they would all talk about possible ways in which the government could be made less forgetful!

This shared search for effective modes of action was in part a fulfilment of Aruna's dream and her own long quest. The change from Tilonia to Devdoongri was the most profound shift in perception so far in her life. In shifting from the IAS she sought to improve what she could do within the same given understanding of development. In coming to Devdoongri she was using all the lessons learnt in Tilonia to see development itself from a different perspective. Years later she wrote:

> In the case of both the government and Tilonia, I saw my role as that of the initiator. I was a 'catalyst', the 'agent for change', the one who 'intervened for change'. In other words, the perception was that of myself as the leader, in so much as the action that followed was ultimately traced back to a set of actions for which I was responsible. It may have been an idea or a set of ideas. Gradually I began to understand that the perceptions and ideas exist in different forms in people's minds already. What is really needed is the time and space and opportunity for putting them into action. My role was now severely limited in my mind.
>
> If leadership was to be different, then the organization would also have to be so defined so as to enable the people to manage things themselves. The leadership in people's organizations has to come from the local area. The issues, the direction, the priorities must be decided by them.

So what, in this scheme of things, was Aruna's role?

I was going to an area where I was an outsider. I would never be able to understand the area quite as well as a local person. But I also had a special set of experiences and a critique of development processes born out of varied experiences. I was born into a class which still remained powerful and dominated decision making. I provided links with an understanding of that class. So I was useful to the local people.

I had developed a personal preference for simple ascetic living. I felt that one could not work with the poor unless one lived with them as one of them. It was important for me to share the lifestyle physically too. It was important for me to lead a life in harmony with myself, to see work and living as a continuum. This kind of lifestyle facilitates a different kind of communication, where the people see you as more accessible. Finally, when the people who you work with, see the mutual dependencies for living and security, there is a much greater sense of equality that permeates relationships.

With every passing day at Devdoongri, the seeds of such relationships were sprouting and taking root. The canvas of the story was ready to stretch wider, move further and include new friends like Lal Singh from the neighbouring village of Sohangarh.

## Lal Singh: the joy of finding kindred spirits
Lal Singh's placid presence was usually infectious. But as he faced the hostility of Thakur Hari Singh's armed goons, even

Lal Singh may have felt a surge of panic. What had he got himself into? The Devdoongri *sathis,* friends, had warned him that challenging the thakur could mean trouble. But the actual attack came unexpectedly. The thakur's men had burst into Sohangarh brandishing swords and *lathis,* which was enough to frighten most people. Then they had come in search of Lal Singh, and his friend Bhanwar, as the perceived leaders of the new spirit in Sohangarh. To their utter surprise Bhanwar did not turn and flee into the house but stood his ground and even tried to reason with them. Hari Singh's men gaped at Bhanwar for just a moment. They were about to split his head open with a sword when a shout went up and virtually the whole village came rushing towards Lal Singh's house. Most people grabbed the nearest object that could be handy as a make-shift weapon. The thakur's men beat a hasty retreat.

The quiet sprawling village of Sohangarh, some twelve kilometres from Bhim, had never witnessed such happenings. The peace had been disturbed by a new spirit among some Sohangarhis. It wasn't quite a revolution. They were just determined to retrieve a large tract of the village's common lands, which Hari Singh's family claimed as their private property.

Once upon a time the Maharana of Udaipur had ruled this area, through local thakurs and smaller rajas. This particular stretch of the ancient pathway was always somewhat difficult to control. Travellers were often looted in these parts. In independent India this area fell in the northern corner of Udaipur district, and later in the newly formed Rajsamand district. Nahar Singh, the former local raja, still had a sprawling residence beside a small lake at Devgarh, some twenty-five kilometres from Devdoongri. But now he worked for a living, as a teacher at the elite Mayo

College in Ajmer. His younger brother dabbled in politics. By 1989, the former Raja's sole claim to fame was that his sister's husband, V.P. Singh, had become the prime minister of India.

Hari Singh, who held over 1,500 acres of land, was among the smaller thakurs who still bowed reverentially to the Raja-saheb. Under the land-ceiling laws much of this land no longer belonged to Hari Singh's family. His claim was maintained by threats of violence which the rest of the village did not challenge.

For most of the people in Sohangarh, agriculture was no longer a viable activity. Over the years, as families grew, land-holdings were divided into small plots, some even less than an acre. Being entirely dependent on the monsoon, crop yields were far from generous. So, like most of his neighbours Lal Singh had travelled down the black tarred road when he was barely twenty. He found a job as a police constable in Udaipur and may have continued there till he retired.

Some time in the late-70s, Lal Singh joined a hunger strike by constables, who were refusing to work as domestic servants for the police officers. Dismissed from the job, Lal Singh returned to Sohangarh and made a living by ferrying milk to Bhim, doing the odd construction work and tilling his land. His experiences in Udaipur had taught him that Hari Singh's arbitrary ways were wrong. But where did one begin to challenge even a small power like the local thakur? This question came alive for Lal Singh when he came to know the new family in Devdoongri.

Around the time that Shanker, Aruna and Nikhil were working to make Jait Singh's old house habitable, Lal Singh used to cycle from Sohangarh every day to sell milk in Bhim. One day, instead of making the left turn at Chalis Meel to return home, he cycled on for another quarter of a mile down the highway to Devdoongri. Someone had sent him a message that a new family there needed help to put up a roof. Thus, Lal Singh became a daily visitor to the house with the fledgling bamboo and gulmohar. As the rough clay tiles went into place over the new room, which was to serve as a kitchen, life histories and dreams were shared.

Mahatma Gandhi was not quite a household name in these parts. But he occupied a special place in Lal Singh's family. His parents and his uncle and aunt had once tended cows at Sabarmati Ashram when it was still the home of the Mahatma. Though they all eventually returned to live as before in their village, Sohangarh, some of Gandhiji's simple confidence in the ability of ordinary mortals to fight moral battles, must have infected them and been transmitted to Lal Singh.

The spontaneous and trusting Lal Singh accepted the transparent goodwill of these unusual people. He could understand that a person would prefer to live in the village, rather than be cramped and caught up in the bustle of some city. But he wasn't sure if this unusual family's making Devdoongri their home would make any difference to the village, as they seemed to hope. Then, one evening, Shanker and Nikhil returned with Lal Singh to Sohangarh and together with many of his family members and friends were up till late in the night. The outsiders spoke of various places where people had formed *sangathans* to struggle for their rights. The people of Sohangarh spoke of seemingly impossible dreams.

Would it ever be possible to earn a livelihood in the village, so that men wouldn't have to squander their youth travelling down the black tarred road? Would the women and old people who stayed behind and toiled at the government's famine relief works ever get the full minimum wage which was their right? The government spent so much money but the schemes were all decided far away by other people. When would it ever listen to the people and let them make their own decisions about local schemes? How will *hamara raj*, people's rule, ever be possible if the MPs and MLAs of all political parties never actually do anything for the people in the village? Thus, countless others, like Lal Singh, wondered—are we destined to remain helpless spectators in the world at both ends of the black tarred road?

The meeting finally dispersed only when the damp night chill began to settle over the circle of people squatting in the village square. Shanker and Nikhil settled down for the night at Lal Singh's house, feeling happy with the gathering. Within minutes Nikhil was blissfully asleep on the hard ground, covered by a muddy much-used *goodadi*, a quilt made from old sheets and rags. Shanker couldn't help contrasting this scene with the comforts of Air Marshal Dey's large and sparkling clean bungalow, in the ministerial area of New Delhi, which till recently had been Nikhil's home.

Once, half way across the world, at a college near Washington DC, Nikhil was asked by fellow students to give a talk on the problem of poverty in the Third World. The meeting was held in a large canteen shortly after lunch. The huge garbage bins were brimming with disposable plates, cups and half-eaten meals. At the appointed moment Nikhil got up, walked over to one of the tall bins and toppled it over. As the other students gaped at him Nikhil pointed to the food strewn all over the floor and said: 'We can solve the

the problem of poverty in the Third World if you can solve *this* problem.'

Nikhil's father was posted as the Air Attaché at the Indian embassy in Washington at that time. Unlike the children of most other embassy staff, Nikhil and his sister had no desire to stay on in the United States. Nikhil went through the motions of a Bachelor of Arts degree at the George Mason University, but then suddenly quit a few weeks before the end of the last semester. The degree was going to be of little or no use to him, where he was going. Returning to India, Nikhil spent a year travelling all over the country spending time with activist groups of assorted ideological hues. This journey had no specified destination or easily definable parameters. He wanted to work in a village, ideally a place of lush green fields and slopes.

The semi-arid plains of Rajasthan never featured in Nikhil's dreams about the future. But one day, a friend and relative, Laila Kabir Fernandes, invited him to join her on a trip to SWRC Tilonia. Nikhil went along not expecting SWRC to contribute any clues for his search. There Nikhil met Aruna and in talking with her heard echoes of his own search. Later, that feeling grew stronger when he met Shanker and slowly pieces of the puzzle began to fall into place. It was a few years more before the search ended in the shade of a lone gulmohar at Devdoongri—which was now more a home than any of the plush homes that were part of Nikhil's early life.

## Sohangarh: surprise stirrings of rebellion

Mishraji, the tall and lean English teacher in Bhim, was astounded as he learnt about the life journey of the Devdoongri family. There was much about them which baffled him. So Mishraji looked bemused, on that bright sunny day in 1989, as he observed the happy gathering under a tent, just outside Sohangarh and reflected on the marvellous surprises of life. Who would have ever thought that these simple villagers in an area which had never heard of 'revolution', let alone of Marx and Lenin, would unite to successfully, peacefully, wrest land from a Hari Singh. Mishraji's long years of unbearable loneliness in Bhim seemed to melt away.

Economic necessity had driven R.N. Mishra from his home, in revolution-familiar Bihar, when he was just twenty years old. He had found a niche as an English teacher in the government-run high schools of Rajasthan. A long-time resident of Bhim he was respectfully called 'Mishraji' by people of all ages, classes and ideology. He could lambaste his fellow teachers for their right-wing views and still be repeatedly elected president of the teachers' union.

While prospects for any kind of revolution in the vicinity of Bhim always looked dim, Mishraji had kept his dreams alive in ways that changed many lives. In most schools where he was posted it was *revolutionary* enough that he actually taught the students and was forever engaged in trying to help their growth. Though he was an avowed and, as he insisted, unrepentant Stalinist, Mishraji didn't preach any fixed dogma to his devoted and ever-affectionate students. But he passionately urged them to see beyond their narrow self and fight against all injustice.

Even after several months of growing friendship with the Devdoongri family Mishraji was still puzzled by them. None of the familiar labels seemed to fit them. They belonged to no party or identifiable ideology or any of the proliferating NGOs (non-governmental organizations). There was nothing academic or researcher-like about them but they did have a grant of Rs 30,000 from the Ministry of

Human Resource Development's Department of Education, to study issues related to the participation of poor in the government's poverty alleviation programmes. But soon these unanswered questions retreated to the background, for their simple life in the mud house touched Mishraji deeply. Later he discovered that all four of them, Shanker, Anshi, Aruna and Nikhil, took a minimum wage out of the grant money. In 1987 this came to about Rs 420 per month for each person.

For all his growing fondness, Mishraji had remained skeptical about the Devdoongri family's hopes for getting anything started in this sleepy area. Yet, Mishraji instinctively shared the activists' conviction that an ethical basis of life and work could be converted into an ideology. Certainly there was no divide between their personal ethics and social morality. But could this ethical strength itself create a movement? Didn't one have to *give* the people an ideological frame to fight their oppression? But these questions didn't entirely preoccupy Mishraji, he was too busy being involved in the emerging struggle. And the living proof of unfolding actions was more compelling than any unresolved theoretical questions.

Here were hundreds of people assembled to celebrate the formation of the Shramik Mahila Vikas Avam Anusandhan Samiti, Sohangarh. This body was made responsible for nurturing, and ensuring collective use of, the land which had been released from Hari Singh's control. Yet again, Mishraji marvelled at the combination of factors spread over time and space which made this possible.

Back in the late-70s, during the post-Emergency euphoria, the Janata Party government in Rajasthan had started a practice called *Prashasan Gaon ki Aur*, that is literally, 'Administration goes to villages'. This required every sub-divisional magistrate (SDM) to periodically take his office to the villages. The SDM would arrive, with due notice to all the villages in a *tehsil*, and hold a kind of 'court'. Citizens could bring up their concerns and the SDM would take action on any matter within his jurisdiction, sometimes settling it on the spot.

In the winter of 1988, the SDM at Bhim announced that he would hold a *Prashasan Gaon ki Aur* session in the panchayat of Tal. Lal Singh and his friends at Devdoongri immediately saw this as a knock of opportunity. Here was a chance to get that grazing land out of Hari Singh's control. But first they needed the *khasra*, plot, number of the land and other relevant details from the patwari. This is usually a difficult, even impossible, task. Luck smiled upon them in the form of an innocent and willing patwari who opened up the records and shared the relevant information.

Now they were armed with the necessary details, plus Aruna's knowledge of the bureaucratic procedures. So it was that a motley group of people from Sohangarh put their application before the SDM's day-long 'court' at the Tal panchayat, with a mixture of hope and scepticism. Could the status quo of decades really be challenged?

The SDM surprised most people by ruling that the land clearly did not belong to Hari Singh. But the land did not automatically revert to the village as a community. It now 'belonged' to the people via the state. Besides, the village of Sohangarh was not an entirely cohesive entity. As the impact of this ruling filtered through, the people of Sohangarh stood divided. Some were loyal to Hari Singh and others celebrated the release of the land. This division was smoothed by forming and registering the Mahila Samiti and transferring the land to this organization. It was here that the fierce leadership qualities of Bhuriya came to the fore.

Bhuriya's wrinkled face and bony hands could not veil her iron will. Like her son, Lal Singh, Bhuriya rose up with courage to struggle for change. But Bhuriya's being, her struggles and her language, were alien to the world of those who wield power. Even the Devdoongri family had to build bridges before entering Bhuriya's world.

Work in the fields, rearing children and dealing with social duties and injustices were all part of a continuous rhythm of life. So Bhuriya could pass with ease from relating the problems she grappled with as a member of the panchayat, to the incontinence of her grandchild all in the same breath. If Aruna praised the creativity of her life, Bhuriya would smile indulgently, peeping from behind the *odni* falling over her face. As Aruna later wrote:

> Her idiom is not ours. We experience impatience and boredom. We do not have the mental concept of time that she has. Though we may share the larger inheritance of India, we see time as linear, she as cyclical. The hurry and bustle of our minds and our conscience is to catch up with it. Hers, an inevitability of the cycle of life—apparent not only in life and death, but in the daily chores of living and in facing the upheavals of life.

This process of building bridges across divergent perceptions rode tandem with more material matters. With help from the Devdoongri family, the Samiti earned a grant from the Wastelands Development Board. This paid for a protective stone wall around the land and the planting of 20,000 saplings of mixed species of trees and bushes. The people of Sohangarh built the wall themselves and then added some basic watershed enhancement devices, like trenches and *bunds*. Grazing and fuel-wood collection were curtailed in the initial period, allowing the land to bloom undisturbed. Subsequently the *beeda*, as this grazing land is called, was opened up for judicious and collective use.

Within two years, the *beeda* became a lush oasis that stood out like an apparition in those semi-arid plains. It is now a source of regular firewood and fodder for members of the Samiti, about three-fourths of Sohangarh. Subsequently, the rest of the *beela-nam* ie. non-classified unoccupied government land, was taken over by the forest department and is now part of a joint forest management scheme. Like villages elsewhere, the people of Sohangarh believed that they suffered frequent famines because they had allowed the forests, that once surrounded their land, to dwindle. So, the burgeoning green *beeda* on the edge of Sohangarh had both a literal and symbolic beauty.

Meanwhile, at Devdoongri, the lone gulmohar grew taller; its branches swaying along with the bamboo. They fed on the soapy water trickling out of the bathroom and that which drained from the stone slabs on which dishes were washed. Everyone in that unusual household washed their own dishes and encouraged all guests to do the same. A district collector, or other *bada babu*, washing his own teacup on a whistle stop to the Devdoongri family was initially quite a spectacle. Some, like Mot Singh, never quite got used to it. Others, like Chunnibai, slowly and affectionately grew reconciled to letting Nikhil or Shanker wash their own dishes even when they came to her house.

## Dadi Rapat: the struggle for minimum wages

Chunnibai's body burnt with fever. Lying on a tattered *goodadi* on the mud floor of her dark home she spoke in a rasping voice. The fever had been plaguing her for almost two weeks by then. Shanker asked if she had been to the Primary Health Centre (PHC) at Brar. No, answered Chunnibai with a silent shake of her head. Going to the doctor at the PHC in Brar required too much money. The doctor saw more patients at his 'clinic' in the residential quarters, where patients had to pay for both consultation and medicines.

Chunnibai and her husband Mohan had a small piece of land but it didn't provide them with grain for even half the year. They depended on earning wages at the government's famine relief works and this wasn't much. Mohan was no longer a young man. He didn't have the energy to travel down the black tarred road. His sons were doing that now, but there was no certainty about the money they could send home.

After some gentle cajoling, Shanker persuaded Chunnibai and Mohan to give the PHC a try the next morning. He went along to ensure that Chunnibai got the attention and medicine that anyone should be entitled to at a PHC. Chunnibai was not sure this could happen every time she was ill. But she no longer believed that it was impossible to change things. The experience at Dadi Rapat had shown this.

Dadi Rapat was the name given to a large 'famine' site near Chunnibai's village, Talai. Decades ago, bureaucratic jargon had introduced the word 'famine' into the local language. As the summer approached, people would talk of 'famine *kab khulegi?*' They wanted to know when the famine relief works would begin.

The story of Dadi Rapat dates back towards the end of 1987, when Anshi and the children had just moved to Devdoongri and the family, having completed fixing their home, was feeling settled in. In those days Chunnibai,

Mohan and scores of others were digging sand at a worksite of the irrigation department called Dadi Rapat. The sand was being carried some distance to bolster the bunding of a local tank. They should all have been earning Rs 11 for a day's work, which was stipulated by the government as the minimum wage. But the men rarely got more than Rs 7 or Rs 8 and the women got Rs 5 or Rs 6.

Nikhil, Shanker and Aruna heard about this and started to investigate. At first it seemed that the problem lay in how the work was measured. The workers had no say in the matter and the junior engineer (J.E.N.)'s word was final. But, if the payment was made according to the work done then why did they all have to be present for the full eight hours? Nikhil, who had recently taken a law degree, knew that there were court judgements which clearly stipulated that wages may be determined on the basis of either piece rate or time rate, but *not* both.

Soon the Devdoongri team was busy discussing all the details pertaining to the work at Dadi Rapat. After several meetings it was decided that when a fresh round of digging started all the 140 workers would participate in the entire measurement process and make sure that the work was completed so that the full wage could be paid. Since wages are determined for a whole team of workers, and not individuals, this became an experiment to infuse a new collective spirit in all the teams and ensure that they completed the entire work assigned to them. The J.E.N. acknowledged that the work had been completed to measure, but still they were each offered only Rs 6 per day instead of Rs 11.

To most of the workers this was only inevitable. No famine relief work ever paid the full amount. That's just the way it was. But suppose the people refused to take this payment and held out for the full amount? This suggestion, from the Devdoongri activists, appealed to Chunnibai and several others. Let's do it, they decided. Initially, all 140 workers refused to accept the truncated wage but it was only Chunnibai and Bhanwar Singh, one other worker, who stuck it out to the very end.

This non-cooperation surprised people for miles around Dadi Rapat. Why should the government care if these people didn't take the wage they were offered? Yet, the local authorities were visibly rattled by this non-cooperation. The 'rebel' workers were often seen protesting in front of the SDM's office in Bhim. Newspapers carried regular reports on the struggle for minimum wages. And the Devdoongri family knocked at the highest doors in the bureaucracy demanding answers.

The bureaucracy, they found, treated such works as a kind of dole intended to ward off starvation and chose to ignore the Minimum Wages Act of 1948. By paying less, the bureaucrats argued, more people get at least a minimum resource. But then, Chunnibai and many others retorted, '. . . you are not doing us a favour. Such famine works have always taken advantage of the exceedingly cheap and surplus labour available during droughts to build the infrastructure on which the economy runs.'

Of course, most people who toil at famine relief works do not see the work this way. At one time, even a latent firebrand like Chunnibai had seen her own work as worthless. If asked: 'What do you do?', most workers answered: 'I lift and throw mud.' The struggle at Dadi Rapat began to change this. It was not just a question of another two or three rupees. Chunnibai and others were as much convincing themselves about the worth of their labour as they were pressurizing the administration to recognize this and pay them the legal due.

For a year there was no breakthrough and the struggle at Dadi Rapat remained in limbo. Then, in April 1989, the famine commissioner was persuaded to visit the site along with the executive engineer, which in itself was an unprecedented event. When the commissioner agreed that an injustice had been done and Rs 11 must be paid to all, there was jubilation. Perseverance and determination had paid off.

A crushing disappointment then followed. In spite of this order, the irrigation department decreed that it would pay only Rs 9 and not a paise more. But, by then, the same struggle was being waged at virtually all the famine relief works in the area. As more and more people got involved, Minimum Wage became a political issue in that area. And this was only the beginning. Eventually a labour court decree gave Chunnibai and Bhanwar the full wage to which they were entitled.

The path from the road to the gulmohar house was now well marked. More people visited that house than any other in the shadow of the *dev doonger*. The family within could barely keep pace with the speed of events. They had been so sure that for at least a year or two they would just settle into the flow of everyday life and understand the concerns of people in the area. Making the house into a home had filled much of the first year in Devdoongri.

In that year Shanker and Anshi's eldest daughter, Kammo, qualified in the entrance exam of the newly opened Navodaya Vidyalaya in neighbouring Ajmer district. Neelu and Vikas, her younger siblings, settled into the local school a short bus ride from Devdoongri. Anshi emerged as the chief of domestic logistics, with the rest of the household dutifully performing their assigned tasks. It was Anshi who fielded the intense curiosity of neighbours. Perhaps Anshi was the one member of this household that the neighbouring women felt was closest to being like them.

The events at Sohangarh and Dadi Rapat had dissolved all plans to just flow with the local current. The friendships forged by this family were releasing energies that altered the nature and strength of the current. Within three years of their arrival at Jait Singh's empty house, the ripples of these energies were shaking up life in Bhim.

## Mazdoor Kisan Shakti Sangathan: a dream takes shape

Bhim, the *kasba*, has nothing in common with its giant-like namesake, the second Pandu brother. It has a population of about 15,000 and serves as a negligible watering stop on the national highway No. 8. But it is important as a local market centre for a few score villages located in an area that touches the four districts of Rajsamand, Pali, Ajmer and Bhilwara. A sub-divisional headquarter, Bhim is the kind of nondescript posting that most government officers try to avoid.

The dull uneventful life of Bhim was disturbed on 1 May 1990, when a stream of over 1,000 people, marching in an orderly double file, swept into the town shouting slogans:

*'Mazdoor Kisan Shakti Sangathan—Zindabad, Zindabad!* (Long live the Mazdoor Kisan Shakti Sangathan!').

*'Jab tak bhookha insan rahega, dharti par toofan rahega,* (As long as people are hungry, the storm of struggle will continue)'.

*'Bhrashtachar—Hai, Hai,* (Corruption: Down, Down)'.

*'Nyaya-samanta ho aadhar, aisa rachenge hum sansar,* (We

will forge a world rooted in the principles of justice and equality)'.

The slogan which sent shivers up many a shopkeeper's spine was: '*Yeh badi havellian kiski hain—hamari hain, hamari hain*, (Whose are these big houses: Ours, Ours)'. This was probably also what later earned the Devdoongri activists the label of 'Naxalites'.

There was Lal Singh, ever calm, slowly marching along, sometimes stopping to just watch the gathering and reflect. Mishraji's ever-purposeful stride had an added briskness that day and a veritable bounce of excitement. Who would have thought that the International Labour Day could take this form in *Bhim*? Somewhere towards the latter end of the procession was Aruna walking with the women, happily shouting slogans, watchful of how the *morcha* passed through the marketplace. Shanker was roaming the length of the procession, leading the slogans.

Earlier that morning hundreds of people had gathered under a tent, pitched on a *maidan* just outside Bhim, and founded the Mazdoor Kisan Shakti Sangathan (MKSS). Banners carrying the carefully designed black-and-red emblem of the Sangathan were fluttering along the length of the procession. The MKSS emblem showed two fists, one male and one female, raised in unison.

Where did this orderly gathering suddenly spring from, many spectators wondered. What most people in Bhim did not know was that for several weeks before that festive day, a team of fifteen men, including Shanker, Devi Lal, Lal Singh and Nikhil, had taken a *nukkad natak*, street play, to twenty-seven villages spread over the districts of Rajsamand, Ajmer and Bhilwara. Shanker and the team had improvised small skits which ingeniously depicted the nascent struggles over land and minimum wages, and showed why a sangathan had become necessary. United in action and purpose the people would have some hope of trying to cure the government's chronic deafness and figure out how their village should be developed. The crowd that gathered in a *maidan* on the edge of Bhim on 1 May, came partly in response to this travelling play.

'This work we have taken up is not some individual work, it is common to people all over the world,' Devaram of Dhapda village was telling the inaugural gathering of the Sangathan. A sangathan like this was necessary, others added, because none of the existing institutions—jati panchayats, political parties, religious organizations, government agencies, village panchayats—could help them fight for justice. The 1000-odd people who had come together to form the Sangathan were defying the pervasive feeling within their communities that ordinary villagers couldn't change anything.

Tej Singh, an elderly friend and mentor of Lal Singh, had once single-handedly fought Hari Singh years ago. Now he leaned heavily on his stick and spoke with fervor: 'I am with you even if I can't walk.' As though smiling at his own missing teeth and grey, frail countenance, he said: 'Never fight for yourselves but for your neighbour. He is not human who can sleep while his neighbour remains hungry.'

Surinder, from the village of Kalalia, in Pali district., spoke of the chain of misery that runs from here to the city. A worker at the Jawaja Centre of the SWRC, Surinder said: 'We don't want to leave this area and go out; we must get work here so we don't have to work ourselves to death in the mines of Bijolia.' 'Once dacoits lived in jungles, now they live in bungalows,' said someone else. Another person recalled history and drew inspiration from Gandhiji's call for a united struggle against British rule.

Chunnibai went behind the mike and delivered her life's maiden speech, with her *ghungat* falling almost to her waist, clenched fist confidently raised in the air. A stranger observing the gathering could have mistaken her for a seasoned 'pro'.

Then there was Chunni Singh, with the stride of a valorous soldier and deep facial scars to match. Chunni Singh came from Palona, a village some forty kilometres on the road towards Beawer. As a boy he had once worked in wayside dhabas. As soon as he was big enough to lift weights, he had found work at a construction site in Rawatbhata, earning twenty-five paise a day. The scars on his face were the remnants of the fights he kept getting into, often on a point of principle.

Chunni Singh could easily have used his courage and daredevil ways to become a local bully. He chose instead to be a kind of Robin Hood. While he worked in Gujarat, Chunni had often waylaid and threatened mill-owners and managers to ensure that the workers were paid their dues.

Stories about the Devdoongri family had slowly filtered through to Palona and Chunni Singh had felt drawn towards them. Now, he was wrapping up the Sangathan's inaugural meeting and preparing the mood for the procession: 'The administration oppresses people; let us reverse that. Now we march into Bhim to tell the people who are not with us and ask them to join.'

That day, members of the new-born MKSS formally pledged themselves to diligently struggle for a full minimum wage and resolved to accept nothing less. But the Sangathan's concern was not to be limited to minimum wages. It also resolved to struggle against corruption and exploitation. Development work for any village should be decided upon by the people of that village. The Sangathan demanded that the government must provide productive work for people near their own village. The government must also ensure proper health and educational facilities.

The *vishal*, grand, public meeting in the Bhim bazaar placed all these issues before the people of the town. As Mishraji rose to address the rally, most of his acquaintances expected a revolutionary 'communist' message. But Mishraji spoke simply of a struggle by ordinary people, against the structure that makes good men corrupt. 'Let us rise,' he urged, in his usual fiery manner, 'against the everyday corruption all around us.'

There was, of course, the soft-spoken Lal Singh, who as always looked both shy and quietly confident: 'We people have longed to do something like this but always hesitated. With some suggestions and encouragement now we have started this . . . Yes, we are all harassed about poverty but none of us can do anything alone.'

The meeting ended in a jubilant mood. Somewhere in the dispersing crowd was a slightly hunched-over Mot Singh, who had watched the event from the fringes. He wasn't one to take a lead or shake things up himself. But he offered a graphic justification for the Sangathan: 'All parties throw us a stone coated with jaggery and expect us to keep sucking it happily. As long as we do that, nothing will happen. We must throw away that stone and form a people's party.'

### Hunger strike: a singing dharna

Narayan was in tune with this perception. But he disagreed with his uncle's decision to distance himself from sangathan-like actions. Narayan found joy in being with his now well-known neighbours. Like his friend Devi Lal, Narayan found a reflection of his own dreams in the ideas and actions that flowed through the home with the gulmohar. So he decided not to go down the black tarred road like his cousin, Mot Singh's son. He completed school, with some tutoring from Nikhil. Then he gave more and more of his time to the Sangathan's work.

Soon, Devi Lal and he were working together on many errands and duties. Narayan found that this growing friendship bothered his mother and father. For them, the sangathan and all that was fine so long as it occupied its own limited place but it just wasn't done to eat and drink with Devi Lal. Ram Singh, Narayan's father, enjoyed considerable power and influence within the hamlet of Devdoongri. It was unacceptable that his own son should be breaking basic rules. Thus, sometimes Narayan was forced to listen patiently as his father urged him to give up all this work. At other times, Narayan tried to explain to his father the needs of changing times. But, finally, Narayan did just what he thought was necessary.

There was clearly no danger of the *tehsil* headquarters being stormed. But the SDM was taking no chances. The heavy iron-bar gates of the *tehsil* office were shut tight at night. But the two harmless-looking police constables on an all-night vigil were more often than not to be found under the tent protecting the MKSS dharna, where merry singing continued late into the night. This was no ordinary late-night *bhajan-mandali*. The tent beside a grand old tree, sheltered fourteen men and three women of the MKSS who had been on a hunger strike for five days by then. The strikers ranged in age from young Devi Lal to the wrinkled Bhuriya. All the strikers had worked on some famine relief site and been denied the full minimum wage. They were determined not to eat or leave that spot till their full wage was paid.

During the day there were speeches and *krantikari* songs

to keep the public's attention focused on the dharna. This was no sleepy dharna like the ones people were used to seeing, where the agitators idled away time playing cards or dozed in defiance of buzzing flies. The MKSS volunteers kept the dharna site alive by using their collective talents to inform, communicate, and attract others to the cause. In the process, some of the most powerful communication and experiences were being forged. Some of the most enduring and effective songs and skits evolved during such dharnas.

'Why this struggle?' a hand-bill of the Sangathan asked in bold letters. The wafer-thin hand-bills, printed on cheap pink paper, were circulating all over Bhim. The question was answered by a brief and succinct statement of how workers were made to toil all day without any assurance of how much they would earn. The dharna had three demands: payment of full minimum wage; the wage criteria must be either time rate or piece rate; the work must be measured on individual and not group basis.

With each new day, Shanker became more frantic. He began to wish that he was the one on hunger strike. Watching Nikhil, Bhuriya and others starve was much harder than running around managing the logistics. Jait Singh, the Devdoongri family's landlord, was otherwise never very involved in the Sangathan. But he couldn't bear to see these people starving. From the third day he just sat at the dharna-site all day and stopped eating.

Many residents of Bhim watched the event closely, quite sure of finding that the strikers were sneakily eating on the side. Some doctors, apparently impressed by the cause, offered to file false reports and urged the strikers to take some nourishment. As it became clear that these strikers were truly hungry and simply would not cheat, emotions began mounting among the townsfolk.

Slowly, and at first imperceptibly, the hunger strike was changing the Sangathan's relationship with the town of Bhim. The stoic perseverance of the starving protesters gave the Sangathan more prestige in the eyes of bystanders who might not have been very impressed by the 1 May rally, a few months earlier. The Sangathan succeeded in also widening the issue by emphasizing that poor wages also mean poor purchasing power.

On the sixth day of the hunger strike, the shopkeepers and traders of Bhim held a meeting and declared their support for the dharna of the Mazdoor Kisan Shakti Sangathan. Their threat to observe a *bandh* the next day had the desired effect. The SDM immediately met a delegation of the strikers and agreed to pay the full wage to all workers within two days. Amid much jubilation the strike was then called off and all the strikers were lovingly fed fruit juice by their anxious *sathis*.

This promise was not, however, fulfilled and the Sangathan learnt an important lesson. A year later, in April 1991, they again chose the 'weapon' of hunger strike and this time refused to get up till they actually had the wages in hand. By then the administration had also geared itself to handle such strikes. On the fifth day they lifted the five strikers and force-fed them. Aruna and Mamta Jaitly, an active supporter of the Sangathan from Jaipur, replaced the strikers. After two more days, the strike was converted into a dharna and eventually the full wages were paid.

Gradually, the Sangathan abandoned hunger strikes as a mode of protest because it created a desperate urgency to reach a settlement. Hunger strikes may be resorted to, they felt, only when no other peaceful means would work and the system is completely adamant. A hunger strike also required the protesters to have a strong moral authority for only then did it put pressure on both the administration and public.

In 1991, the struggle for minimum wages got a major boost when an article by journalist Usha Rai about events around Bhim, drew the attention of S.R. Sankaran, secretary, Rural Development in the Central government. Sankaran immediately sent a team to investigate the non-payment of minimum wages in Rajasthan. Payment of full minimum wages, Sankaran pointed out, was a condition of the Jawahar Rozgar Yojna, an important employment programme. As soon as the team submitted its report, Sankaran issued an order withholding a hundred crore rupees instalment of JRY funds to the Rajasthan government.

## Mazdoor Kisan Kirana: challenging the 'market'

The first light of dawn dappled playfully over the *chabutra* of the Devdoongri house. Anshi brought Kaliya the goat out of her room, which doubled as a bathing place for the family and tied her to the *babool* tree in the backyard. Nikhil sat hunched on the edge of the *chabutra* with a transistor held to his left ear trying to catch the BBC morning news. As Kaliya began nibbling on her breakfast of dry hay, the BBC Hindi service crackled to life and announced great changes in distant *Roos* (Russia). Nikhil didn't hear the swinging wooden gate of their compound bang shut or see Narayan quietly saunter in and sit close by, intent on picking up the radio news. The great USSR was falling apart and it was not going to be a *samajwadi* country any more.

As soon as the news bulletin ended Nikhil switched off the transistor and got up to share the morning news with the rest of the household. Anshi had just finished sweeping the kitchen. Vikas was preparing to go to school. Shanker had just returned from the well with a pot of water. The, as yet, imperceptible ripples of a big shift in history held their attention momentarily.

This will change things for all of us, Nikhil mused. How? asked Narayan. Now there is no challenge to the American capitalist system, and that is the way Manmohan Singh is also taking us, Nikhil said.

The year was 1992, the MKSS was just over a year old. All around it, in India and the world, history appeared to have gone into hyper-drive with the collapse of the Soviet Union. The waves of change rippled through Bhim with opponents of the MKSS mocking its activists saying—'your dreams have collapsed . . .', 'the communists are finished . . .', 'your party has lost . . . ', 'the free market has won . . .' Even if the comments of detractors were overlooked, very real problems loomed large. The new Narasimha Rao government was dramatically shedding even the half-hearted claims of India being a semi-socialist state. Now, there was a 'new economic policy' based on the belief that the profit motive and the private sector offered the only solutions for India's economic ills. And then there was also news of an amorphous entity called GATT. It seemed that this would affect everyone, but just how was difficult to understand sitting in Sohangarh or Bhim.

Yet, some things were clear enough. When she heard about the Indian government taking big foreign loans, Chunnibai asked: 'You told me that I should not pawn my jewellery and mortgage my land. I know and you know too that it leads to complete slavery, bondage and economic servitude. How come the "intelligent" leaders have done the same to the country? Can you explain such conduct?'

Chunnibai would have been even more baffled if she could have fully deciphered the 'double-speak' of the rulers. For even while the 'new economic policy' dropped old socialist jargon, it still claimed to eventually benefit all. As Aruna saw it, if one took the government's declared intentions seriously, then it would appear to be spearheading a revolution against itself. For most of its actual functioning and effect were the very opposite of all the socially-radical jargon in which its documents were framed.

However baffling and overwhelming the forces of history may sometimes seem, the discussions at the Sangathan's internal meetings always reaffirmed a simple faith that the motive of collective welfare can mobilize many more people than private gain. This is how we would like things to be, many wondered, but can it actually work?

The Sangathan's third birth anniversary brought on a new kind of excitement. Let us not have just the usual rally and speeches, many Sangathan workers suggested. Let's make it a *mazdoor mela* where the fun and frolic of a fair mixed with politics. So there were stalls selling *jalebis, pakoras, kulfi,* other sweets and tea at half the market price but of better quality. Inexpensive clothes were available at rates offered to wholesalers in distant towns. And all this enterprise was run by MKSS members on a no-profit basis.

Along with these shops were stalls with information about labour rights. During the public meeting, people were urged to give their opinions and suggestions on how the problems of the area and its people could be solved. There was a profusion of suggestions. Clearly, the will to change things was strong.

At that point the Sangathan also wanted to work with other groups to create the blueprint for an Employment Guarantee Act in Rajasthan. It hoped to do this by involving interested economists, academics and lawyers. But even the sympathizers advised that it would be impossible to press successfully for such an Act at that time. The Government of India's Secretary for Rural Development, S.R. Sankaran, had himself said as much when he visited Bhim in mid-92.

Under the Jawahar Rozgar Yojna (JRY), the country's largest employment programme, families below the poverty line were supposed to get at least a hundred days of employment. But such families were getting only six to fifteen days of employment in a year. Moreover, the World Bank was putting pressure on the Government of India to waive the protection of the Minimum Wages Act, for employment programmes.

Since the realm of policy-making was far beyond the Sangathan's influence, let alone control, it decided to tackle things closer to home. They could set up and run a fair price shop. They could take over a Public Distribution System outlet in Devdoongri village. Some could take up the manufacture of cement roof tiles, others could produce note books for children. Eventually, they might even set up labour cooperatives that could bid for road and building contracts.

They remembered Gandhi's words: 'No machinery in the world can compete with these villagers who need no other machine than their own willing hands and feet, and a few simple wooden instruments which they can devise themselves.' But how did this truth get translated into action on the threshold of the twenty-first century? Aruna and Nikhil travelled to the power centre in Delhi in search of sympathetic intellectuals. Among others, they found their concern echoed by L.C. Jain who explained that in India 'industrial development' has ignored the concept of 'industrialization'. Thus, artisan activity has never been recognized as industrial activity.

How to convert this understanding into action was the

most troubling question for the Sangathan's activists. They realized that it is not easy to simultaneously fight and create. Perhaps it is better to fight for the revolution now and implement change under more conducive conditions. But Aruna, Nikhil and Shanker were sure, as they later wrote, that:

> . . . The powerful networks that exist on the international plane make local spaces the best launching pads for a different ideology. When a variety of forces are being used to literally 'buy' the minds of people, action alone can speak louder than monetary power. Very often such creative action, which fundamentally questions the values of the establishment, is the most effective way to expose it. It is not enough to have collective strength. There is a need to understand how best to use that strength, to develop a paradigm which is particularly suited both to the collective, and the conditions which currently exist . . .
>
> . . . The principles underlying the MKSS's role as a protest and pressure group had to be transferred to its new function as an economic collective intervening in a conventional market, subject to all the forces which exist in a free-market economy. On the other hand, the MKSS is not a philanthropic organization. The MKSS does not see itself as doing *tyag* or *sewa*. Though this is how it is often described by some members of the dominant group. Because in so doing, the act is deprived of its intention to effect long-term change of a fundamental nature. More important, the MKSS presented an alternative value base. In this case the economic enterprises

were not set up for profit. The challenge was to have an alternative value base from which to operate and control economic relationships.

There was no way in which the Sangathan could alter the market forces which accept individual self-interest as a fundamental value. But it could act in ways that challenged and rejected these notions. This meant not only believing but also giving living proof of the imperative of collective interest through group action. How could self-interest and group interest be matched, related and connected?

Aruna had begun her education in the business of collective economic enterprises years ago when she ran the crafts centre at SWRC and worked with the leather craftsmen. That work had led her to the question:

> Why do we talk of the poor forming cooperatives to fight a capitalist market where everything is spelt out as individual profit and gain? As soon as the leather workers got some benefits, the cooperative's inner strength began cracking ... (thus) I learnt that no income generation activity could be scaled up. The artisans had to look for an outside market if they produced re-designed goods. The outside market demanded a pattern of marketing and credit in which the per-capita amount required was too high. Above all, income-generation activities of this sort emphasized individual profit. The incentive for production and income would therefore draw the craftsman away from making any kind of political demand locally, or even looking at local political-developmental needs. The Harmara leather workers have prospered, but their social

conscience for collective action has, if anything, come down. They are now ready to make charitable gestures, but cannot think of using their economic clout for real change in the village. . . . (Moreover) a venture that covered such a small proportion of the rural unemployed/under-employed enjoyed so much publicity and popularity just because it caters to the rich and elite. Employment and work cannot be reduced to handicrafts production and sale.

The entire ethos of the Devdoongri endeavour was quite different. In September 1992, the Sangathan held a three-day workshop of thirty of its active workers at the village Chapli, to decide on a course of action. So far the Sangathan had only taken up issues of collective protest and pressure on the development administration. Now, the Sangathan's leading workers were reflecting on how this collective strength could become the means of gaining at least a bargaining position in that larger 'market'.

The earlier struggles had already ensured that work was no longer considered just a drudgery to be endured in order to earn a few rupees. It was now part of a struggle for another way of life. 'This enabled people to rise in their own self-esteem and bring out their very best,' Aruna, Nikhil and Shanker wrote in 1993. 'Contributing to the general well-being of others has brought abundant confidence. It is this aspect, more than any other, that led the MKSS to believe that there is tremendous potential to form a new set of relationships through work.'

The question now was how to launch a venture which defied the concept of profit motive as the basic prerequisite for all enterprise. And this had to be done while ensuring that the Sangathan did not itself become a vested interest. So

the first safeguard was that the benefits remained open to all, that it benefited a large number of people and that entry into the new management group was not restricted. It was decided that the Sangathan:
– must take up economic activity in the mainstream;
– must ensure that capital is collected in a conventional manner without the component of grants, etc., though soft loans may be necessary;
– institute various controls to ensure that there was no misappropriation in such a venture;
– the enterprise should be labour intensive, not harm the environment, provide benefit to the poor of the area, be collective in nature and management.

There were a number of specific suggestions on the kinds of businesses the Sangathan could enter into—a fair price shop, a roof tile-making unit and a ration shop. Why roof tiles? There had been a time when all homes in such villages were built at virtually no monetary cost. The rocks, used to make walls, were easily available, mud came from the local tank beds and roof tiles were made of fired clay and then rested on wooden rafters. But firewood was now scarce and most people could no longer make their own roof tiles. Most villagers still cannot afford the cement and concrete *pucca* structures. Thus, a silent housing crisis has crept up on thousands of villages like Devdoongri. If roof tiles could be cheaply and locally manufactured that would solve much of the housing problem.

So the Sangathan set up a committee to examine the viability of a collective tile-making business. It was estimated that if the Sangathan ventured into all these businesses, it would need a seed capital of around Rs 1.20 lakh. This was a large amount and there was no question of going to any of the funding agencies which are ever keen to give money to NGOs working for empowerment of the people. There was also no possibility of seeking a bank loan for such an unconventional venture. No, the money would have to come from within the community. The money was finally raised, from people in villages around Bhim, as interest-free loans for a period of two years. Two categories of contributors were created and the venture was made contingent on raising at least a thousand Rs 10 loans and a hundred Rs 100 loans.

The Sangathan raised about Rs 80,000 from about 2000 local villagers and another Rs 50,000 from fifty supporters in Jaipur, Delhi and other cities. The Mazdoor Kisan Kirana store opened in Bhim on 16 November 1992 with an investment of about Rs 1,30,000 and two full-time workers. Both of them had over five years experience in such a job. The shop provided cheaper, better quality groceries to the people of Bhim and surrounding villages and succeeded in earning the targeted net profit of 0.45 per cent. In the first year, the shop had a turnover of about Rs 36 lakh.

## Demolition in Ayodhya: A tough stand in Bhim

A *lathi*-wielding crowd of a few score men menacingly inched towards the Mazdoor Kisan Kirana store. Some of them carried saffron flags and shouted slogans pledging their loyalty to the cause of Hindu Rashtra. They approached the Sangathan's store with a mixture of aggression and uncertainty.

While the Sangathan and its community had been busy with the excitement of the Kirana store, history was quietly moving towards an event that momentarily overshadowed all happenings on the Indian subcontinent. The newspapers had been reporting the assembly of thousands of *kar sevaks* in Ayodhya for the 'liberation' of the place known as

Ramjanmabhoomi. Even sleepy Bhim had contributed a handful of *kar sevaks* to the boiling cauldron of Ayodhya. But most people in Bhim paid scant attention to these developments. Waves of propaganda about the Ramjanmabhoomi campaign had swept through towns like Bhim, all over North India, several times since 1989. So plans for yet another *kar seva* seemed routine.

But on the afternoon of 6 December 1992, there was a buzz in the Bhim bazaar about an assault on the medieval structure of the Babri Masjid in Ayodhya. Most people thought that the *kar sevaks* had once again climbed atop the mosque and made a few holes in it. This had happened before in 1990. Certainly, no one expected to awaken on 7 December to find the radio reporting that the Babri Masjid had been completely razed to the ground and the rubble cleared away.

The news ripped through the Devdoongri household like the shockwaves of a shattering blast. Stunned disbelief was followed by anger and then a gnawing sadness. It felt like a death in the family. But there was no time to mourn. There might be trouble in Bhim, so enough members of the Sangathan must stay near the Mazdoor Kisan Kirana store. By afternoon all the Left political parties and trade unions had called a national bandh, on the next day, to condemn the demolition of the Babri Masjid. For the first time since it had opened, about three weeks earlier, the Sangathan's store downed its shutters on 8 December. It was the only shop in Bhim to join the anti-demolition bandh.

The rest of the Bhim bazaar was shut on 9 December, in response to the national bandh called by the BJP and its pro-demolition allies. The BJP workers found ready support from most of the traders. They knew the Mazdoor Kisan Kirana store would pose a problem and so they approached it gingerly. About twenty Sangathan members were assembled at the store in anticipation. A blackboard outside the shop still carried the earlier day's notice explaining that the Sangathan was joining the national bandh in order to condemn attacks on *all* places of worship.

The group of bandh-promoters stopped outside the shop and requested that the Mazdoor Kirana show solidarity with the rest of the marketplace which was now shut. But we closed yesterday, the shop workers explained. A moment of uncertainty followed. Then the BJP workers moved on, either because they weren't spoiling for a fight or due to the poor odds of winning a tussle with such impassioned opponents. And so the Mazdoor Kirana, which stayed open, was gradually joined by a couple of other shops. By late afternoon a good part of the Bhim bazaar was doing business as usual.

This fleeting incident had a lingering political impact. It established the Sangathan's presence as a strong force that others hesitated to challenge. But it was in the economic arena that the Mazdoor Kisan Kirana store really created a minor storm in Bhim. Its mere presence was disturbing enough to the rest of the market, but in addition it also announced its low prices over a loudspeaker all day long. Some of the shopkeepers tried to counter this by installing a rival loudspeaker that blared music at a much louder volume. But this battle of the loudspeakers only drew more attention to the Sangathan's shop.

Within three months, prices in the Bhim market fell by ten to fifteen per cent. A kilogram of edible oil was now cheaper by Rs 3, jaggery was cheaper by fifty paise and sugar by seventy-five paise per kg. The activists of the Sangathan beamed with pride. They had proved that the market could be used to benefit the poor. They felt that the shop also overturned the notion common among the upper classes that the poor are incapable of managing money and running a business.

The panic-stricken Vyapari Mandal of Bhim decided to boycott the Mazdoor Kisan Kirana store and instituted a fine of Rs 5051 on any wholesaler who did business with the Sangathan shop. But the boycott was virtually impossible to enforce. Six months later, a second shop was opened in Jawaja, some twenty-five kilometres away and soon after that another one at Brar.

Reporting on these shops in the *Economic Times* in May 1993, Bharat Dogra wrote that the shops had finally shown a way out for the small and marginal farmers who had to sell their produce cheaply and buy their basic necessities at high prices. But the activists were painfully aware of the limitations of such a venture. As they told Dogra:

> We have tried to step out into finding ways around the middlemen in the larger wholesale market, but we have found ourselves out of our depths. Nevertheless, there is a determination to persevere. We know that the larger markets are even more manipulative than the ones in Bhim. We have seen the stranglehold middlemen have on them. But we have seen that exposing the internal contradictions of a so-called free market is a very effective path to a greater share for its exploited 'consumers'.

For the Sangathan, the greatest satisfaction lay in its having taken such a big risk and succeeded. The highest stake in the Kirana stores venture was not money but the hard-earned credibility of the Sangathan, which had till then never dealt directly with money. It never paid people's fare to come to meetings nor served free meals. It had deliberately chosen not to acquire any assets and remained poor like its members. The Sangathan had no vehicles, no office, no affluent contributors, nor any conventional political aspirations. The shops were the first venture in which the Sangathan had paid workers.

Thus, underlying the excitement over the shops had been a great sense of trepidation. There was the risk of bankruptcy, of dishonesty among those who worked at the shop. But the shops worked and thus became a quantum leap in the growth of all involved, particularly for the collective persona of the Sangathan.

Six months later, Chunni Singh attempted to explain the importance of the shops to the crowd of spectators gathered around the May Day rally at Bhim. He called upon the local traders not to see the shops run by the mazdoors as a threat, but to see themselves as victims of a system that would soon finish off the small traders, so that only 'bigger *seths*' would prosper.

Mot Singh was by then a veritable skeleton, watching these developments from the sidelines. It took Nikhil and Shanker several weeks, working in tandem with 'Mehsus Ba', to persuade Mot Singh to see a doctor in Beawer. Knowing that 'Mehsus Ba' was Mot Singh's mocking and affectionate distortion of 'Mrs' was the signal of an outsider's proximity to the man and his special lexicon. The doctor in Beawer confirmed what many people in Devdoongri had long suspected. Mot Singh was suffering from tuberculosis. Over the years, Mot Singh's racking cough had worsened, and his body was reduced to bare bones.

Mot Singh had never become actively involved in the

·Sangathan. But as a neighbour and friend he was part of the Devdoongri family's daily life. When some of his favourite visitors were around, he would amble over early in the morning with some *moolies* or corn from his field. So Nikhil and Shanker had an almost filial right to insist on taking Mot Singh to the hospital in Beawer. The doctors were not hopeful but offered various kinds of treatment that would keep Mot Singh at the government hospital in Beawer. No thanks, Mot Singh said firmly. He preferred to die in his own hut. His friends did not try to dissuade him. They knew that the ill-equipped and poorly-stocked public hospital would not offer much relief to Mot Singh. A few months later, he died quietly in his home beside the big tarred road.

Over the years, the Devdoongri family had seen many men in their forties and fifties return from the city, to die at home. But watching Mot Singh's premature end had brought them even closer to the pain. Aruna's reason and resolve to stay calm fought a losing battle with anger and sorrow. Every time she visited Delhi the media and corridors of power were ever more preoccupied with talk of Human Rights. But hunger and death due to poverty was not seen as a denial of rights. Now no one even mentioned poverty alleviation; instead, now there was only talk of 'social safety nets'.

Like millions of others all over India, Mot Singh had slipped through these invisible nets and fallen to a slow, early death. Most young men accepted this fate even as they struggled to somehow defy or delay its course. But for Narayan and Devi Lal there was a warning and inspiration even in the fading embers of each such life. They realized that only collective solutions could help build a better tomorrow. The success of the Mazdoor Kisan Kirana had sent their imagination and energies soaring over uncharted realms. Much more now seemed possible.

Why not devote this confidence to tackling corruption? This was the obstacle which uniformly thwarted the simplest aspirations. Under the Jawahar Rozgar Yojna every panchayat received over a lakh rupees annually, directly from the Central government. Why couldn't the people of each panchayat collectively compel the local officials to account for these funds?

## Public hearings: away with corruption

In the winter of 1994 a *natak mandali* of the Mazdoor Kisan Shakti Sangathan toured villages of the Kot Kirana panchayat of Pali district with the idea of organizing a *jan sunwai*, public hearing. It was already well known that this panchayat had the most daring cases of corruption relating to funds for public works. With their usual mixture of songs, skits and jokes, Shanker and his *mandali* gathered crowds in every village. They depicted the audiences' despair over the theft of money allocated for development projects in the village and presented their strategy to change this. For a start, the *natak mandali* suggested, we have to stop feeling helpless. Let us gather in a *jan sunwai*, a public forum, where we can share all available information about misdeeds in local works and then demand accountability from the officials.

On the appointed day, hundreds of people gathered under a tent pitched in the school compound of Kot Kirana village. The muster rolls of some recent works were read out and immediately there was an uproar. People rushed up to the mike to say that though their name was on that list they had not received a single day's employment. Some of the people named on the muster roll had been dead for years.

There was a unanimous demand that the gram sevak, who made the payments, and the junior engineer, who certified that work was done and payments made in his presence, both be taken to task.

When bills and vouchers for the unfinished *patwar ghar* in the village were read out there was uproarious laughter. The papers showed payments for roofing material, doors and windows, while the structure stood close by devoid of a roof and with gaping holes where doors and windows were shown on paper. As the laughter died down, anger took over. Soon after the public hearing, the acting BDO, an IAS officer under training, filed a First Information Report (FIR) against the junior engineer and the gram sevak. A few weeks later a *jan sunwai* in Bhim revealed the existence of a fraudulent company that had siphoned off Rs 36 lakh over one year, through illegal payments in just one block. The owners of the company were family members of the block officials.

Renuka Pamecha was an old hand at conducting public meetings. On 25 April 1996, she was chairperson of the fifth *jan sunwai*, held at village Thana in Bhilwara district. Renuka, an efficient housewife, mother and college teacher in Jaipur, had spent over twenty years fighting for the rights of women and helping other struggles for justice. She had just the presence needed for a credible chairperson of a *jan sunwai*. Her manner was firm, if necessary even loud, but never harsh. She was thoroughly earnest and yet the inherent humour of her smile kept her from seeming intimidating.

'Yes, there is a lot here to make us angry,' she spoke into the mike. 'But merely shouting will only make matters worse. Let us present all the details one by one and then decide what action should be taken. The *jan sunwai* is not a summary trial to be followed by an instant punishment'. The block development officer and gram sevaks, who were present, looked relieved by the reassurance. The officials had been ordered by their boss, an unusually sympathetic Collector, to attend this *jan sunwai*. It was the first time that local government functionaries were in attendance.

This was one of the several reasons why the *jan sunwai* at Thana evoked a special excitement. About three weeks earlier, the chief minister of Rajasthan, Bhairon Singh Shekhawat, had made a statement in the state Assembly that local government functionaries would have to make photocopies of all documents available to the people. That was partly why the BDO and his juniors were present. Even more importantly, the sarpanch of the Thana panchayat was an active member of the Sangathan. Ladu Singh was the first Sangathan activist who had successfully contested an election. This fifth *jan sunwai* also showed the maturity of the process. To a large extent the public hearings had been an experiment for the MKSS. But its foundational principles had been clear:
– the power, legitimacy and sanctity of the public hearings would emanate from the people, not from any judge or panel, and;
– the gathering would truly be a *hearing* and not a court or an agitational body. The priorities of the hearing would be set by the questions raised by the assembled collective.

On both these counts, the Sangathan could safely say it had succeeded. Yet, with the Thana *jan sunwai* the process also reached its limits in that particular phase. The five hearings had succeeded in attracting wide publicity, thanks to journalists who came from Jaipur, Udaipur and even Delhi and Mumbai. This was partly what compelled the chief minister to make that statement on the floor of the Assembly.

But meanwhile the local functionaries and bureaucrats at all levels also strengthened their resistance to this pressure to reveal documents. Even Ladu Singh, who as sarpanch was an elected representative of the village, could not get information from all functionaries in that panchayat. Merely a chief minister's statement was not enough. A formal written order was essential before government functionaries at all levels would cooperate with information seekers. A year later, in April 1996, the Government of Rajasthan had still not issued this order. The dharna in Beawer followed.

## Beawer dharna: struggle for the right to information

Beawer may not be very famous outside Rajasthan but it can lay claim to a modest share in the history of social struggles. Many of its citizens speak with pride about Shaheed Bhagat Singh and Chandra Shekhar Azad taking refuge in Beawer at the height of their struggle. This industrial town on the Delhi-Ahmedabad rail-line has also been a base for communist workers of various hues in Rajasthan. In 1994, the city saw a spontaneous citizen's agitation when the water supply was cut off for a week.

The MKSS's dharna at the city centre, Chaang Gate, from 6 April 1996, must have initially seemed odd to the townsfolk. Here was a militant gathering of about 200 to 300 peasants, from a radius of about a hundred kilometres, who had no conventionally recognizable demands. They seemed to have no identifiable vested interest and were demanding neither food, nor shelter, nor clothing, nor wages, nor jobs. Of all things they wanted photocopies of records on the panchayat level government works. All day, and late into the night, they talked, sang and chanted about little else.

'*Sona chandi? Mein nahi maanga!* (Gold, silver? That's not our demand!)'.

'*Mota bangla? Mein nahi maanga!* (A big house? That's not our demand!)'.

'*Bangle mein gaadi? Mein nahi maanga* (A car in the house? That's not our demand!)'.

'*Gaadi mein kutta? Mein nahi maanga* (A dog in the car? That's not our demand!)'.

Finally the *sutradhar* would ask: 'So what do you want?'. Promptly came the answer:

'*Panchayat ka lekha jokha! Mein maanga* (Records of the panchayat—that's what I want)'.

'*Muster-roll ki copy! Mein maanga* (Copies of the muster rolls—that's what I want)'.

'Bill, voucher! *Mein maanga*'.

'Photocopy! *Mein Maanga*'. And so it went . . .

Within four or five days of this, people began to stop by to pick up literature and ask questions. They wanted to know more about the Mazdoor Kisan Shakti Sangathan, whose name was emblazoned on bright banners all over the dharna site. Why was this Sangathan demanding photocopies of government records? The answers came in many voices as each man or woman who sat in the dharna eagerly explained the purpose of their effort.

'You are demanding of a system of office, where rot has set in, that it place its soul before the people. The trouble is no one can refuse this demand—while at the same time giving you what you are asking for would (for the officials) be like committing suicide.' The speaker was one of the numerous citizens of Beawer who regularly visited the dharna, listened and added their voice from the podium of the dharna.

Just before sunrise, while most people at the dharna site were still sleeping, a man would arrive, sweep the dharna site clean, drop five rupees in the collection box and quietly leave. Another visitor, a young man who could only move about in a hand-operated tricycle, would come every day to listen for a while, deposit ten rupees in the kitty and return home.

For days the people of Beawer had watched simple villagers arrive from long distances carrying small, preciously assembled contributions of grain. Soon, a steady trickle of anonymous contributions began to flow to the dharna site from the citizens of Beawer. Vegetable vendors gave free vegetables. Poets composed poems, a band that used bagpipes regularly came to play in solidarity. Sign-painters did free banners. In all, the dharna collected Rs 46,000 in small cash contributions, gathered twenty quintals of wheat from surrounding villages, six quintals of vegetables and several trolleys of fuel wood. These resources were used to feed the 200 to 300 people who were steadily at the dharna site for almost six weeks.

On 14 April, the followers of Babasaheb Ambedkar gathered, as always, to celebrate his birthday in a public meeting at Chaang Gate. But they chose to use the same *pandal* in which the Sangathan's dharna was located. Thus, the SDM, who could not refuse to attend a celebration of Ambedkar Jayanti, found himself on the stage of the dharna, sharing a podium with Aruna Roy, who spoke on behalf of the MKSS. A fortnight later all the major trade unions of Beawer took an unprecedented decision to celebrate 1 May collectively at the dharna site, starting with a *prabhat pheri* early in the morning.

The popular support was due to the uniqueness of a

non-partisan agitation which made no demands for any one section of society, but asked for something that was common to all. Beyond the basic one point demand for photocopies was a more detailed frame of demands which every citizen related to and agreed with:

– social audit of all government works is essential;

– accounts must be made available in a detailed and systematic manner. Greater thought must be given to the form and procedure of such an audit as it has the potential of being far more effective than just the financial auditing;

– the presentation of these accounts and other information must explicitly be made the responsibility of a particular official;

– once misappropriation is proved, the *gram sabha* must have the powers to enforce corrective action;

– at the block and district levels there is need for larger forums for social audit because here questions relating to the nature of development programmes will also have to be discussed.

These demands seemed local but by logical extension they threatened the entire political status quo to its very core. The dharna was no longer local news. National television networks sent teams to cover it. Veteran journalists came to support and give their blessings. Prabhash Joshi, then editor of *Jansatta*, saluted the men and women of the dharna as the 'Rajas' of democracy demanding public accountability from the *sevaks*, ie. government servants. Nikhil Chakravorty, the editor of *Mainstream*, compared the demand for right to information with the national movement leaders' demand that the British account for every penny that they snatched away from India.

So, it was from a position of strength and confidence

that, four weeks later, the MKSS decided to intensify the pressure and start a second dharna at Jaipur. Now, the songs and jingling slogans of the MKSS wafted across the lawns of Statue Circle to the secretariat buildings close by. Ten days later, on 15 May, the government, in principle, conceded the demand for photocopies. A committee was appointed to work out the details. But the report of that committee was marked 'confidential'. Thus, the Sangathan braced itself for yet another pitched battle.

Eventually, on 15 July 1997, after over two years of struggle, the Government of Rajasthan finally issued a notification granting people access to copies of panchayat level records. For several months after that, district officials denied receiving the notification. So the Mazdoor Kisan Shakti Sangathan waited another six months. In January 1998 it held two public meetings, one at Kukarkheda and the other at Surajpura.

The Sangathan's triumph lay not merely in the fact of these public hearings where people came armed with xerox copies of relevant development records. The true test of its success was the smooth, polite and non-vindictive nature of the proceedings. Even as various frauds came to the surface, the guilty sarpanches were allowed to respond without heckling. Basanta Devi, the sarpanch of Kukarkheda, was compelled to admit, and apologize for, a fraud of one lakh rupees. She agreed to return the money to the panchayat's kitty.

At the time of these public hearings, India was preparing for its second mid-term poll in two years. Journalists covering these hearings wrote about them as evidence of democracy at the grassroots. For activists of the Sangathan this success was tempered by the sadness that such actions were not multiplying as far and wide as they hoped. Groups elsewhere were holding similar hearings, some on specific issues. But the possibility of a wave of public action, demanding accountability from those in power and challenging the status quo, still seemed like a dream.

## On the national stage: fame and challenge

Aruna looked exhausted. Stepping out of the second class compartment at the Mumbai Central station she and Nikhil joined the flow of passengers heading for the exit. By 1997 the Devdoongri family's life had changed dramatically. The quiet, slow-motion rhythm of Devdoongri or Sohangarh was now a memory. The fame of the Beawer and Jaipur dharnas in 1996 put the Sangathan on the national scene. Soon a National Campaign for the Right to Information had evolved. This kept Aruna and Nikhil on the road for most of the year. They travelled to different parts of India, meeting with other activist groups, journalists and policy-makers to build a movement for the Right to Information.

Aruna was never comfortable under the spotlights. But the very success of the Sangathan made this inevitable. The outside world did see her as the leader of the Sangathan, no matter how often she corrected people about this. So Aruna agonized over the public honours conferred on *her*. In late-96, a letter arrived in Devdoongri informing Aruna that a high powered jury, headed by the former Supreme Court Chief Justice, P.N. Bhagwati, had selected her for the Diwaliben Mehta Award.

'I cannot accept this award,' Aruna replied. 'However, if the award is given to the Sangathan it will be cordially accepted'. The sponsors of the award, a family of gems merchants, were astonished by the request but agreed to go along with it. They gladly offered to fly Aruna and one other person to the award function in Mumbai. Again, Aruna declined. Would it be okay, she asked, if instead eight people travelled second class by train to attend the function?

Lal Singh craned his neck to follow the full length of the skyward building of the Taj Hotel. All his life he had heard of the tomb at Agra. Now here, in Mumbai, was a hotel by the same name. Others in the animated group of visitors had many questions. Did it really cost Rs 5000 to spend one night in the smallest room of this hotel? But Lal Singh just stood there and stared in a cold daze. He was happier being bundled into a taxi and going on to a press conference where they would tell the Mumbai journalists about the Sangathan's work. After all, *this* is what they were here for, not the bewildering wonders of Mumbai.

That evening Shanker went up on the stage of the plush Y.B. Chavan Auditorium in South Mumbai to receive the award, on behalf of the Sangathan, from the former President of India, R. Venkatraman. In his brief speech Shanker did not attempt to elaborate just how far the world of Devdoongri was from the reality of Mumbai that had put Lal Singh in a daze. Instead, Shanker briefly and sweetly conveyed a sentiment which many of his fellow-workers often voiced: 'Why can't we have a government that is really *ours*, the people's?'

**Gulmohar in bloom: expanding frontiers of the 'possible'**
Seen from a car or bus, zooming down that endless strip of tar, the scattering of homes below the *dev doonger* looked no different than it had ten years earlier. Those who lingered a bit might spy the fully grown gulmohar and the bamboo swaying in the breeze. Only those who lived there would

miss the presence of Mot Singh and his animated chatter as he rested by his well. Those rushing by would not notice the liveliness under the shade of the grand old neem tree. The Sangathan's office stood on the fringe of that shade and was often bustling with activity.

The phone at the gulmohar house was another never-before addition to Devdoongri. There was still no electricity in there. The evening hours were brightened by a solar-powered portable tubelight, gifted by a friend. Otherwise, the home of that unusual family looked much the same as it had when they first arrived there. It was the people who had changed.

Kammo and Neelu, Shanker and Anshi's daughters, were now young women in the final years of college. The once tiny Vikas was now a gangly teenager preparing to graduate from high school. Anshi worried even as she fended off family pressure to marry off her daughters. A college education for girls was unheard of in their entire clan. The older and more educated they became, the harder it would be to find them husbands, Shanker's mother wailed persistently.

Shanker's effervescence remained undiminished through all the problems and tensions, whether at home or in the Sangathan. The expanding activities around Devdoongri and outside, over ten years, kept him merrily energized, thus preserving his boyish buoyancy.

Nikhil seemed like a fully naturalized villager. He now felt somewhat out of place in the plush urban social setting into which he was born. If a Lal Singh or Narayan felt a strong sense of identity with Nikhil, it was because they had shared so much of each other's daily and mundane existence. The drama and excitement of work in the

Sangathan was an added joy, but not the foundation of their friendship.

Some lives were entirely transformed. Ten years earlier Devi Lal would have found it difficult to imagine that he could get a college degree and even aspire to become a lawyer.

Narayan had been resigned to attaining the humble status of a '10th fail'. Being a '10th pass' was important to Narayan but it was a small part of the experiences that made him a confident young man.

In 1996, Narayan had enjoyed a visit to Mumbai, where he and Shanker attended a meeting of activists from rural Maharashtra. Narayan was brimming with an intensely intelligent curiosity about the workings of the stock exchange, the Reserve Bank of India and notorious personalities like Harshad Mehta. Narayan had come a long way from the awkward boy who had diffidently hung around the house with the gulmohar. But like Shanker and Lal Singh, he was eager to leave the big city and get back, down the black tarred road, to his own home.

Narayan and Devi Lal happily worked together, taking on more and more vital duties within the Sangathan. They learnt to simply ignore their families' disapproval of such a camaraderie across caste lines. But their growing confidence and joy was clouded by the constant awareness that other young men in countless villages like Devdoongri were still caught in the sapping gravitational pull of that black tarred road. Both of them were aware that much more needed to be done in countless villages like Devdoongri.

This occasional gloom was pierced by stubbornly persistent rays of hope. What once seemed impossible was already a reality. They now *knew* that the frontiers of the possible are never fixed. Constantly stretching these frontiers was now both the goal and a way of getting there. It is this timeless journey to which the *dev* atop that little hill, stands as an aloof sentinel. Yet perhaps, sometimes, when a Nikhil or Narayan goes by, even this detached witness rejoices.

\*

*The mid-morning sun was streaming through the back door of Bapu Kuti. Aruna and I entered through the other door and lingered for a few brief moments before heading on to a meeting. Over the years Aruna often told me of her many differences with Gandhi. But the austere simplicity of Gandhi's life touched her deeply. The beauty and power of these qualities always energized her. Now, as we passed through the Kuti, none of this needed saying.*

*We walked a few score yards to a long hall at one end of the Sewagram Ashram. There the first national convention of the Rural Workers Campaign was about to begin. About 300 activists, representing a wide variety of political action groups, non-governmental organizations and trade unions, had assembled to launch an ambitious campaign in November 1995.*

*Together they hoped to fight for the rights of India's rural labour force. This task has never been easy. The liberalization and globalization policies since the early-90s made it even harder. As distant market forces make deeper inroads, people have less and less control over their natural resource base. Their struggle for survival has, therefore, become much harder. Thus, the convention included activists who were fighting for the land rights of the landless and others who are opposing projects which led to privatization of common property resources.*

*Aruna was part of a small group of activists who had worked for over a year and a half to draft a charter of demands and launch* the Rural Workers' Campaign. The charter echoed the needs of groups like Mazdoor Kisan Shakti Sangathan. Among other things, it demanded enforcement of minimum wage laws, access to information, community-based control over local natural resources, effective land reforms and adequate health, education and housing facilities in villages.

Even as this charter of demands was forwarded to the Central government, some activists wondered if this was an effective mode of action. Without mass mobilization at the ground level, such a charter could wind up being a mere token. Such methods do not even begin to challenge the distant economic forces which are setting the terms of even the smallest local 'market'. So what do we do?

There are no clear answers to this question, only a determined groping for answers. Thus, a Lal Singh listens patiently to all the analytical and strategic wranglings at such meetings and then voices a simple hope. Perhaps, some day, a local success like the Mazdoor Kisan Kirana stores can be a reality at the larger level. 'Can't we find a way' Lal Singh asks wistfully, 'of somehow creating our own "market" where the small producer or cultivator like me can trade directly with others like myself and keep the big merchant out?'

# T. Karunakaran
## From 'Worryland' to 'Merriland'

*Bapu Kuti was playing host to friends old and new. They sat in small clusters under the generous shade of the trees planted half a century ago by Mahatma Gandhi and his friends. Even as meetings at Sewagram Ashram go, this one had an exceptionally varied mix of persons. There were scientists, philosophers and aging Gandhi-lovers from at least three continents. A large contingent of peace activists had come from Italy. There were a few, young, khadi-clad Americans on a Gandhi pilgrimage who had just stumbled upon the international gathering. And there were a few score young Indian students and activists.*

*Among them was the frantically busy Professor T. Karunakaran. The short, wiry and ever-beaming 'Karuna' had devoted several months to help organize this international conference in January 1993. The event was commemorating the birth centenary of Joseph Cornellius Kumarappa, the Gandhi-inspired economist who wrote about an 'economy of permanence' four decades before 'sustainable development' became a fashionable term. Karuna was there to render service to the memory of his 'guru' and exchange working notes with kindred spirits on how the economy of permanence can be a reality in the twenty-first century.*

*Amid technologies created for rapid obsolescence and*

*economies thriving on waste, how did Karuna have the confidence to insist that an economy of permanence is not only possible but imperative and even inevitable? For one, he sees the world quite differently. What are generally seen as 'developed' and 'developing' countries he sees as 'ruined countries and racing-to-be-ruined countries'. Karuna has a complex formula for how India can opt out of this race.*

*This formula relies neither on state-run development programmes nor on the Wall Street variety of 'market'. The answer, Karuna believes, lies in social entrepreneurship which would tap the creative energies of the 'last man'. The essence of Karuna's dream is conveyed by the name of the schools he initiated—Mazhalaipoonga, which means Merriland in Tamil 'as opposed to hurry-land and worry-land which is what most of life is becoming.'*

*To understand the origins of Karuna's Merriland dream we need to travel back in time to a thatched roof home which in its simplicity and austerity may not have been very different from Bapu's kuti or Kumarappa's mud home, still preserved at Maganwadi, Wardha.*

\*

## Poovenkudi

T. Karunakaran and free India were both infants at the same time. Karuna arrived in this world on the day after Christmas in 1946, just eight months before that fateful midnight's hour when India kept her 'tryst with destiny'. He was born the son of a marginal farmer in Poovenkudi, a village about eighteen kilometres from the town where the goddess Kanyakumari presides over the southern-most tip of the subcontinent.

The family elders told little Karuna stories about how

their ancestors had fallen foul of the Travancore rulers some centuries ago. Since then their *jati* had been relegated to the lowest rungs of the social hierarchy. Both men and women were forbidden to wear cloth above the waist and were compelled to render several free services to the upper castes. Thirumalayaperumal, Karuna's father, added to his meagre farm income by collecting and selling coconuts. Like all marginal farmers, Karuna's parents lived in a wood and bamboo house with a thatched roof. His mother, Muthulakshmi, would spin cotton yarn on a charkha. It was Karuna's job to carry the yarn to the khadi centre, where it was woven into cloth.

The 1950s were filled with an optimism which made little boys like Karuna different from their ancestors. Sure, the boys still took the cattle out for grazing every day but this generation also went to school. Sometimes the boys would herd the sheep into a small valley, from which the grazing animals could not stray. This left them free to play. They would go leaping from tree to tree. The boy who managed to climb the highest branch would win the right to question the others about lessons learnt at school. That was the beginning of Karuna's learning. His father and mother, like their forefathers before them, had never learnt to read or write. So, when young Karuna went way beyond becoming merely literate and turned out to be a brilliant student, his whole clan felt proud. Karuna was the first person in his community to enter an engineering college.

## College in Madurai

While Karuna was studying for a Bachelor's degree at the Tyagaraja Engineering College in Madurai, independent India was preparing to celebrate the birth centenary of the father of the nation. Mahatma Gandhi was not new to Karuna. All through school Karuna had been winning prizes and these were usually books by or on Gandhi and Acharya Vinoba Bhave. Once he got over his initial awkwardness in the big-town culture of the college, Karuna led a Gandhi study circle which set about making a critical assessment of the Mahatma.

Along the way he also read Karl Marx and was not terribly impressed. But, Karuna discovered within himself a natural socialist. It was Gandhi's concern for *daridra-narayan*, the last man, which brought together the Gandhi study circle of about forty young men. As Karuna later recalled: 'We were putting Gandhi in the dock and yet trying to inherit him.'

Preparations for the Gandhi centenary brought Jayaprakash Narayan to Madurai for a consultative meeting at the Gandhi Museum. Karuna and about thirty other members of the Gandhi study circle gatecrashed into the meeting where elderly speakers were droning on and on, heaping the usual floral and verbal tributes on the Mahatma.

Suddenly Karuna could bear it no longer. He sprang to his feet and shouted: 'Is this any way to celebrate the Gandhi centenary? We should be planning action in the villages. That is what Gandhi wanted us to do.' Later Karuna was surrounded by fellow-students congratulating him for saying what they felt. The next day, 'I faithfully took all my corps to JP, I used to adore all such people. JP administered an oath to us (the students) that we won't take a dowry when we marry,' Karuna recalls wistfully.

Karuna's other passion at that time was Hindi. In spite of the Tamil Nadu government's ban on teaching Hindi in schools, Karuna learnt the language and stood first in the Rashtrabhasha exam of the Dakshin Bhasha Hindi Prachar

Sabha. But at the same time, he opposed the violent and arrogant imposition of Hindi by the north. So when 25 January 1964, was observed as an anti-Hindi protest day, Karuna was out on the streets, wearing a black suit, and agitating. The prize-winning student of Hindi became one of the first persons to be wounded by the police and hospitalized in the anti-Hindi agitation.

## On to the Delhi IIT

The spontaneous group of young Gandhi enthusiasts at the Tyagaraja College scattered after graduation. But the trajectory of Karuna's life was more or less fixed. By now he had begun to build his vision of 'World Citizenship—outside casteism and above religion'. It bothered him that free India had failed to provide '*roti, kapda, makan*'—food, clothing and shelter—to all its citizens. Karuna suspected that this was partly because the Indian psyche was too deeply trapped in fatalism and the *varnashram* to visualize a truly equal society. Karuna was always sad to see questions about religion and caste on any application form. He unfailingly answered such questions with one word—'Nil'.

When Karuna had first nervously showed up at the engineering college in Madurai someone asked him if he had also applied to the Indian Institute of Technology (IIT). Karuna had no idea what that was. Four years later, Karuna knew about the prestigious IITs and was ready to seek admission there. Having gained entrance to the M.Tech course at the Delhi IIT, Karuna travelled north for the first time.

In the urban ambience of the nation's capital Karuna looked, and was made to feel, the odd one out. He was the small-town chap other students found strange and made fun of. Most of the other students were urban middle-class youth with B.Tech degrees from the same IIT. The way Karuna dressed, spoke and thought was all out of tune with the en route-to-USA culture of most of his fellow students:

> While most of the other students studied the subjects merely from an examination point of view, I was interested in pushing the discussion either to the foundations or to the frontiers. I even had an on-going dialogue with a senior professor on the philosophical approach to the subject. This made the other 'elitist' students jealous and some of the teacher-candidates were frustrated. Then two strongly-built students were made to sit on either side of me and whenever I stood to ask a question I was pulled down.

But his tenacity did not go unnoticed or unrewarded. Within three months, a renowned professor was guiding him personally. No one laughed when Karuna was elevated directly to the Ph.D programme, without completing the M.Tech degree.

Karuna took a Ph.D in systems engineering with special focus on mathematical system theory. His Ph.D examiner, a famous systems philosopher from the University of California at Los Angeles, deemed Karuna's thesis comparable to the best at Massachusetts Institute of Technology (MIT) or Cambridge. Endless possibilities in the West now beckoned him. Karuna was faced with a choice that most IIT graduates make at some point. Should he go to the West and work at the frontiers of theoretical science or should he stay in India? If he went to the USA, he could work in the field of artificial intelligence or systems modelling related to satellite launches, among other things.

But somehow the idea of going abroad held no special allure for Karuna. The one place he really wanted to visit was China, and no one was offering to send him there. Karuna's primary interest lay in what he considered 'more challenging development problems'. His systems training could as well be used in the socio-technical context to work out the systematic use of water resources, rural industrialization structures, employment development, people's action, etc. So, Karuna opted to stay in India and at the IIT, but focused his creative energies on villages and the millions who live as he had in childhood.

This did not stop opportunity from knocking—in his case more than once. But even as time went by, Karuna couldn't shake off the feeling that it would be 'funny' to go abroad to work on mathematics. 'India should be strong in mathematics even if not in instrument-oriented subjects,' he thought. So, after completing his Ph.D, Karuna became a visiting lecturer at the Mathematics Centre of Madurai University and later, in 1973, was a visiting fellow of the School of Mathematics of the Tata Institute of Fundamental Research, Mumbai.

Even while he worked on mathematical equations and formulas, Karuna's central preoccupation was the rural economy. Convinced that urbanization and urban-biased politics have wrecked the village economy, he sought pragmatic ways to counter this and achieve something. But achieve what? Years later, at the threshold of the twenty-first century, Karuna would reply in state-of-the-art terms: 'Sustainability, equity and a mutually nurturing co-existence.'

For this to be possible, people must be able to reach the

power centre and not merely be at its mercy. But how could this happen? As he searched for answers, Karuna found his most steady source of inspiration in Gandhi's disciple J.C. Kumarappa. 'My naive thoughts and vague theories always coincide with shadows of the profound poetic, philosophic thoughts of Kumarappa. I consider him my elder brother and I sincerely wish that his dream world should come true.' Yet Karuna was careful not to hero-worship his philosophical mentor. 'JCK', as Karuna refers to Kumarappa, 'was a die-hard idealist, totally uncompromising, while mine is a pragmatic utopia. JCK appeared to be a rational theist, I am a firm atheist.'

Before searching for solutions, Karuna attempted to understand why the simple vision of plenitude for all eludes modern society. This led him to identify a central villain, or 'poison', known as 'economies of scale':

The cost of a consumer product has two components: one, the fixed cost which includes overheads; and two, variable cost depending on the volume of production. 'Economies of scale' is the idea of increasing the volume of production with a view to reducing the overhead cost per unit and also to enhance quality. The increased volume of production, presided over by machines, and the resulting need for marketing, suited the colonial powers but it is totally unsuited to a country like India. The 'high volume production' is logical where raw materials are brought from outside to *a* point and then the finished products are shipped off to other countries—at the same time reducing the labour needed, through mechanization and automation. But in our country these high-volume industries would mean more transport of raw materials and re-transport of finished products which would have inherent environmental and social costs.

. . . The hundred dollar question is, is there a philosophy that can challenge this concept of economies of scale?

In order to pursue this question more systematically, Karuna shifted to the Chennai IIT in 1982. There he could work closely with the IIT's Centre for Rural Development, an interdisciplinary centre established to carry out rural development through employment generation. This gave Karuna an opportunity to train himself in a wide variety of disciplines. Over the years, he taught electrical engineering, mathematics, control engineering, management and civil engineering relating to water resources. The focal point of all these varied interests was to gain experience that would help him learn about employment-oriented industries. He also trained himself in regional planning, employment planning, women's development, training organizations, low-cost housing and entrepreneurial development.

Here Karuna, or 'T.K.' as friends and students called him, came to be known for the freshness of his ideas which stemmed from his combination of training in engineering and other areas. The fact that he used these talents to understand the structures of poverty and find answers, won him a faithful following among the students. Many of them enthusiastically joined his various projects in rural areas.

Gradually, over the years, Karuna found an answer to the 'economies of scale' problem. He called it 'networking'. This was a concept of a multi-tiered structure of rural industrial activity which would foster a village-centred economy that is sustainable and eco-friendly. This networking, Karuna insists, would be viable 'even in the market economic terms of Adam Smith' for it would produce cheaply and competitively. It could thus effectively challenge the prevalent concept of 'globalization'.

## Practical Swadeshi
Practical Swadeshi would be another way of describing networking. This means recognizing that a fully self-sufficient village is no longer possible at the end of the twentieth century. But clusters of villages could work together to attain self-sufficiency through cooperation. Each network of clusters would generate all essentials of life and even export certain items to other networks. A viable network could be formed at the district level, building on the block-level sub-networks.

'We have to strive for a path that is between the idolized village industry and multi national companies,' says Karunakaran. All 'universal' products, starting with food, clothes and shelter, should be made in the village. But a pace-maker, for example, is not universal and can therefore be made in the cities. Gandhi's concept of Swadeshi was that the more universal a product is, the closer should be its domain of production. 'Gandhiji identified twenty-four major categories in rural industries, but these are now archaic. I have built a system on the basis of the contemporary reality and its needs.'

As chief techno-economic officer at IIT Chennai, Karuna and his team identified 350 types of consumer goods, falling in twenty-four major categories, which can be easily produced in the villages. Most of these goods are either personal or household items, for example, utensils, soaps, kum-kum, matchboxes, clothes and shoes. These details were worked out partly through experiments undertaken by a group which, in 1984, registered a society called STEP—Society for Total Employment Planning. This society brought together committed academics and 'social servants'. It aimed to provide a platform for development of thought and action, 'since institutions like IIT were not always ideal for rural development activities'. Karuna was the first president of STEP. The underlying assumption of all these efforts was that the key issue is not rural *employment* but rural *activity*.

This is all very well, but how does this understanding help a landless labourer or a marginal farmer? At present, those who own the land and assets also avail of all production opportunities. The landless and poor farmers have neither the information nor the energy to compete.

This happens, Karuna found, when both information and energy are concentrated in the hands of a few. The emerging structure is then, inevitably, exploitative and oppressive. Karuna suggests that we think of the village community as a pyramid with the mass of people at the base and the block development officer at the top. At present power and resources flow from top to bottom. The block development officer (BDO) has both the Plan information and the monetary resources, while the people are reduced to mere recipients. Instead, Karuna suggests that the control over natural resources, as well as monetary and decision-making power, be vested with the community itself. The BDO should merely play the role of providing certain information and coordination.

Once this is done then Karuna's 'real change agents' enter the picture and the road is cleared for Rural Technology Centres and Social Entrepreneurs. The Rural Technology Centres (RTC) would give skills and a technological advantage to the landless and under-privileged, rather than making them mere recipients of dole in the form of poverty alleviation programmes.

Instead, the RTC would promote a new type of economics through Social Entrepreneurs. Just how this happens has been worked out by Karuna on flow-charts and diagrams that could compete with the detail and complexity of any engineer's blue print. 'In the name of taking science and technologies to the villages, we seem to be transferring "test tube ideas" and other laboratory concoctions to the villages. It should be a transfer of the *attention*. A technologist's task is not to take his fixed methods and lab to villages but to focus his attention and see what emerges in working along with people.'

Many of Karuna's village projects during his years at Chennai IIT, were based on these principles. When he was offered a chance to move his work to the rural areas on a full-time basis, Karuna jumped at it. This took him to the Gandhigram Rural University, at Dindigul, where he set up a Rural Technology Centre.

## Valayapatti
The town of Dindigul is clustered around a lone rock hill that incongruously sticks out on the plains some sixty kilometres north of the temple-town of Madurai. The Gandhigram Rural University occupies a large tract of land along the highway on which maniacally-driven buses hurtle back and forth throughout the day and night. Across the road is the town of Chinnalapatti, famous for its art silk and cotton handloom sarees. Just beyond the University lands, at the foothills of a nearby low-lying mountain range, is the village of Valayapatti.

Valayapatti lies across a stretch of scrub land and a

couple of shallow streams, about two kilometers from the Gandhigram campus. Green fields garner the edge of the village and among the crops, at one side of the village stands a square carved column of gleaming jet-black stone. On it is depicted the life of Khanappan Nayanar, an archer and hunter who is revered as a Shaivite saint. His descendants, the Valayars or archers, settled the village which is therefore called Valayapatti. The intricate beauty of the carving on that old stone column shows that once, many generations ago, the people of this area had a much finer and higher level of skills. It also tells the tales of times when nature was more bountiful.

Now it appears that nature needs the help of Valayapatti's people. All around the village, young tree saplings are guarded by thin thorny twigs. Children at what the village calls the 'World Citizenship School', run by the Rural Technology Centre, mark not only their own daily attendance but that of the fledgling trees in their family. Disco film music usually blares in some part of the village during the day. Several homes are being repaired and others are being built anew. But Valayapatti was not always like this.

When Karuna first arrived on campus, in January 1988, he was warned that Valayapatti was a filthy and dangerous village. 'Stay away from it'. That was all the urging Karuna needed to rush to Valayapatti and make it the centre of his experiments. Once upon a time the Gandhigram University had attempted to 'uplift' Valayapatti through various welfare projects and eventually given up. Karuna felt such experiments failed because they did not seek to tap and release the latent creative, entrepreneurial energies of the local people. Determined to do that, Karuna set out for Valayapatti.

The warnings had not been exaggerated. Karuna did find Valayapatti unbearably filthy and mired in endless quarrels among its residents. Most of the people there were unemployed. They made a living by cutting and selling wood from the hills near the village. The primary industry of the village was brewing and selling of country liquor. This led to frequent brawls and fights that often landed some residents behind bars at the local police station.

So Valayapatti presented itself as a perfect test case for Karuna's reformist zeal. He turned down the professors' quarters offered to him by the University and went to live in the village instead. Among his early friends in Valayapatti was Panchvarnam. This young woman had watched her mother struggling to bring up six children after her father abandoned them. Now Panchvarnam herself was separated from her husband. At the time when Karuna appeared on the scene, Panchvarnam was yearning to acquire some means by which she could earn a living. For a start, she thought, it would be good to learn how to write her own name and to read the bus signs.

Panchvarnam was not alone. Many other women also wanted to read and write. So Karuna began by starting a village literacy centre, with an initial enrolment of twenty-four women. Many of Karuna's students faced a great deal of opposition at home. But their determination and enthusiasm soon proved infectious. Karuna's literacy classes became the focus for envy and the men protested, demanding to join the class. Soon, there was a World Citizenship School and a Merriland night school, run by the staff of the Rural Technology Centre. As the circle of involvement gradually grew, some unexpected flowers bloomed.

Tangadurai was till then known as one of the village's

most hardened drunks and liquor brewers. One day he stormed into Karuna's class and demanded to join its charmed circle. Gradually, as he interacted with the class, they discovered that when he was sober the burly Tangadurai had soft smiling eyes and the deepest dimples. It turned out that Tangadurai had attended school up to class four and over the years he had composed eighteen songs. The appreciation of his class fellows and the refresher course in stringing letters together to make words and sentences opened a new dimension in Tangadurai's life.

With this new self-confidence, Tangadurai and others moved on to explore other forms of work. Gradually, as this happened, the liquor business went into decline and the brawling stopped. Tangadurai became the major communicator for the village through his songs and other folk arts. He learnt cement masonry and today builds homes. He learnt the necessary skills at the Gandhigram University's Rural Technology Centre. Others learnt how to make furniture and marketable products like pickles and tutti-frutti. The latter is made out of papayas which grow aplenty around the village. The raw papayas are cut into tiny bits, dried, sweetened and coloured to become tutti-frutti, which is then sold to bakeries in nearby Dindigul town.

Karuna labelled all these enterprises as Sarvo—Societal Action for Reconstruction Vigilance and Organization. At first, people were reluctant to come for training but later there was a veritable avalanche of participants. Soon there were Sarvo Fruit Products, Sarvo Snacks, Sarvo Ferro Cement, Sarvo Coir Products and even a Sarvo Bank—which helps to raise funding for small projects within the village community.

These various Sarvo activities had many spin-offs. Several young men became manufacturers of steel furniture.

About half a dozen youths set up shops and restaurants. Valayapatti, which once had a dearth of milk, soon had its own mini 'white revolution'. Within three years, one of the residents was running a successful dairy farm, holding more than eight buffaloes. The children in the World Citizenship School became more confident. Parents who once laughed at the idea of sending their children to school, now made education their first priority.

For Veerachalam, one of the village elders, the trees around Valayapatti were the most powerful evidence of the changes. Earlier all families went into the hills to cut trees. After the Sarvo enterprises came into being, only forty per cent were still cutting trees. The number of head-loads of wood, being cut from the hills near-by, came down from 130 a day to about fifteen. Instead, the village collectively planted over a lakh trees on the surrounding hills.

For Karuna, the Valayapatti effort was a success because it was a 'development initiative' that released local energies, instead of being an 'aggressive intervention' that just injects resources and 'expertise' from the outside. If a crime-ridden village can be so transformed, Karuna argued, it should be easier in other places.

### Social entrepreneurship
This is what Karunakaran triumphantly calls 'social entrepreneurship'. The endeavours in Valayapatti are a small example of the kind of economics which alone, Karuna believes, can ensure employment for all—something which the prevailing economic system clearly cannot do. In 1972, the organized industrial sector in India employed eleven per cent of the workforce. By 1996, this figure was down to seven per cent. About fifty-seven per cent of the total workforce in India is self-employed.

Karuna's concept of 'social entrepreneurship' recognizes that along with the state-owned public sector and the private sector, which runs most large modern industries, there is a 'people's sector' made up of the craftsmen and other small producers at the village level. These three sectors are closely inter-dependent. Currently, the terms of trade are set largely by the private sector and weighed against the entrepreneurial energies of the 'last man'. How can this be changed?

The work in Valayapatti is part of the answer. It is a small illustration of the concepts Karuna has articulated in copious detail in his book, *Rural Growth Networks*. Anticipating that the scheme will seem complicated to many readers, Karuna points out in the preface that poverty alleviation is a complex task and 'I can only point out the fundamental systems law: "complexity can be combated only through a strategy of matching complexity".'

*Rural Growth Networks* is a blueprint for delivery systems that would effectively develop the 'target group', in this case, those who are below the poverty line. Existing government programmes like the Integrated Rural Development Programme (IRDP) have not worked, according to Karunakaran, as most of the would-be beneficiaries do not have the required combination of entrepreneurial skills in production, marketing, accessing raw material and finance. Thus, the transfer of inadequate resources to ill-equipped people below the poverty line ends in large-scale failure.

The concept of Rural Growth Networks (RGNs) is a means for creating a new, more workable, equation. The solution is based on the assumption that since one kind of technology has brought about inequality, disparity and massive unemployment, it is time to try other forms of technology to solve these problems. For this, people must have training and social preparation, along with the political will to safeguard such processes from 'disruptive forces'.

The objective of the RGNs is 'to help develop the rural economy by insulating it from the normal exploitative forces'. This is to be done by making the RGN an agency for organizing employment, income generation and asset-building mechanisms for those who are incapable of organizing these for themselves. The RGN would also be a meeting point of the governmental agencies, financial institutions, entrepreneurs and beneficiaries of government programmes. The key to making it work is that the infrastructure must be owned and managed mainly by the people themselves, primarily those who are currently below the poverty line. Any surplus can then be ploughed back into the community for health, education and other facilities which enhance the quality of life.

This three-tier system visualizes House Level Activities, Village Work Centres and Rural Growth Centres. Together, these various levels would empower village-level producers and eliminate logistical hurdles and exploitative middlemen. For example, a weaver's trade depends on many factors. The loom may be self-owned and located at home but the supply of yarn is controlled by businessmen and master weavers. Associated services like warping, sizing, bleaching, dyeing, polishing and printing are also usually controlled by private investors. The weaver is thus reduced to being a piece-rate wage earner. Even most cooperatives have not been able to do away with middlemen.

Under Karunakaran's scheme the Village Work Centre (VWC) would create the necessary supportive infrastructure on the basis of collective ownership and serve several home-based weavers. Higher level facilities and processes, like printing and marketing, could be located at the Rural Growth Centre (RGC) which would serve a whole region. So, for example, in the case of dairy farming, the animals would be reared at home, the milk collection would be at the VWC, and the chilling, processing, tinning, marketing and feed-mixing would be at the RGC.

This approach was followed by traditional cobblers in one part of Tamil Nadu. If these craftsmen produced and attempted to sell their goods individually, they were not able to compete with the products of the big shoe companies. But when six cobblers of a village got together, they succeeded in marketing their goods more effectively. The cutting of the leather is done at a centralized centre and then the cobblers take the shoes home to stitch and finish the footwear. Since they are directly involved in running the whole enterprise, they are not reduced to being mere wage-earners but remain self-sufficient craftsmen and entrepreneurs.

Of course, this system can work only if there is true Panchayati Raj, that is, effective decentralization of decision-making and more powers to the village collective. As Karuna sees it:

> I feel that for the true spirit of Gram Swaraj to come out, the grassroots bodies should have a hold over the topmost decision-making bodies like Parliament and state legislatures. I have recently suggested that instead of the Rajya Sabha there should be a Panchayati Sabha of district level panchayat representatives, so that the wisdom of the grassroots can guide the destiny of the nation even on things like GATT and CTBT.

Thus, the core of Karuna's concept for social and economic renewal is that:
– instead of economies of scale and centralization there would be networking through Rural Growth Networks;
– instead of entrepreneurship of the capitalist variety, there would be social entrepreneurship or 'sarvodaya';
– instead of urban development there would be viable communities and block level self-sufficiency and ecologically sustainable habitats;
– instead of 'blind globalization' there would be 'universal or rational swadeshi';
– instead of education fostering inequality there would be 'education for world citizenship'.

**Reflections**

Looking back on a quarter century of striving, Karuna feels that his works have been 'sincere and wishful rather than vigorous and rigorous'. Though his field experiments have been small and sometimes incomplete, Karuna has the satisfaction of seeing many of these efforts replicated at the larger level. The University Grants Commission has declared Karuna's B.Sc. level course design in rural technology as a model for the whole country. The Dindigul market has responded by accepting the Sarvo products. Four of the low-cost house models designed by Karuna are now being widely replicated. And this, he feels, 'is much more than I deserve'.

Some of the students who came in contact with Karuna during his IIT days are now part of an intense group of young alternatives seekers who have abandoned careers in engineering to explore ways and means of ensuring livelihood opportunities for all. Many of them have been inspired not only by Karuna's unflagging persistence but also by his refusal to use any 'extraneous' means like personal friendship and clout to push even noteworthy causes.

Karuna's self-image is that of an 'evolutionary who accepts all the villains and wise men of the past as my elder brothers. The reconstruction strategies of Gandhiji conceptualized in the 1940s may not work fully well now, since we have already done much irreversible damage (to the enivronment and economy). What I have done during the past eighteen years or so is basically to identify the antidotes, field-try them on a small scale and also to visualize the replication—from message to movement.'

Shambu Prasad, one of Karuna's former students, admires 'his amazing ability to plan out things in great techno-economic detail. Karuna would surely have done better but for his excessive use of systems jargon. Few people have his abilities. Imagine a person like him working in Kerala with all the people and the atmosphere right for the people's planning exercise. In fact, many of his ideas might have taken better root where the political atmosphere was right.'

Karuna acknowledges that there has been 'many a slip between the cup and lip. Many times I felt unprepared and at other times the institutions to which I was bonded thwarted the attempts. If I were prepared to take risk of a higher level and if I were a lot more daring, I could have enabled my models to unfold themselves better. Thus I am to blame.'

In a conventional sense, Karuna or his senior fellow-traveller C.V. Seshadri, may not seem very successful. This is partly due to the lack of a general atmosphere in which their efforts could be lapped up. And perhaps that atmosphere comes only from an intense political movement.

## The future

Karuna's enthusiasm for rigorous and successful ground level models is tempered by the limitations of such efforts. The last fifty years have seen many excellent micro-level experiments all over India. But they have not added up to significant macro-level changes.

The Gandhigram Trust itself is a classic example of well-meaning schemes for craftsmen and rural poor, which never multiply widely enough to change the larger picture. As late as 1994, the Gandhigram Rural University itself did not offer courses in organic and natural farming, because it functions on rules made by the University Grants Commission. Besides, the teaching staff comes from conventional educational institutions which are unfamiliar with the Gandhian perspective.

Venkateswaran Padmanabhan, who headed the Gandhigram Trust, worked well into the mid-90s in the hope that some day macro planning would be shaped by the micro-data that local experiments were accumulating. Padmanabhan, a veteran Gandhian and colleague of J.C. Kumarappa, drew sustenance from the belief that since both the capitalist and communist world have failed there is more space for non-violent concepts of development.

But it is not clear if this space was being sufficiently and effectively cultivated. For example, the Kumarappa Centenary gathering at Sewagram in January 1993, represented a small fraction of the international community at work for shaping a different world. But there appear to be few active linkages and interaction among such people on an on-going basis. Most of them have a conceptual affinity but are probably not working together for any tangible goal. So, does it all amount to just 'wishful' thinking?

Karuna is acutely aware of the limitations of doing intense hard work in pockets:

It is not like Gandhi's struggle in South Africa or India. Now, having visualized the problem globally, we are all perplexed. What we need is to visualize the *new order* in terms of Global Agenda, National Agenda, Regional Agenda and Economy of Permanence at the individual level. Presently, the Gandhians are only reacting to certain realities staring at us, i.e. North-South equations, multinationals etc. but there is lack of a framework to visualize the new order whereby we forge transcontinental linkages among multicultural communities for sustainable development and peaceful coexistence.

Also, there is a hesitation to confront foundational issues like land rights and there is a lack of optimism and inner strength. This is possibly because India disowned Gandhian models and now many constructive workers depend on foreign funds to keep their activities alive.

So, how will the dream of a total transformation be fulfilled? Once upon a time Karuna believed that the liberating 'eco-tech era', which combined innovative technology with ecological wisdom, would be spearheaded by the Scandinavian states or the USA. But on closer examination he found the near-ideal states like Sweden and Denmark under the grip of high-tech tension. This is partly the toll of having lost family and community structures.

Thus, Karuna refers to the so-called developed world as 'ruined countries' and the 'developing' world which emulates that model as 'rushing-to-be-ruined countries'.

In the early-90s Karuna was hopeful about the emergence of alternative lifestyle movements in the USA. But now 'the growing unipolarization of the world and emergence of organizations like WTO has given another lease of indulgent life to this unfortunate country (USA) to continue to play its Big Brother role and ruin itself and others ultimately.'

What then is the role of activists like Karuna? How are they going to be more effective at the larger level? As Karuna sees it, such activists must find ways to 'help India to learn from its own mistakes and skip ruinous experiments through use of the wisdom imbibed in its cultural heritage.'

There is an ever-growing number of people working at the grassroots and seeking answers to the same questions that have bothered Karuna all his working life. It does sometimes seem to Karuna that this fraternity is like the blind men trying to decipher the shape of an elephant. Each has grasped a part of the truth but they are yet to put this experience together and forge the political instruments to free every *daridra-narayan* from having to struggle for the bare necessities of daily existence.

Like many of his peers Karuna sees the next ten years as a decisive decade not only for India but the world at large. If the persons working for change are to fulfil their potential, Karuna feels, they must emerge from 'their little ego shells, understand the dimensional complexity of each problem and strike a partnership in action with others who have complementary resources. Then there will be a synergy effect and the resulting force will lead to the dawn.'

\*

*When the exiled Prince Rama of Ayodhya went into the forest he first made his home at Chitrakoot. A place by that name, in eastern Madhya Pradesh, is a major pilgrim centre of north India.*

*In 1997, Karuna found himself at Chitrakoot as the vice chancellor of the Mahatma Gandhi Rural University located there. The task of building up an institution he found in 'ruins' was somewhat daunting. But the prospect of working amid throngs of pilgrims enthralled him. Here is an opportunity to catch the attention of millions and communicate the ideal of social entrepreneurship. Who knows what shape this germ of an idea might take as it spreads further and wider.*

*But first Karuna has to deal with the disapproval of his colleagues who are aghast and cannot fathom why he wishes to live in a nearby village instead of the vice-chancellor's bungalow!*

# Ravindra Sharma
## A Silent Dawn

*Three men, all clad in dhotis, entered the Bapu Kuti. The oldest of the three stood sharply erect. His movements were slow and graceful. Adjusting the* angvastra *on his shoulder the man wandered about, quietly taking in the furniture-free spaces of the Kuti. One of the younger men bounded about excitedly exclaiming and admiring tiny details. His face was lit by a luminous smile that spoke of an irrepressible enthusiasm for life. The other young man wore a sombre expression and an improvised turban of crumpled, aging white cloth. Long, uncombed locks escaped from the turban, tumbling onto his neck. He could pass for a fledgling sadhu.*

*The older man, the one they called 'Guruji', nodded admiringly as he completed his tour of the Kuti. He did not know much about Mahatma Gandhi. Though he lived less than half a day's bus-journey away from Sewagram, 'Guruji' had never felt the need to visit the famous ashram. Yet, this simple home, made from local materials, complete in its simplicity, struck a chord in him. The Kuti interested him more than the proceedings of an international conference, to which his chelas had dragged him.*

*Amid the crowded schedule of sessions on world peace and economy of permanence, I slowly got acquainted with Guruji, and found that he is otherwise known as Ravindra Sharma. His frequent references to a place called Kala Ashram began to weave a spell of wonder. The two young chelas turned out to be renegades from the Chennai IIT. Now the mystery deepened further.*

*A year later, in the winter of 1994, I took up their invitation and made my way to Kala Ashram in the company of Uzramma, a member of the Kala Ashram fraternity. Our bus, from Hyderabad, arrived in the town of Adilabad in the pitch dark hour before dawn . . .*

\*

## Growing up with Budubudukalodu and Gosamolu

Ravindra Sharma clings to memories of songs which greeted the dawn in his childhood. Adilabad was a smaller town then. There were few people and hardly any noisy modern gadgets. The nights could be deathly quiet. Little Ravindra would sometimes lie awake and wait. Then, while all of nature rested, the rhythmic 'duk, duk, duk, duk . . . ' of a small hand-held *damru* would arise faintly in the distance.

The mysterious and hazy form of the Budubudukalodu would appear from the direction of the cremation ground and disappear down the road, to the steady beat of his damru. The boy understood that the Budubudukalodu was roaming through the town warding off ghosts and bidding farewell to the spirits of the night. It was now about three in the morning.

A little later the Gosamolu, a husband-wife team, would pass by singing *bhajans* to an *ektara*. Then, just before the first rays lightened the sky, came the Haridas. He danced with *ghungaroo* on his feet, gently making music with an earthen pot on his head, singing Rag Bhairavi. It was the Haridas who awakened the gods from slumber to greet the new day.

By then the townfolk were stirring and so the Haridas was the first minstrel to get *bhiksha*. Well into the morning, with the sun shining bright, came the Jangam, who could be a single man or a pair or trio, singing the praise of Shiva. They too collected *bhiksha* as they went along. Closer to noon came the Kathi-palodu, a magician with animals, usually a bullock or bear. And so on, as the day moved full circle a variety of singers, minstrels, water-diviners, medicine men and travelling merchants filled the life of Adilabad with colour, song and meaning.

Once every fifteen days or so, the then resident Budubudukalodu and the Gosamolu would come around for *bhiksha* before moving on to another town or village. And alert ears, like little Ravindra's, would eagerly listen out for the Budubudukalodu and Gosamolu—to catch a glimpse of them in daylight.

As dusk pulled the curtain on yet another day somewhere in Adilabad young people were dancing the Kolatam in a joyous group. At other times rapt audiences watched the enactment of stories from the Bhagvatam or Ramayana.

Minstrels and Pauranic story-tellers have enlivened villages and market towns like Adilabad for centuries. A particular Budubudukalodu or Gosamolu may pass away but the continuity of their dawn music was unbroken, undisturbed. To little Ravindra it seemed as perennial as the chirping of birds and the wind in the trees. In different ways each of the minstrels linked everyday life with the hereafter, with the infinity of the cosmos. But even as Ravindra watched, the Gosamolu and his like were disappearing.

By the time Ravindra looked about at his world with the full awareness of an adult, Adilabad was waking to a silent dawn. Most people may have taken this as being inevitable in the flow of time. But this silence hurt Ravindra. He knew that with the minstrels an entire civilization, a way of life, was fading. It was leaving behind an eerie vacuum. The standardized, long-distance broadcasts of All India Radio were no substitute for the presence of a Gosamolu. Now life and art, art and beauty were moving further and further apart.

## Once upon a time in Adilabad

Once upon a time the dense Dandakarnya forest covered the space where the roads and buildings of Adilabad now stand. It was through these parts of central India that Lord Rama and Lakshman are believed to have wandered searching for Sita, in the epic tale of Ramayana. This legend is faithfully and lovingly kept alive. In many villages people still enact episodes from the Ramayana or other Pauranic legends. This means more to them than the material reminders left behind by the ebb and flow of time, like the ruins of a Jain monastery which lie near the place now known as Adilabad. The tumble of masonry and broken idols is ignored by most local residents.

What the people of Adilabad do know is that some 400 years ago two Vaishnav *muths* were established in the area. The present market settlement of Adilabad emerged around the walls of these *muths* about 150 years ago. At the turn of the twentieth century, Adilabad was a humming urban centre with the clickty-clack of thousands of handlooms. A wide variety of craftsmen fed the local economy with their products. In those days the Nizam of Hyderabad ruled the area. The British influence was fairly negligible. The first modern roads and railway lines began to be laid in this region some time in the 1940s.

This construction attracted merchants and entrepreneurs from far corners of the country. Thus, young Lahori Ram Sharma, of Layalpur in the Punjab, came to seek his fortune in Adilabad. Some day, he planned to return home wealthy and live among his own. But history had other plans. While Lahori was working as an engineer, laying railway lines, the British were in the process of leaving and two separate nations waited to be born. Suddenly Lahori's home lay in a 'foreign' country. Shortly before the formal declaration of Partition and the formation of Pakistan, in 1947, Lahori's entire family made the long journey south to Adilabad, carrying just the bare essentials.

Almost half a century later the aging Lahori and his brother would still tell this story with a deep sense of relief. Other families who waited till much later were caught in the madness of brutal communal riots. While retaining their distinct flavour of speech and dress, the Sharmas slowly merged into Adilabad and, setting wistful regret aside, got on with life. It was into this joint family that a son was born to the second Sharma brother in 1952. They called him Ravindra.

The boy was less than five years old when the family noticed that he had an intense preoccupation with creating images and playing with colours. Little Ravindra spent hours in the homes of the 'low-caste' Nakashi artisans, watching them carve and paint wooden figures. After such visits, Ravindra's grandmother always poured a bucket of water over him, for purification, before letting him into the house.

In those days, Adilabad was still a sleepy little town, though it was now a district headquarter. The local Narayanswami and Gopalkrishna *muths* still played a central role in the annual cycle of seasons and festivals. The Mahant of each *muth* would emerge outside only four or five times a year to seek *bhiksha* among the people of Adilabad and surrounding villages.

These were days of great excitement for all children. But Ravindra's absorption in the elaborate paraphernalia of decorations and *torans*, which honored the Mahant, was quite extraordinary. He carefully followed the Mahant's ceremonial procession, passing under the beautiful *torans* in each neighbourhood. Householders would welcome the Mahant into their homes, reverentially wash his feet and then place some grain in his *jholi*. That token *bhiksha* was accompanied by a promise of how much grain the household would contribute to the *muth* that year.

On Dussehra the Mahant of the Gopalkrishna *muth* would head a procession sitting in a *palki*. Virtually the whole town would join the procession which went to a particular *shami* tree on the outskirts of the town. There the tree would be worshipped. Then people would pluck some of its leaves and the procession would head back to the *muth*. The leaves were treated as symbolic of silver coins and exchanged among the citizens of Adilabad. The Dussehra evening was spent visiting neighbours and paying respects to the elders and gurus. Decades later, Ravindra still had vivid memories of these scenes. He treasured the mental images of brilliantly-coloured turbans in many different shapes.

At the age of eight, Ravindra found a teacher in the traditional art of wielding a *lathi* and was an expert by the age of twelve. This earned him the title of 'Guruji' and soon he became a young personality to be reckoned with. The title stuck for life and, in future, people of all ages always addressed him as 'Guruji'. At sixteen he was running his own *akhada* or gymnasium. Ravindra also discovered that he had an uncanny skill for telling people's fortunes just by studying their face. Soon people were asking him for sacred threads and mantras that would solve their problems.

At that time the economy of Adilabad, like many such urban centres, still revolved primarily around local resources. Those who had land grew their own grain and some cotton. They depended on the market for purchasing tea, jaggery, salt, etc. But as Ravindra grew up, the economy and society of Adilabad were changing rapidly.

Old trades and industries were dying. The products of local artisans were being replaced by mass-produced goods of the modern 'market'. These decisive changes brought to Adilabad new residents who had no hereditary links with either the *muth* or the Budubudukalodu or Gosamolu. New equations of commerce and power were taking shape. Eventually, by the late-80s, the annual Dussehra day procession was led not by the Mahant but by the District Collector.

## Gale-force winds of change

These changes baffled and disturbed Ravindra, but he was not quite sure why. He concentrated on exploring life around him and evolving a distinct personality of his own. Ravindra completely gave up the western style pants and shirts which all the other male members of his family wore. He took to wearing a cotton dhoti and kurta and applied elaborate *bottu* on his forehead.

Most of his time outside school was spent roaming the villages around Adilabad in search of craftsmen, sculptors, painters and other artists. He loved to watch them at work and tried to learn their skills. Along with his closest friend, Nishikant, Ravindra spent long days lost in the mystery and beauty of the ruins of the old Jain monastery. At that time the ruins were still rich with statues and other stone carvings. Later, as Adilabad became commercially busier and more outsiders came into the area, the ruins were slowly plundered of the pieces that had been lying undisturbed for almost a thousand years.

Ravindra and Nishikant would often take a small bullock cart and set out in search of the 108 *devalayas* that once existed in that region. Over the years they located sixty. Ravindra remembers these wandering days with a sense of almost magical happiness. Wandering into a village the boys were always quickly adopted by someone, fed, housed and even given fodder for their bullock. Ravindra recalls fondly that their hosts were equally delighted by these visits. In village after village, they found a living culture of *'atithi devo bhavah'*, which treated the guest as a God.

There were some ground rules to this wandering. Ravindra and Nishikant never returned to Adilabad by the route they had travelled out. They ate in any village only after making at least one new acquaintance or friendship. As Ravindra outgrew his teens and acquired a muscular physique, this process of making friends took a while.

Here was a man of medium height with heavy shoulders and a long black mustache. He wore a deep red *tilak* on his forehead and carried a saffron-coloured cloth bag. The moustache gave him the look of a tantric sadhu, some one who meddled in *mantra jadu*, like magic. That *jhola*, or bag, aroused suspicions. It could easily be filled with charms and tantric paraphernalia. And it didn't help matters when this young man with a powerful presence asked people about old temples in the area. Perhaps he was here to steal idols or gold ornaments from the temple deities. So it took a while for young Ravindra to put strangers at ease. For some, getting to know him, was a bit of an anti-climax since that *jhola* contained mundane things like a torch, tooth-powder, a *lota* and some sheets of paper.

At that time, in the mid-60s, many old social habits were

still alive in these villages. When a traveller arrived he would rest at the village *chabutra*. The kotwal would greet the traveller and ask to which caste he belonged. The traveller would then be directed to his caste-brothers in that village, who took turns at feeding the stranger for as long as he stayed.

One village, Devapur, consisted entirely of people who lived on *bhiksha*. They roamed from village to village, telling stories and living on the alms people gave them. Each family had its own fixed terrain to cover and they did not encroach on another's area. The multi-dimensional skills of these story-tellers had been cultivated over centuries. There was the *Shakunjatak,* who told fortunes with the help of parrots. These travelling fortune-tellers traced their lineage and knowledge back to Shakuni of the Mahabharat.

As Ravindra observed more closely, he learnt that a story-teller must also be a good instrument player, dancer and actor. People of the *Sharda Kalu* community acquired all these skills and told stories of local ancestral heroes and mythic figures in village after village. The session would begin late in the evening and as night melted into morning, tales of valour, adventure and the endless quest for eternal truths were enacted with fervour. In the old days, when they were secure in the patronage of their respective community, these *bhiksha vritti* story-tellers performed with the accompaniment of elaborate costumes and props.

The more he saw, the harder Ravindra worked at soaking up these fading cultural riches. He kept detailed notes on the various social customs, art forms and people he encountered. In some things, like the Kolatam folk dance, he was also an avid participant. One of his friends Kishtopanthalu, knew thirty-two songs each accompanying a distinct style of Kolatam.

In Adilabad, a grand old man called Yellapatata became Ravindra's mentor. The sheer presence of Yellapatata's regal dignity was a joy for Ravindra. This aging artist taught him the wonders of colours and painting. Slowly, an informal 'school' evolved around Yellapatata, with Ravindra as the star pupil. Often they would meet at the *muth*, which served as a natural *adda*, hang-out, for these artists.

As the twentieth century moved inexorably to its close the electronic transmission of images at cinema halls, and later television sets, began to take over. More and more people became merely spectators rather than being participants. Daily life became more mechanical and self-centred. Then the concept of *bhiksha* began to lose its power. Now the *bhiksha vritti* story-tellers began to seem like 'beggars'. The traditional patrons faded out and none took their place. Besides, there were now fewer people interested in spending a five full evenings on live story-telling.

Ravindra could see that the flow of *kaala*, time, did not favour the old skills. But still, he felt distressed that most artists were not able to evolve creatively with the times. Instead, the pressure and confusion of change brought greed to the fore. More and more material demands were added on to the ritual story-telling. Now the *puja* to the *kul-devta*, an essential part of the *katha* tradition, became very expensive. If the wedding of Rama and Sita was being enacted, a full *dahej*, dowry, was required from the village.

In the old days the performers had dealt with the village mahajan and decided which stories would be told and how much would be spent on the whole event. Now no one was clearly in charge of such matters. Or, as Ravindra saw it, '*sab chowdhry bane hue hain*', everyone had become self-important. Besides, now people were spending more money on themselves and the immediate family. There was less and less set aside for collective social purposes.

These developments badly hurt the local craftsmen and artisans. These indigenous industries had rested on an intricate pattern of interdependence among artisans, and between them and society at large. Social customs and festivals were evolved to ensure the economic well-being of the artisans. For example, in Adilabad, there was a festival some weeks before Diwali in which groups of people went dancing in the streets and threw stones at the roofs of homes. This inevitably broke at least ten-fifteen tiles in each home. Then just prior to Diwali as people cleaned and painted their homes, these tiles were replaced. Each family would have the tiles made by the local potter. The festival became an excuse for not only cleaning and renewing the house but also giving business to the potters.

In this way, every festival required some new purchase from the craftsmen. The wives of potters, *dhobis* or barbers were often asked to inaugurate new works in the community or in a family. Their participation was considered auspicious. This also lent prestige to the artisan families. Instead of cash the medium of exchange was goods like grain, cloth and other necessities. A close interdependence was thus ensured between the farmer and the artisan.

Now, as Ravindra watched, the artists and artisans whose skills had been handed down from generation to generation, whose lineage stretched over two millennia, moved towards a slow collective death. Art forms and crafts that enriched everyday life, were being swallowed up by the all-powerful flow of *kaala*. To Ravindra it seemed as though, one by, one the many different kinds of light and colour essential for a full life were being extinguished. This approaching darkness appalled him. With it came a pervasive feeling of anxiety and a nagging heartache.

As he grew more worldly-wise, Ravindra realized that this vanishing act was part of something powerful that was seeping into the innards of Adilabad. This force recognized no borders. It was a gale which came from far away, knocking down everything in its path. Some called it modernization. Different ways of living were being blown away in a race to get 'ahead'. But ahead of what? Ravindra asked himself. As he looked around life seemed to get duller and somehow alienated.

Even a romantic dreamer like Ravindra no illusions that he could change the course or speed of this storm. After all, who can fight *kaala* itself! Now one question obsessed him. How should he live amidst all this change? What should *he* do?

Ravindra nurtured these questions and kept wandering in villages around Adilabad, in the spirit of a *bhikshu*, living on whatever hospitality was spontaneously offered to him. Often he was invited to share the meagre meal of the impoverished craftsmen or peasants. Thus, he lived with, and learnt from, scores of different craftsmen — potters, goldsmiths, drum-makers, leather craftsmen, weavers and sculptors. When night fell someone would take him under their thatched roof, or he would curl up under a tree in the village centre.

### A twenty-year oath

Once, during winter, Ravindra was staying overnight at the home of a metal craftsman. As the night deepened it grew bitterly cold but his host had no covering either for himself or his guest. The only tattered blanket in the home was covering the man's sick wife. The host stayed awake to keep a small fire going and invited Ravindra to lie close to the warmth. Lying awake, huddled before the flickering flames, Ravindra made a vow to himself that night. He would devote twenty years of his life to helping such craftsmen. No one could hold back the tide of time but he would build a sanctuary for them, a place to seek solace and work at their craft—a Kala Ashram.

Since his early wandering days, Ravindra had felt the need to save the memory, save the fading practices and crafts. So he took copious notes about everything, documenting even details about the toys of the region—how they were made and the games children played. Creation stories among the different communities and castes particularly fascinated him. If nothing else, Ravindra thought, the Kala Ashram would salvage some token remnants of the fading civilization.

Much of this documentation was on loose sheets of paper which Ravindra had piled together and put on a shelf at home. No one in the family knew quite what Ravindra was always scribbling or what its significance was. So, while Ravindra was away at college in Hyderabad, the papers were gradually used for assorted purposes, such as toilet paper for the babies of the house and to pack meals. By the time Ravindra noticed what was happening most of his documentation, like its subject, had also vanished.

In 1970, much to his family's relief, Ravindra managed to pass the tenth class exam which made him a high school graduate. He was quite mystified with his own success. But he had somehow managed to momentarily curb his dread of Maths and English, the *phirangi bhasha*, foreign language. By then he was no longer telling fortunes or dabbling in the realm of *jadu* and mantras. It just didn't feel right and gradually this occult dimension faded out of his life.

Ravindra was now ready for some modern qualifications. So he joined the School of Fine Arts and Architecture in Hyderabad. There he became obsessed with the search for a distinctive artistic style. He restlessly roamed the streets of Hyderabad 'like a dog'.

'Why modern art?' he asked himself. 'Why shouldn't we work within our tradition and do something new in that?' He also embarked on an emotional journey that was not fully within his grasp or control. Soon, he was overwhelmed by a terrible restlessness that was both an artistic and emotional crisis. He felt dizzy and at one point was bedridden for two weeks. When he first arrived in the metropolis, Ravindra weighed seventy kilograms and had the body of a *pahalwan*, wrestler. Within a year he was a pale image of his old self.

Through all these agonies, the twenty-year resolve remained firmly in place. As soon as he returned to Adilabad, Ravindra began the search for a place to locate the Kala Ashram. Since the group of friends who were committed to this idea had always interacted closely with the mahant and swamis of the *muth*, they first approached them to spare a little space. The management of the *muth* offered them a structure which was leased out to an Urdu school. If they could get the Urdu school out of there, the structure was theirs. Ravindra would have no part of this.

Just across the road from the Sharma household was an old, high-roofed structure that had once housed a cotton ginning plant. The building stood on a large empty compound which had its own well. The location was suitable and with little persuasion the owner agreed to rent the structure. Thus, in 1979, the loose group of young friends and elders who shared Ravindra's ideal started the Kala Ashram.

Many shared in the evolution of the Kala Ashram

dream. But Ravindra had firm views on all the essentials and insisted on running it *his* way, as the *guru*. It could also be run as a collective of friends, but Ravindra was convinced that this would not work. In a *guru-shishya* relationship there is a clear understanding about following someone and thus a stronger sense of direction.

Guruji also resolved not to ask anyone, either local people or government, for funds. He wanted to stay as far away as possible from government 'development' projects. Those who helped to form the Ashram promised to give one per cent of their income for its expenses, which did not amount to much.

There were many people in Adilabad, outside this inner circle of the Ashram, who were willing to contribute funds. But Ravindra would not take money from just anyone. Money given as charity, as a favour or begotton by some trick was unacceptable. Only the money of those genuinely committed to the idea, who shared its ethos, was acceptable. The scale and scope of the Ashram was left to depend on how much could be mobilized within this criteria of acceptability.

In 1982, the outside world beckoned once again and Ravindra took off for Baroda to study metal casting at the M.S. University. The Kala Ashram was left in the nurturing care of Nishikant and Yellapatata.

Amid the mostly city-bred students, Ravindra was the odd one out. Other students did not wear dhoti-kurtas or speak unadulterated Hindi with such perfect diction. Judging by his attire and traditional idiom, derived from the Vedas and Pauranic literature, many fellow students suspected Ravindra of being 'an RSS type' or at any rate much too 'Hindu' for the cosmopolitan atmosphere of the art school. So initially Ravindra made few friends.

In this lonely state the angst, or 'ghosts', that had plagued Ravindra since the Hyderabad days returned in full force:

> Even after going to Baroda for a year and a half I couldn't work. Many times I thought of going back to Adilabad. But I was irked by a friend who said, 'What have you ever done?' That egged me to stay on and work. For six months I spent a lot of time staring at a banyan tree, saw it change leaves and wondered why we are not able to self-renew like it does. Then I abandoned all the old ideas. [What matters is] to focus on one's experience and to express it, to give it form . . .
> Then one day, as I lay resting, I suddenly had a flash. It was 4 a.m. but I got up and went to the school and started working, making different shapes. These were appreciated and bought by someone. That gave me a push and then I started really working. I went back into my childhood and asked myself: are we creators? I could recall things from when I was four years old. I remembered making objects with clay, colour threads and metal pieces. I realized that *this* was my own, *original* work. Everything else I had picked up and learnt. I gradually built up from that and built back to the present.

Now Ravindra found a new interest in other artists' work. He developed a special admiration for Nasreen Mohammedi, an artist of rare genius who then taught at the M.S. University. 'She (Nasreen) loved my work. For a long time she kept putting off coming to see my work. When she finally came, she gave it full attention. She taught me how to *look* at work.' This approval and support boosted Ravindra's spirits and work. Such interaction gave a maturity and richer context to Ravindra's favourite question: what is art? Now he longed to go home to Adilabad and stay put.

## Kala Ashram as sanctuary

Returning to Adilabad, Ravindra devoted himself full-time to the twenty-year 'mission' of the Kala Ashram. At last 'Guruji' was back where he belonged—his energies somewhat tapered and mellowed. The joint family household of the Sharma clan welcomed him back into its fold and set about arranging his marriage. The bride hailed from a Punjabi family settled in Gujarat. A quiet, gentle presence, 'Bhabhiji' of the entire Kala Ashram clan, she merged into the background.

Ravindra's life revolved around those who sought his company and shared a heightened sense of beauty in everyday existence. Ravindra had learnt through his travels in villages that the experience and realization of beauty was an intrinsic part of life, not a symbol of pleasure or something to be seperately 'sought after'. So now, young people flocked to him for he helped them to see beyond the mechanical repetition of rituals and instead understand the symbolic and metaphysical significance:

> The washing, clothing and dressing of an idol or *shivalingam* is an aesthetic experience which prepares, creates the atmosphere in which we pray. Or perhaps this experience in itself is an end, the experience of beauty, *saundarya bhav*? After all we had nine kinds of *bhakti*, why then did we need to worship idols?

Over the years the Kala Ashram accumulated a collection of local artifacts. There are silk embroideries of the Mathurias, various wooden deities, ceremonial headdresses of the Gonds, jewellery in cast silver or brass, local tools, implements, household vessels and musical instruments. Some of these are old pieces collected by Ravindra and others have been commissioned to be made in the traditional way.

Since the Kala Ashram can only house a 'living' museum, this collection is like a magnet for craftsmen and artists of traditional communities. Since most of these artifacts are no longer available in society at large, some come to Kala Ashram to borrow them for use at ceremonial occasions. Others come to work and replicate these, now rare, artifacts. Thus, Kala Ashram has become a repository of peoples' history. It fulfils some of the functions which the Nakashis, traditional story-tellers, once performed—like repairing the old picturized story scrolls or painting new *patts* if necessary. Some craftsmen and artists come just to hang around, be together and sometimes work on a particular piece with 'Guruji'.

The Kala Ashram has also been enriched by the regular presence of children, exploring and experimenting with their creative energies:

There is no imposition. If they wish to they can learn about traditional forms and methods or they can work entirely with their own imagination without any 'instructions'. I realized that that's all you should do with children—let them do their own thing, express without limits and outer influence. They can discover formal stuff later ... My point of resolution with the self became my starting point with children when I taught them.

What is a painting? It is the division of a space by some lines. When you begin to add rules to it, it becomes an illustration, that's not creative painting.

As the years sped by, the twenty-year resolve of the Kala Ashram found realization in many forms, which were also scenes from the life of Ravindra Sharma.

There he was as art teacher in a special government school for Kolam tribal children. This was the start of his involvement with the government. Shortly after he returned from studying in Baroda, the then Deputy Collector of Adilabad urged Ravindra to take on the job. Of course 'Guruji' refused a *job* with the government. But he did want to teach the children. So he did the work, not for a salary but, for an honorarium of Rs 600.

Meanwhile, modernity continued its assault on Adilabad. No matter how much he trained himself to act, not react, Ravindra was disturbed to find odd lumps of clay and other aesthetic horrors passing for Ganapati idols at the time of Ganesh Utsav. Thus, Ravindra began an annual practice of crafting eleven statues in all the various poses and moods traditionally associated with Ganesh. These were presented at an exhibition where he took pains to explain the symbolic significance of each idol. This was his way of educating the community about the traditional aesthetic and how its symbols encode messages for a richer daily life.

Eventually, as the decade of the 1980s neared its close, Ravindra abandoned this practice. Some people were now more interested in the politics that could be woven around those innocent idols. 'Hindutva' was the name of their political agenda and 'Guruji', they expected, would be a natural partner. So one day:

> They called me to address one of their meetings, with a request *'ki humko gali mat dena* (don't abuse us in your speech)'. At the meeting I started by asking: 'Who is a Hindu here?' There was a baffled silence. Then again I said: 'All Hindus please stand up.'

Since the gathering looked both confused and uneasy, Ravindra went on to explain that a true identity has its ingrained manifestations through symbols and a sense of self-confidence. So, a male figure carrying a *damru* and *trishul* with snakes wrapped around his neck and arms is instantly identifiable as Shiva. A male figure holding a *chakra* on one finger is clearly identified as Vishnu.

'What do you have (on your person) to show that you are Hindus?' Ravindra asked his audience, most of them dressed uniformly in modern pants and shirts. Ravindra's point was that: 'if you have distinctive characteristics you don't need to assert or shout out loud about who you are. It is only when you are not confident that you need to make all these assertions.' It is only those who are alienated from their cultural roots and don't know their own heritage who are making a noise about being Hindu, he added.

Ravindra was equally scathing with other ideological groupings. In 1990 some friends from Hyderabad invited him to work as art director for 'Komram Bhimu', a Telugu film based on the life of a tribal hero. Many members of the film unit belonged to the Marxist tradition and strongly disagreed with Ravindra's love of the pre-modern, mythic and Pauranic traditions. Heated arguments inevitably erupted on the sets. 'We were on location near a lake,' he recalled, with a wicked gleam in his eyes. 'When we would all go for a bath together in the lake I would loudly chant while bathing " . . . Jai Manu Smriti . . . " just to irritate them.'

It was not, however, all in jest. Ravindra is, in all seriousness, radically opposed to the modern view of the caste system as an unqualified evil. 'If it had been a set of terrible oppressions, people would have never accepted it,' Ravindra argues passionately. 'They would have killed the creator of such an idea.' Yes, but didn't Buddhism successfully challenge caste and was therefore run out of India? Ravindra countered: 'If Buddhism died or was sent away, it wasn't right for us. What makes me angry is the denouncing of traditional practices by *phirangis,* foreigners, or in the language and terms of *phirangis.* Yes there are problems today but why blame them on the whole of tradition. The caste system was not itself a problem. There was a richness in the multiplicity of functions, their inter-linkages, their aesthetic variety and intensity.'

Even though he grew up in the heartland of Andhra Pradesh's vigorous Naxalite movement, Ravindra has remained untouched by such contemporary struggles. 'Somehow my attention has never gone to such movements. Yes, my father kept in touch with local politics, he can tell you all about it.'

From Ravindra's window to the cosmos, the Naxalite seems like a speck in the complex interplay of darkness and light. Oppression and injustice are understood in the language of eternal principles. In one of the dusty alcoves of Kala Ashram stands a stark metal statue of the Chamunda. Ravindra's hands have wrought a riveting effect in that naked female skeletal figure wearing only a garland of human skulls, belligerently crushing a corpse underfoot with scorpions crawling in her stomach. Chamunda's burning rage and excruciating anguish leap at the observer, inducing an eerie chill. For Ravindra, the Chamunda symbolizes the power and anger of the *nirbal*, oppressed. 'Hunger can create such anger, and destroy the powerful *asura*.'

For all his strong opinions favouring the 'logic' of caste or gender relations, Ravindra is not a rigid perpetuator of orthodoxy. He does not hesitate to befriend those who inhabit the fringes of social acceptance. Two of his closest friends in Adilabad are Dharamchand and Bela Jain, who fell in love in defiance of community norms. Dharamchand comes from a conservative Marwari family which was shocked when he chose to marry a Christian woman. It took many years, and perhaps the aura of Dharamchand's prestige as a doctor, to gradually win acceptance for their marriage within the middle class of Adilabad. Ravindra was one of the few people who befriended them in their time of isolation. So he is like a member of their family and they are his loyal supporters.

But even friends like Dharamchand and Bela could not change the fact that within middle-class Adilabad few people took Ravindra seriously. This only changed, momentarily, when Ravindra and Kala Ashram were featured in a programme on national television.

The wide range of Ravindra's interaction is due to his faith that a person's views or opinions are inherently limited, often even shallow. But a civilization and culture are grand and deep, like an ocean. One must strive to *see* the difference between short term 'issues' and the larger truths which make a civilization:

I ask all who come here to leave their '*mat*', ideology

134

or dogma, aside. There's place here for people of all persuasions—Gandhians, Marxists-Leninists, whatever . . . You see your times and your surroundings from your own perspective. All of them were great people in their own context but we have to find our own way. All I ask is that you look within for your self and your path.

## Arrival of new friends

On Dussehra day a lanky, broadly-smiling young man walked into the Kala Ashram. P.B. Srinivas, a graduate of the Chennai IIT and more recently of the Calcutta Indian Institute of Management (IIM), was staying at the Circuit House in Adilabad. It was one of the busiest days of the year at the Kala Ashram. A variety of preparations were under way, for the festivities of *Vijay Dashmi*. Srinivas was fascinated by the burst of activity he had walked into and waited patiently for 'Guruji' to lend him a ear.

Ravindra was not immediately impressed with the young man's introduction. It appeared he was travelling to different parts of Andhra Pradesh on a fellowship from the Council for Advancement of People's Action and Rural Technology (CAPART), in Delhi. This fellowship programme gave such young professionals a chance to spend time in rural areas and understand the problems of development first-hand. Thus, Srinivas had landed up at the District Rural Development Agency (DRDA) in Adilabad with a plan to work on bamboo crafts. It took a few more meetings for Ravindra to gauge that Srinivas saw this fellowship as an intermediate step before dropping out of the system that had trained him.

By the time he got the B.Tech degree, Srinivas was quite convinced that the modern scientific knowledge he had acquired was only helping to destroy India. He was also clear that until the rural craftsmen and farmers become the basis of economic organization in India, poverty can only increase. Besides, as people lose touch with their own culture, restlessness and alienation are increasing. Even as he studied for an MBA at the Calcutta IIM these questions plagued Srinivas. This restlessness took him to the Harsud rally in September 1989, where thousands of groups and individuals from all over India had gathered to protest against 'destructive development'.

A chance meeting with Vinoo Kaley, the bamboo activist from Nagpur, gave a major boost to Srinivas' search and pointed him towards the CAPART fellowship and eventually, Adilabad. Srinivas was not sure what he would do with his future but for now there was a burning need to learn something of the *samaj*, from which he found himself estranged. 'Guruji' and the Kala Ashram were the ideal place to house this search and consider the sign-posts of several different paths to the future. Through Srinivas, Vinoo Kaley and later Uzramma of Dastkar Andhra, were drawn into the world of the Kala Ashram. Soon Ramakrishna, an IIT batchmate of Srinivas who sported long unruly hair, also arrived at Kala Ashram and both young men became absorbed in the day-to-day life in Ravindra's orbit.

Till he came to Adilabad, Srinivas had known of Gandhi and J.C. Kumarappa through their writings and was intellectually inspired by them. The Kala Ashram offered him living examples of the Gandhi-Kumarappa path. To Srinivas it seemed that Ravindra was following that path without knowing much of Gandhi and virtually nothing about Kumarappa.

Ravindra's extensive experience of the artisan world, even two decades after Independence, had taught him that the factory, or workshop, was alien to India. The indigenous industries depended on the skills of mobile craftsmen. They worked with simple and efficient instruments which could be easily carried around. From these they wrought a vast variety of creations—be it sea-faring wooden ships, stone temples or household necessities. Artisans thus made optimum, artistic and imaginative use of local resources. This local self-sufficiency was not only ecologically sound but it also nurtured a high level of culture and skills among the people at large.

Under this system of production there was no wastage in transporting resources over long distances and there was limited damage to the environment. It also prevented the concentration of wealth in the hands of a few factory owners and ensured, naturally, a wider distribution of material resources.

As Srinivas and Ramakrishna became familiar with Ravindra's worldview they felt it was important that he meet other fellow-travellers. So, at their insistence, Ravindra travelled for the first time to Sewagram Ashram in January 1993. Ravindra had never before felt the need to make the five-hour bus journey to Wardha, just across the state border in Maharashtra. At Sewagram, he found himself at a large international conference to mark the birth centenary of J.C. Kumarappa, the Gandhi disciple who worked out the details of Gandhi's vision of an economy of permanence.

The proceedings of the conference were of not much interest to Ravindra. But Gandhi's mud, wood and bamboo hut delighted him. There was an instant sense of identity with the Bapu Kuti:

> The modern cement house sets off a chain reaction
> leading to accumulation of more and more material

objects. A person gets so absorbed in making money to compile these objects, that he has little time for the spiritual dimension and loses all touch with nature. From the construction of the house to making of what we wear, we get completely cut off from the larger social good. This atomized individuality is now creeping into village life also.

Traditionally, Ravindra realized, a greater degree of spontaneity and simplicity was known to be more conducive to a richer life. The emphasis was not on *quantity* of resources but on their diversified and multi-dimensional use. For example, the same room of a home could be used as an office in the mornings, a dining room at noon, a sitting room in the evening and bedroom at night—just by folding mattresses and replacing them with *chataies* or *chowkies*. These changing arrangements and the altering play of sunlight in the room changed its mood and character throughout the day. Today, tonnes of steel and wood are used to permanently fix the character of a room.

Ravindra was articulating what many others had felt instinctively. The interaction with 'Guruji' gave activists like Vinoo Kaley and Uzramma a more nuanced grasp of their own mission. Ravindra's account of village life in the 1960s reinforced their hunch that the traditional industries had supported a large segment of the population. Much of the dehumanizing impoverishment was a fall-out of the modern mass-producing industries. For young men like Srinivas and Ramakrishna the sheer intensity and passion of Ravindra's mission was an inspiration. And then there were some who came from the core of the 'mainstream' to seek out Ravindra, like a government officer and later a fledgling corporate executive.

Shortly before Srinivas and Ramakrishna made Kala Ashram their temporary home, Ravindra had befriended a dynamic young government officer posted with the Integrated Tribal Development Agency (ITDA), in Adilabad. The school in which Ravindra taught art was run by the ITDA. Chinna Veer Bhadru, a sprightly young man with a zesty laugh, shook the set up as soon as he arrived—bringing about greater efficiency and quality in the ITDA schools.

Chinna Veer Bhadru grew up in an atmosphere where children were sharply critical of Gandhi and he flowed with that stream. But the principal of his school was a *'pucca* Gandhian' committed to implementing the ideals of truth and non-violence. Under this influence, Chinna began to rethink and read Gandhi's autobiography in Telugu. Numerous questions and ideas raised by Gandhi now nestled in his mind.

When he became a Class II government officer, he was determined to try and apply some of the values and concepts he had learnt from Gandhi. In one posting he explored the possibility of introducing the charkha as a means of overcoming the dire poverty of a tribe of adivasis. At every stage in this endeavour Chinna was faced with insurmountable hurdles. But he pitched on and delved deep into a book containing Gandhi's ideas on khadi.

Thus, when Chinna found Ravindra and the Kala Ashram, it was a meeting of kindred spirits. Soon the team of Srinivas and Ramakrishna were working with Chinna to introduce charkhas in the ITDA schools. The children easily took to spinning and began to enjoy it. The idea was to give a kilogram of cotton to every student for spinning. A half of the yarn they produced would be used to make two sheets for the student and the rest of the cloth would belong to the weaver, as his wages.

In two months about a hundred students from twenty-five schools participated in this experiment. But soon, Chinna was transferred and the experiment foundered on the rocks of bureaucratic obstacles. Shortly after this Srinivas moved on to his family home in coastal Andhra to run a business and Ramakrishna returned to Chennai to do research on the problem of cotton spinning in the handloom sector.

A steady stream of other young people from cities continued to drift through Ravindra's world at Kala Ashram. Some were fascinated with his personality and others were puzzled by his worldview. Among them was Parvez Davar, an IIM graduate who came to Adilabad on a project funded by the Confederation of Indian Industries.

Involvement in government schemes eventually seemed like a burden to Ravindra. Yet he seemed to get more and more entangled. By 1994, the ITDA had built a special art school for adivasi children and insisted that Ravindra take over as principal. He had also accepted government funding to build a campus for a local art museum and training centre.

## The tangled web of unfulfilled aspirations

On a bright winter morning of 1994, Ravindra was busy grumbling and organizing the inauguration of the Girijan Kala Ashram at Adilabad, the art school set up by the ITDA. His assistant was a young man from a Lambada tribal family, who had hung around Kala Ashram as a child and now runs a private school for tribal children.

On display was the most astounding exhibition of paintings and sculptures, quite different from the mundane stuff usually found at school exhibitions. The mostly abstract works seemed to be inspired by a Dali or a Picasso. If Ravindra was challenged to honestly admit how much of a hand he had in each work he replied firmly: 'not even a touch, they worked on their own.' The mere fact of the children's art gave him joy. He was not particularly moved by an outsider's insistence that some paintings carried seeds of greatness.

However, these successes could not shake off a sense of gloom that nagged Ravindra. He looked back wistfully on his once, firm conviction about relying entirely on the resources of the local community. Then, as he pondered over how much the Kala Ashram was now enmeshed with the government, Ravindra sometimes felt defeated. He saw the increasing grip of the state as part of the same phenomenon that is destroying cultural and economic collectivities. Without those collectivities, even a sanctuary like Kala Ashram cannot save the arts and crafts that Ravindra worships. So he became sadly reconciled to playing the role of curator, preserving odds and ends in the form of a museum.

Sometimes it seemed that the Kala Ashram had failed to serve even as a powerful example. The structure of the government-funded art centre and museum had been designed by Ravindra as an illustration of aesthetically pleasing, geographically appropriate and low-cost architecture. The structure used the arched clay cone roof innovated by the Centre of Science for Villages in Wardha. The clay cones were made by a community of *kumbhars*, potters, in Adilabad.

Shortly after this work had been completed, the kumbhars received a small government grant to build new homes. The money was sufficient to build homes with the clay cone roofs, which the *kumbhars* could make themselves. But the entire community preferred to go deep in debt and build concrete roofs. Ravindra felt baffled, and somewhat crushed, by this decision. Why couldn't the *kumbhars* see that the modern innovative clay roof of the Kala Ashram was cheaper to build and cooler, more comfortable, to live under?

Perhaps because clay tiles in any form are associated with weakness and poverty. Only a concrete roof is considered *'pucca'*. It is a step up the social ladder. For the *kumbhars* the Kala Ashram's locally-produced, aesthetically-pleasing structure had the value of an artifact. It would not be something to replicate or emulate until, perhaps, the District Collector and Dr Jain were to live in such homes.

Meanwhile, Ravindra continues to nurture dreams and plans. He has loads of work do in metal casting. The in-depth study of funeral rites is another long-pending project. The aesthetic of preparing the body for the pyre, fascinates Ravindra. The iconography of the *gram-devta* and various related forms of worship also plead for his attention. Even some of these interests could easily fill a lifetime.

Yet Ravindra does not find peace. As the twenty-year period of his resolve draws to a close, he finds the Kala Ashram woefully inadequate. He still dreams of the Kala Ashram becoming a catalyst for a gathering of all the *bhiksha vritti* people. They could display their practices and settle new arrangements with their respective community. But this has to be done, Ravindra is sure, only by offering assistance and not by becoming their leader.

This sentiment is echoed in the initiatives of friends like Vinoo Kaley. So, in September 1997, Ravindra was lured out of his self-imposed internment at Adilabad to attend a *manthan*, a gathering, of artisans from all over India. The *manthan* was planned as a step toward the formation of a Karigar Panchayat. This was a long-cherished dream of Vinoo, Ravindra, Uzramma and many other friends. Through this gathering they attempted to play a catalytic, supportive, role and hoped that the emerging panchayat would be a forum where the artisans could evolve their own collective strategies.

Over 250 artisans from twenty states gathered for the event. There were ship building artisans from Kerala, iron smelting adivasi craftsmen from Jharkhand, other artisans from Manipur and Assam to Gujarat. Here was a possibility for the artisans to feel more confident about their skills and find their place under the sun in the twenty-first century. Present to lend their support to this artisan endeavour were Madhu Dandavate, deputy chairman of the Planning Commission; Surendra Mohan, chairman of the Khadi and Village Industries Corporation (KVIC) and several prominent academicians.

Even as he participates in such efforts, Ravindra is aware of the inherent limitations. Some part of him is still caught in a struggle against the all-powerful *kaala*, time. There seems to be a latent longing to check the flow of time. Perhaps this is why he is sometimes despondent. Then he reminds himself that: 'This is a period between two civilizations, the old has died and nothing new has yet replaced it. If we can just hold on to the *saundarya drishti*, aesthetic vision, of the old and save it in parts, maybe this can help to build the new.'

\*

*So, Ravindra remains diligently at his post in this twilight zone. He is not tilting at windmills to bring back the Budubudukalodu*

*or the Gosamolu. They are gone in the flow of time, never to return.*
*The silence of their absence cannot be filled by recorded music and*
*the one-way transmissions of satellite television. Ravindra lives by*
*the faith that eventually new creative energies may arise and the*
*eternal play of light and darkness will find new expression in every*
*village, every town. The silent dawn may yet be filled with new*
*music, if Ravindra's faith proves to be greater than his single*
*lifetime.*

*This may be possible if enough of us examine our own role in*
*this civilizational journey. We can start, Ravindra suggests, by*
*accepting responsibility. And as usual, he says it best through a*
*story:*

*Once a vulture was flying with its prey, a snake, hanging*
*from its claws. As the snake struggled for life it spewed*
*out its poison. The poison fell into an uncovered pot of*
*milk which a guwalan was carrying on her head. The*
*guwalan delivered the milk to the village mukhia's*
*house where the cook made a kheer out of it. This*
*poisonous kheer was then served by the mukhia to a large*
*number of guests, all of whom died. The yamdoot, agent*
*of Death, who came to collect these souls was confused*
*about how to record the responsibility for these deaths. So*
*he went to Yamraj, the Lord of Death, and asked on whose*
*account these deaths should be registered: the vulture, or*
*the snake, or the guwalan, or the cook or the mukhia, or*
*the entire village? Assign the responsibility of these*
*deaths to all of them, replied Yamraj.*

*Today artisans and artists are dying. Who is responsible*
*for their death? You, me, the economic system, today's*
*values or all of this together? Think about it and tell me.*
*I want an answer.*

# Kahelgaon
## Daring to Seek Mukti for the Ganga

The platform of Bhagalpur station was overflowing with passengers. Picking my way through people squatting or lying on the platform, I reached the ticket checker's office. The TC found my request for a reserved seat, on any Patna-bound train that night, somewhat pointless. He was quite sure that I would not be able to board in such a crushing crowd. An unprecedented Ashwamedh Yagna was being held in Patna the next day. Hundreds and thousands of people were converging to the capital city for this event.

An hour later, two friends helped to somehow push me through the throng and on to the train. The seats were already packed to twice their capacity. As the train moved, most of the people who boarded at Bhagalpur sat down in the aisle. A few stations later, even the aisle was so packed that people stood crushed together. I began to fear that some people may suffocate. Crouching beside me, on the lower berth, was a frail old woman who looked like she might pass out any minute.

Why, I asked myself, are people putting themselves through this? What can be so important about attending the Ashwamedh Yagna in Patna? It was another matter that the fellow passengers found my presence equally inexplicable. Why should a woman from Mumbai be travelling alone across Bihar?

*I was returning from Kahelgaon after attending the anniversary gathering of the Ganga Mukti Andolan. Why, I wondered, can such an Andolan not tap even a small part of this irrepressible urge and energy that was carrying lakhs to Patna for the Yagna?*

*

### The river's bondage

As the Ganga winds its way across the plains of Bihar, two determined rock hills stand in its way beside the village of Kahelgaon. Spread out as wide as a lake, the river caressingly flows around the twin sentinels and languidly continues its eastward journey to the beckoning ocean. The fisherfolk who live on the bank close by have named one of those hills after the legendary adivasi archer 'Eklavya'. On 22 February, every year, they gather at dusk on the ghat of Kagzi-tola and row their boats in a reverential *parikrama* of Eklavya and its companion. The birth anniversary of the Ganga Mukti Andolan has been celebrated with such a *nauka jaloos* every year since 1983.

Sometimes, when the wind is uncontrollably boisterous, the boats are linked together with ropes, and rowed in a single file. Songs rise from the men and women sailing the small wooden boats. The wind scatters the melody across the shivering ripples and the voices seem to merge with the ceaseless flow of the Ganga.

After sunset a few women gather on the shore with scores of brightly-coloured paper boats. They place a *diya*, wick lamp, in each tiny boat and with due ceremony reverentially launch them on the river. Glittering like stars in the darkening water, the little lights float valiantly before being swallowed by the river. For generations, all along its course across the northern plains of the Indian subcontinent, the Ganga has been worshipped with such offerings of flowers and light. The eternally generous and caring Mother, she assimilates the sins and longings of millions.

Yet, at the close of the twentieth century the Ganga's children in the fisher-locality of Kagzi-tola, at Kahelgaon, feel driven to work for the *mukti*, liberation, of the Mother herself. The symbiotic identity between the two makes this a struggle for liberation of both the river and its people. For five thousand years, millions of people have bathed in the Ganga to wash away their sins and sought *mukti* from the endless cycle of birth and death and re-birth. How, then, can there be a movement for *liberation* of the *river*?

Kahelgaon is a small town, about thirty kilometres downstream from Bhagalpur. Somewhere nearby a lone, steep mountain sticks out on the plains. For centuries people have called it Mandrachal, the mountain used in the mythic churning of the ocean, when the *devas* and *asuras* competed for *amrit*, the elixir of life. The more historically inclined believe that the mountain may have once been the focal point of an ancient market-place which served as the scene of a prolonged confrontation, and later mingling, of the Aryan and non-Aryan cultures.

Later, in Pauranic times this, area was known as 'Ang-desh', the principality which the Kuru Prince Duryodhan gave to his friend Karna. In the time of Gautam Buddha the area was called Champa. One of the greatest Buddhist universities, Vikramshila, stood just downstream from Bhagalpur. The river folk were then also seafaring sailors who travelled as far as Java and Sumatra. Even then the Ganga must have had an ample spread here, thus enabling Bhagalpur to serve as a major harbour and trading centre.

The desperate poverty of this area is commonly thought to date back to the Mughal period. That is when the *jalkar zamindari* is believed to have begun. This gave ownership over parts of the river to individual landlords, allowing them to collect a tax from fishermen. In 1730, the British formally established their power in Bhagalpur. The Santhal adivasis revolted against the new rulers. Tilka Manjhi, the leader of that revolt was executed by the British. A statue of Tilka Manjhi, now stands in Bhagalpur and the city's university is named after him.

At the dawn of the twentieth century, Bhagalpur was the meeting point for five cultures—Mithila, Bangla, Islamic, Adivasi and Marwari. It was then an important cultural, intellectual and commercial centre with a flourishing cottage industry of silk weavers, which still survives. Thus, the narrow lanes of present-day Bhagalpur are filled with homes which reflect the faded glory of diverse architectural and cultural patterns.

More recently, Bhagalpur has become a byword for the most heinous brutality. In 1981, a newspaper exposé revealed that for several years policemen in Bhagalpur had blinded under-trials and convicts as retribution for their crimes. This had been common knowledge in and around Bhagalpur. A series of investigative articles in the multi-edition daily, *Indian Express*, made it a national scandal. The horror of most urban middle-class readers was further compounded by the fact that many citizens of Bhagalpur approved of the police's arbitrary punishment. The scandal affirmed Bihar's image as an area of darkness.

Of course, the actual life and times of Bhagalpur did not fully correspond to this distant one-dimensional image. The story of the Ganga Mukti Andolan offers glimpses into some of these more varied shades of reality. A part of the story is to be found in a corner room of an old mansion in the narrow lanes of Sujaganj, a locality in the older part of Bhagalpur. That small room serves as the office of Ang Press. On the wall is a smiling portrait of Mahatma Gandhi. Below it sits a tall portly man whose face reflects a tremendous gentleness. Ram Saran is one of the key links in the story of the Ganga Mukti Andolan (GMA).

## Birth of an andolan

For generations, the fishermen of Kahelgaon have risen half-way through the night, long before the first rays of light shimmer over the horizon, and set out in their small wooden boats to harvest the river. But for over two decades now, many have not been able to make an adequate living as the quantum of fish in the river has steadily declined. Thus, they have joined the countless, faceless people who live on the pavements or slums of some large city, breaking stones or lifting bricks at a construction site as casual labourers.

The fisherfolk of Kahelgaon regard themselves as the descendants of the *malaha* who carried the exiled Prince Rama across the Ganga. That Pauranic boatman has been remembered and revered over centuries as a blessed one. But his descendants feel they are a cursed people, poor of mind and perennially victims of circumstance.

Even the practice of *jalkar zamindari* was unique to this eighty-kilometre stretch of Ganga in the region of Bhagalpur. The zamindars charged an average tax of about Rs 5,000 per year on every boat. With 5,000 boats in the area, the total income came to about Rs 2.5 crore annually. The system was ruthlessly administered through *kachheris* run by the armed henchmen of the zamindars.

By the 1980s, the zamindars were not the only problem of the fisherfolk. The once-bountiful Ganga, the veritable cradle of north-Indian civilization, had become an open sewer. All the towns along the Ganga's 2,290 km journey, from Gangotri to the Bay of Bengal, dump their sewage and industrial effluents, virtually untreated, into the river. The falling catch of fish was a consequence of this slow death of the river, a tragedy seemingly beyond the fisherfolks' realm of action.

A struggle against the atrocities of the zamindars seemed more feasible. But even this latent desire to challenge the oppressors was over-laid by a strong sense of helplessness. The fisherfolk believed that they were suffering the consequences of an ancient curse which has forever condemned the community to suffer the indignities of poverty and social oppression. So how did the same people come to even dream of liberating themselves *and* their mother, the river?

The genesis of the Ganga Mukti Andolan was in the revolutionary excitement of Bihar in the mid-70s. In 1974, the veteran Sarvodaya leader, Jayaprakash Narayan, led a students movement against corruption and for a comprehensive social-political renewal which he called *Sampoorn Kranti*, Total Revolution. This wave of idealist energy swept through Bhagalpur carrying on its crest hundreds of young men and women. One of them came from that old mansion in the narrow Girdharishah Lane at Sujaganj, in Bhagalpur.

Ram Saran was born, shortly after Independence, into a prosperous zamindar family. The family's ancestral *haveli* has spacious inner courtyards and a private temple. Women of the house are still rarely seen in the outer rooms. Ram Saran grew into a tall, soft-spoken youth with an intense interest in the world around him.

By the time he graduated from college, with an MA

degree in 1972, the movement led by Jayaprakash Narayan (JP) was just gathering force. Ram Saran was swept along, in spite of opposition from his family. In January 1975, when JP formed the Chattra Yuva Sangharsh Vahini, Ram Saran became an active worker. The Vahini was meant to be a youth force that would work for the interests of the most oppressed or *antim jan*, last person, by peaceful means. The Vahini's age limit was thirty years and its members were prohibited from contesting elections.

The JP Movement momentarily built up an active challenge to the status quo. It helped to create the atmosphere which led Prime Minister Indira Gandhi to react by imposing the Emergency and suspending democratic rights. Thousands of political leaders and activists were arrested. Ram Saran did not go to jail but remained active in the 'underground' work of the Vahini. When the Emergency was lifted in 1977, Ram Saran was working on an adult education programme with the Gandhi Peace Foundation's unit in Bhagalpur. Some of the people in this programme were the fisherfolk from Kagzi-tola.

The fisherfolk would often tell friends like Ram Saran about the cruel ways of the *jalkar zamindars*, water landlords. The henchmen of the landlords were known to slash a man's body and leave him half immersed in the river to slowly bleed to death. The fisherfolk and landless labourers around Bhagalpur had lived with such atrocities for years. Thus, many people supported the blinding of under-trails because they had lost faith in the courts to deliver justice. The same criminal elements were linked with the 'mafia' which robbed the fishermen.

While the blindings of the undertrails had made national headlines, a successful land struggle in Bodhgaya

District, led by the Vahini was virtually unknown outside Bihar.

Two thousand and five hundred years earlier, Gautam Buddha had attained enlightenment under a *pipal* tree beside a stream. That place has since been known as Bodhgaya, today a bustling little town polluted by exhaust fumes of auto-rickshaws and tempos. Since the sixteenth century a Hindu *muth* has controlled about 9,575 acres of land in Gaya district. Most landless peasants of that area laboured for a wage on the *muth's* lands.

In January 1978, scores of Vahini activists went to live among the landless of Bodhgaya, eating the same food and living as members of the community. There followed a string of protest actions challenging the power of the *muth*. By 1981, the movement had succeeded in getting land out of the *muth's* control, for the tillers.

There were many, more ambitious, land struggles all over Bihar at that time. But most of them were led by groups either formally linked with the Naxalite stream, or ideologically inspired by it. Big landlords had created their own 'armies' to crush these armed land struggles. The Vahini activists took pride in the fact that since they did not use armed methods, no counter army was created in Bodhgaya. The emerging 'star' activist of this movement was Anil Prakash.

Anil Prakash was born into a middle-class family of Muzaffarpur, a night's train journey away from Bhagalpur. By the time he was in college, two types of slogans were common in Bihar. One kind was popular with the Naxalite groups: 'Blood, Blood . . . The Blood of Capitalists'; 'One spark can burn an entire jungle'. The other kind of slogans were raised by Jayaprakash Narayan: 'Neither do injustice nor tolerate injustice'.

While he studied for a Bachelor's degree in physics Anil also read the works of Karl Marx. But he was more drawn to Jayaprakash Narayan and plunged full-time into the students' movement. This landed him in jail for six and a half months during the Emergency. There he read Mahatma Gandhi's autobiography. This got him thinking about the importance of seeking goodness within and acting on its strength. But Gandhi didn't seem to offer any answers on how to change the social system. And Anil was restless about doing some thing to bring about Total Revolution. The Vahini answered this need for action and Anil flung himself into the Bodhgaya struggle.

The Bodhgaya movement taught him that non-violence was essential for the success of any such struggle. The Marxist-Leninist (ML) groups, he decided, were not likely to succeed because landlords were instead becoming more powerful. But, 'by our means his [landlord's] weapons are dropped. The ML groups created the Senas. Even the Bodhgaya Mahant tried to build a Kisan Suraksha Samiti (Farmer Protection Committee) but it could not be built . . . We have not learnt non-violence from books but from experience. We have come the full circle from doubt to re-affirmation. And none of us have read Gandhi's full set.'

Some of the fisherfolk of Kagzi-tola had watched the Bodhgaya movement with hope and were now keen to launch a similar struggle of their own. So Ram Saran and other friends in Bhagalpur urged Anil to shift to the banks of the Ganga to confront the problem of *jalkar zamindari*.

### The struggle for mukti

Thus, a dream took shape. This was a longing for creating a new social order, not merely fighting the local goons for small gains. On 22 February 1982, the Nishad Jal Shramik

Sangh, an existing group of the fisher community, convened a meeting at Kahelgaon. This meeting resolved to launch a movement against the *jalkar zamindari*. This was the beginning of the Ganga Mukti Andolan (GMA). On 4 April, 120 people from nineteen villages met at Kahelgaon and agreed to conduct the struggle by non-violent means. As word of this spread, the zamindars and their henchmen laughed. But they soon found that once people felt a sense of unity, through the GMA, they were no longer as afraid as they had been in the past.

Anil Prakash used a powerful example to sharpen the motivation for action:

> Valmiki was a criminal. But when he changed his ways he created an epic poem—the Ramayana. So destructive energies can be converted into creative energies that produce great works. Today there are many Valmikis in our society, we only have to be able to *see* them and give them due recognition and right orientation.

On 23 March 1983, the GMA launched its first *nauka jaloos* from Kahelgaon to Bhagalpur. Its slogan was: '*Jal, bans, auzar hamara, Ganga par adhikar hamara* (The water and fishing instruments are ours, we have rights over the Ganga)'.

A few months later an Eklavya Mela was held on the island, just off the banks at Kahelgaon. The heroism of the self-taught adivasi archer was exalted, but his 'blind devotion to the guru' was negated. Over the years, the GMA would come to define culture as that which gives human beings the strength 'to fight oppression and injustice, to share the sorrows of others and to spread joy, friendship and affection.'

Thus the GMA's domain was not limited to the interests of the fisherfolk. This won it the support of many middle-class professionals both in Bhagalpur and Kahelgaon. However, this changed when the GMA decided to oppose a thermal power plant coming up on the banks of the Ganga at Kahelgaon. Most middle-class supporters saw the plant as essential for the development of the area. But the core group of GMA was determined to challenge this concept of development.

Why, asked Anil Prakash, must the high energy consumption Bata factory replace the local cobbler? Why must sugarcane be processed in large mills to produce polished sugar? *Gur*, or jaggery, is much healthier and its local decentralized production generates widespread livelihood opportunities. Why should there be so many factories spewing toxic wastes into the Ganga? The problem cannot be solved just by treating these effluents. Poisonous pesticides used in fields of the river plain seep into the river, killing aquatic life. The slow death of the Ganga is a consequence of the so-called 'development' in which large thermal power plants are considered essential.

This stand cost the GMA many of its middle-class supporters but the Andolan forged ahead on this track. As Ram Saran often took pains to point out, this was not a mere union. If that had been the case 'we would have called it *Machuara Mukti Andolan*, Fisherfolk Liberation Movement. It is the *Ganga* Mukti Andolan because we are concerned with the holistic importance of Ganga to our life, economy and culture.'

The GMA was trying to become a larger social movement with a vision for a more creative form of development. Thus, the GMA struggled to carry this vision in tandem with its more immediate, and passion-rousing battle against the zamindars. In the following years there were many different actions, including collective hunger strikes, dharnas and other kinds of satyagraha. These actions drew different kinds of people into the struggle. Within five years the GMA had acquired a substantial base in several villages around Kahelgaon. Thus, in 1987, the GMA launched an ambitious *nauka jaloos* from Kursela, further downstream from Kahelgaon, to Patna about 400 kilometres upstream. The long line of boats with fluttering banners and slogan-shouting passengers was a unique sight.

'It is better to die once for your rights rather than to slowly die a little every day at the hands of the zamindars.' The woman who boldly said this was not used to making public speeches. Yet there she was addressing a public meeting on the river bank at Kahelgaon. The gathering was welcoming the *nauka jaloos* which had arrived from Kursela with two boats. Now fifty other boats were anchored close by, ready to join the procession towards Patna.

Sonia Devi, another resident of Kahelgaon, explained why the struggle of the GMA was an imperative:

Now there are few fish in the river and because of that we are going into debt. The atrocities of the zamindars have increased so much that now it seems we will have to drop everything else and just fight this battle, even if we don't have enough to eat. Only then can we get our just due.

People along the banks 'were amazed to see women and men working together day and night in this fearless manner, sailing through the dangerous areas of the Ganga', a chronicler of the movement later wrote in a book titled *Ganga ko aviral bahene do* (Let the Ganga Flow Freely). At many places the procession was stopped by criminals and dacoits who asked many questions about this unique exercise. Most of them were impressed by the demands and purpose of the GMA. Some of them urged the GMA to prepare an atmosphere in which the criminals could return to a life of peace and comfort. 'We have no attachment to a life of violence and theft,' many of them confessed.

It was still very likely that the procession could be attacked anywhere along the way to Patna. But the comfort of numbers and a defiant spirit made the participants unafraid. Shanti Devi, a 55-year-old widow who had been active in the GMA since the beginning, vowed that: 'We will fight, no matter what happens. If I die fighting then like a daughter I will go to sleep in the lap of Mother Ganga.' Another woman, Lalita, said: 'Our struggle is against the gun and bullet, so there cannot be an instant victory. We are fighting and slowly we are also winning.'

For fourteen days the procession sailed slowly towards Patna. The sounds of revolutionary songs floated on the waves of the Ganga attracting attention everywhere. Yogendra, an activist and co-author of *Ganga ko aviral bahene do*, later wrote that 'people along the banks of the river felt that something momentous is about to happen.'

The *nauka jaloos* culminated in a rally at the Gandhi Ghat, Patna, where the Ganga stretches towards the horizon like an ocean. Here, the fishermen took a vow that they would no longer pay tax to the zamindars. But the GMA did not represent the limited economic interest of the fisherfolk. Thus, when the Andolan spoke of people's *right* over the river, it was not enough to lament the villainy of the zamindars. The river itself must be saved.

Thus, for the GMA the rally in Patna was an opportunity to present its perspective and list its demands:

–the government's ambitious Ganga Action Plan, launched in 1985, is a futile exercise. Cleaning the Ganga requires a comprehensive review and reorientation of industrial and urban development policy along the banks;

–instead of large polluting thermal power plants, small power plants must be built in various places. This will mean less displacement of local people and a much wider spread of economic benefits. Given the quantities of cow-dung available in India, bio-mass resources can be effectively harnessed for both energy and fertilizer needs. According to one estimate this could provide almost three times the amount of phosphate and nitrogen being produced in factories;

–in order to solve the escalating problem of heavy floods in the Ganga, the cutting of jungles in the Himalayas must be completely halted;

–'*kapda jal*' must be prohibited. These are nylon nets, somewhat like mosquito nets about 100 to 200 metres long. Fishermen, in some parts of Bihar, had switched entirely to these nets which destroy the breeding grounds of the fish, by pulling in tiny fish and eggs. The nets also drag away a lot of the water-weeds which are essential to the natural cleaning processes of the Ganga;

–the Farakka Barrage must be dismantled. This barrage is a dam-like bridge, across the Ganga, with doors that open and close. It was opposed by some engineers even at the planning stage in the 1960s. Since its completion in 1975, the barrage has been held responsible for causing excess flooding and silting. It has also hit the livelihood of fishermen on both sides because fish cannot move freely across the barrier.

This *nauka jaloos* put the GMA on the political map of

that region. The struggle around Kahelgaon now gathered greater momentum. In December 1989, hundreds of members of the GMA took control of the zamindar's *kachheri*, at Kagzi-tola. This old stone structure was the managerial and symbolic centre of the zamindari power. Hundreds of men and women marched peacefully into the *kachheri* shouting the trademark slogan of the JP movement: '*Hamla chahe jaisa hoga, haath hamara nahin uthega* (no matter how we are attacked, our hand will not be raised in retaliation)'.

By then the strength and determination of the GMA had been established through scores of different actions. The zamindars' henchmen did not offer much resistance. The erstwhile *kachheri* then became the permanent office of the GMA. As Raj Kumar, an activist from the fisher community later recalled, non-violence was first adopted because the outsider activists like Anil Prakash and Ram Saran insisted on it. But now it had grown into a conviction within the community. Six months after this take-over, the Andolan returned triumphantly to Gandhi Ghat at Patna to, once again, make their presence felt in the capital city.

The harsh mid-May sun beat upon the gathering at Gandhi Ghat in Patna. The sweltering heat was accompanied by thirst and hunger but there was a sparkling energy in the voices that shouted slogans: 'Make the whole Ganga tax-free'; 'Abolish water-zamindari'; 'Close down the Bata shoe factory'; 'Break down the Farakka Barrage'. Fishermen, peasants, weavers, craftsmen, students, intellectuals, teachers and artists had come from different parts of Bihar to attend a two-day meeting called by the GMA.

A group of Santhal adivasis opened the meeting with a song which told of a time:

. . . when the jungles were still there, food and drink was easily available. There was wood to make homes. There were enough things in the jungle which we could sell in the market and buy other necessities. Today the jungle has been cut and our livelihood has been destroyed. Now we have neither enough to eat nor wear.

In another song the Santhals urged all Adivasis to get educated and 'give a new direction to the nation.'

Anil Prakash recounted the success of the GMA in eight years of struggle:

. . . For thirty kilometres around Kahelgaon the fisherfolk have stopped paying tax to the zamindars. People who were once intimidated by the guns of the zamindars are now ready to challenge them. There is a new awareness among the people from Patna to Farakka. The mafia of the fishing cooperatives is also being challenged. The Bihar government gets Rs 10 lakh in taxes from the entire stretch of the Ganga. But the contractors of the cooperatives snatch crores of rupees from the fisherfolk. The government must abolish the tax in the interests of the people.

The meeting closed with all participants making a pledge that they would fight against the commercialization of rivers, oceans, mountains, forests, the earth and the air—and struggle ceaselessly to free these gifts of nature. They also resolved to work for a society which is free of exploitation and based on the ideals of equality, cooperation, affection and democratic values.

Later that year, the chief minister of Bihar, Laloo Prasad Yadav, formally abolished the *jalkar zamindari* and all fishing taxes on either rivers or their tributaries. With this victory the GMA entered a phase of uncertainty that induced a strange lethargy.

## Unfulfilled yearnings

The old crumbling *kachheri* was slowly being geared up for the meeting to mark another anniversary. It was 22 February 1994, and the GMA was twelve years old. A raised area with a rough uneven surface served as a platform for the meeting. Beside it was an open verandah, damp from the downpour of rain. All remnants of the old zamindari power had long ago been removed. And some of the old energy for action seemed to have gone too. The anniversary was a lacklustre, routine affair.

Representatives from different villages had gathered for the meeting. There was an underlying sense of regret that another year had gone by and not much had happened to carry forward the mission of GMA. Most of them accepted the low phase with a quiet resignation. Some despaired about it. Others sought to analyse and understand the reasons for this lull.

At one point in the early-90s the GMA was getting letters from people in different corners of the country, expressing solidarity with their cause. The idea of Ganga *mukti* seemed to spread further along the course of the river. What happened to this momentum?

Perhaps, Yogendra wondered, the anti-tax struggle had been too brief and victory had come too soon while the Sangathan was not properly formed in many areas:

Tax abolition and zamindari were directly related

to fishermen's self-interest, but Farakka and pollution seem indirect to them. We need to involve many more fishing villages and make an impact on these issues. But we're not able to actively involve people from other villages. When GMA was at its peak it was hoped that this success would sweep through society, but there wasn't any follow-up. The movement has gone cold due to lack of workers and lack of funds.

There was some self-doubt among the middle-class activists of the Andolan. Had they perhaps taken on too much of the work and responsibility, thus stunting the growth of the village activists? Most of the analytical discussions on larger social and political issues tended to be dominated by the urban activists, where the fisherfolk mostly listened.

As Raj Kishore, himself a fisherman, said:

The GMA has helped some people to understand why fish are reduced—because of factory pollution, Farakka Barrage, over-harvesting, etc. The issue now is how to stop this and then decide on a course of action. Otherwise no one can stop fish from declining and livelihood from becoming more and more difficult.

At such times it helped to reflect on the successes of the Andolan. Working together in the GMA had broken down many of the *jati*, sub-caste, barriers within the fisher community. This intermingling within sub-castes was a joy to Vahini activists, since *jati todo*, caste abolition, had been one of the foundational principles of their politics. But it was a qualified success since they did not succeed in encouraging inter-caste marriages.

However, the active involvement of women, their new awareness and emergence in leadership roles, was a source of tremendous satisfaction for the activists of GMA.

Meanwhile, dacoities once again increased in the area around Kahelgaon. Parvati Devi felt this was because 'the Andolan is slow now, there are differences within. The whole village doesn't join, or support, though all the people here are fisherfolk.'

Raj Kumar Saini lamented despairingly about the emergence of new criminals who are even worse than the old zamindars:

> If the Sangathan does anything about this we will
> be shot at. If we die our children will die; whoever
> takes a lead in this will face death. The government
> must take action. I never had headaches before, now
> I have. They (people) pull back anyone who does
> work. I work so hard but everyone criticizes me.

By 1994, village activists like Raj Kumar were also agonizing about the Dunkel Draft, which they understood was going to mean the worst kind of zamindari by a distant, unreachable enemy. 'Dunkel is such an instrument that it will strip [us] and we won't even know that a robber has attacked us.' In mid-94, the GMA sent a small contingent of its members to join an anti-Dunkel rally organized by the National Alliance of People's Movements in New Delhi. This Alliance is a political platform for formations like the GMA in different parts of India.

Rám Saran pondered that perhaps:

The GMA shared the shortcomings of the Vahini because it took the task of changing society on its own shoulders. Therefore, even in Kagzi-tola, we didn't encourage the local leadership to emerge and take on challenges. Now they're not ready. We, older people, don't have so much time. Anilji is ill. Many workers have left.

Underlying these various observations were complex personal and social factors. By 1993, Anil Prakash had withdrawn from the scene at Kahelgaon and returned to his hometown, Muzaffarpur. He wore the look of a wounded soldier. He felt like 'Arjun at the end of the Mahabharat war when he can't even pull the string of his *Gandiva* bow.' Some blamed the slack pace on Anil's decision to withdraw. But others knew that Anil had gone away partly to deal with a depression induced by the lack of progress in the Andolan.

## The future
The boyishness of Anil's face was undiminished by the newly greying hair. He seemed to be wilting under the sheer weight of his own unfulfilled aspirations. But he retained an unwavering sense of gratitude for the Ganga Mukti Andolan experience: 'What I feel today, has been taught to me by the waves of the Ganga. From Emergency to Bodhgaya there were many experiments but it was along the banks of the Ganga that I got to see society up close.'

Perhaps, he mused, sometimes you have to move back a step or two in order to make a jump. A year later he was back in the fray, travelling to Champaran and helping to organize a *gur* satyagraha. Sugarcane farmers in Bihar are prohibited by law from making jaggery and compelled to sell all their cane to the sugar mills. Under the gur satyagraha, thousands of sugarcane growers began defying this ban and locally manufacturing jaggery.

However, these various local struggles seemed to have little impact on the power structure. At just about the same time a series of multi-crore scams were being uncovered within the Bihar government. Chief Minister Laloo Prasad Yadav, once identified with the JP movement, now seemed like enemy number one to activists like Anil Prakash.

These developments strengthened Anil's conviction that the future lies in people creating their own institutions:

> This will happen through widespread awareness and this is happening in villages, small-small sangathans are coming up everywhere, some are working against liquor . . . Democracy must be rooted in the people, then democratic institutions will be born from among the people. There may be many failings in our society which need to be corrected. But society also has its own mechanisms (of self-regulation). Our job is to remove the dirt and dust from these in-built mechanisms . . . Our job is to make people more aware and then to support their efforts. Even if some institutions and sangathans fail, others are born. This process is going on and GMA is a part of it.

Ram Saran longed to see a formation like the National Alliance of People's Movements gathering strength to enable effective coordination between such andolans all over India. In time, he hoped, out of such coordination may be born a political formation that would make its presence felt at the centrestage of Indian politics. But the fulfillment of this dream requires a regular and sustained effort in which intricate ideological issues are dealt with and differences are resolved. And this inner-task sometimes seems more difficult than battling the status quo.

On the eve of the fiftieth anniversary of Independence, Ram Saran, Yogendra and several of their old Vahini colleagues issued an impassioned appeal to their fraternity. They wrote about how bitterly the dream of a New India has been betrayed by the political leadership. Why, they asked, doesn't the people's anger surface? Why are the intellectuals, writers, social activists so silent? Why is there no collective response? Why don't those who believe in honesty, justice, democracy and equality, arise? Don't we have faith in ourselves?

They could easily have added another question: why don't we have faith in each other? The lament about pervasive social and moral decline was accompanied by a silent realization that many efforts collapse from lack of a team. Anil looked about and found most of his friends and colleagues in deep despair—undermined by a pervasive negativity. When things are gloomy, he pondered, we wind up pulling each other down. But on some reflection he was also able to see that his own shortcomings made true team-building more difficult. In 1995, Anil had alienated several colleagues by almost unilaterally deciding to contest a seat in the state Assembly elections.

So, for the time being, Anil found his own partial answer by changing gears and entering a reflective phase. He spent many months trying to understand the problems created by the Farakka Barrage. Given the enormous scale of the problem, he realized, a movement on the scale of the GMA would be meaningless. Besides, now Anil was not interested in working on short-term campaigns. Now, he longed to do something deeper and long term.

This feeling was born out of the realization that one round of the battle against globalization has already been lost. The usurpation of natural resources and production processes by distant forces has entered a more advanced stage. So Anil set about seeking clues to the cause and cure of the pervasive indolence which he found afflicting much of Bihar and Uttar Pradesh. He is seeking a means by which people can feel energized and enthused about creatively altering their circumstances.

Ram Saran sees this reality with a quiet anguish. His unique gift for not judging others makes him a link between diverse kinds of people. He longs for some process, some elusive magic, which will bring various kinds of activists together to build powerful andolans. But, as the low phase of the Ganga Mukti Andolan continues, Ram Saran gracefully accepts this as a time to just wait and watch for possibilities on the horizon.

Meanwhile Ram Saran never errs from his duty. Every year, early in February, a warm letter unfailingly goes out from that tiny office of his printing press. Ram Saran signs that letter on behalf of the GMA, inviting all friends of the Andolan to come and join the birth anniversary function at Kahelgaon.

The drama of dharnas and satyagraha is now rare. But the gathering on 22 February and its rituals are an intrinsic part of Kahelgaon's culture. During the day, activists from different villages discuss the work of the year gone by and make plans for the future. Even if the numbers at this discussion dwindle, there is usually a good turn-out for the brief *nauka jaloos* in the evening. A few dozen boats faithfully sail in a *parikarma* around the Eklavya hill. Later, when it is dark, the women of Kagzi-tola reverentially send the fluttering *diyas* in colourful paper boats floating down the Ganga.

Acts of devotion are unfettered by the vagaries of political struggles.

*

*Let us return now to that tightly-packed train heading for the Ashwamedh Yagna in Patna. At some point I asked the frail old woman, sitting next to me, why she was going for the yagna. Her fatigue seemed to lift a little as she explained that this was the first, and probably last, time in her life that such a yagna was being held. Then she folded her hands, lifting her eyes upwards, conveying more than words ever could. The effort and discomfort of the journey to Patna is nothing before the merit and peace of being present at the yagna.*

*There was a vast chasm between that woman's sentiments and the despairing disgust of the two young activists who had stood with me at Bhagalpur station a few hours earlier. Watching the milling crowd of pilgrims on the platform, they had lamented about why lakhs of people can be mobilized for a yagna but not for a process like the Ganga Mukti Andolan.*

*A possible answer came my way the next day during a tourist boat ride at Banaras. The boatman gave a lively commentary on the city of Banaras and its exquisitely crafted ghats. Obtruding among these ghats is the large cement structure of a sewage treatment plant, built under the Ganga Action Plan. The boatman pointed it out with gleeful ridicule, and asked his audience: 'When a child shits on its mother, it is the mother who cleans the mess. The Ganga is our mother, who are we to clean her?'*

## C.V. Seshadri

# Gandhi as the Century's Greatest Inventor

A tall man with heavy shoulders stood just inside the main entrance of Bapu Kuti. The sharp white of his crisp cotton shirt and pants echoed the sheet on the narrow mattress that was once Mahatma Gandhi's bed. Moving closer to Gandhi's small writing 'chowki', beside the low, foot-high window, C.V. Seshadri's high, scholarly brow creased. His patrician face bore a faint scowl.

Looking around, absorbing minute details of the simple, strong bamboo roof, the beauty of the black wooden pillars, he let out the ghost of a sigh. How did India reduce the contributions of the century's greatest inventor, Mohandas Karamchand Gandhi, to an archive? Of all the questions that bothered 'CVS' this one may have hurt the most.

This is a Gandhi that most young people don't know. CVS had heard his own son dismiss Gandhi outright because 'that man was obsessed with sex'. So is everyone else, CVS smiled to himself, but Gandhi dared not to hide it.

Adjusting the strap of his shoulder bag CVS ambled out of the Kuti on to the gravel compound. Feet crunching on the tiny rounded pebbles, CVS passed under the grand neem trees beside the Kuti. He headed for Gauri Bhavan, where a bunch of young friends waited to spend the day with him. Brainstorming with young enthusiasts beat brooding over the past any day!

*The winter sun over Sewagram was just a shade too strong to sit under the sky for long hours. So the avid group of young people had gathered in the porch of Gauri Bhavan, a three-sided structure of long halls with a large open courtyard. Besides, here there was ample wall space and poles on which to lazily lean back.*

*This group had spontaneously come together during a five-day conference to commemorate the centenary of J.C. Kumarappa. The most intense and illuminating discussions, we found, happened outside the formal meetings of the conference. Most of us had been enthralled by CVS's ideas and sheer presence, when he spoke in the plenary session of the conference. So, on the day set aside for delegates to tour local village projects, we persuaded CVS to drop out and spend the day with us. Settling down on the cold cement floor of Gauri Bhavan we followed CVS as he led us on a journey through time and the philosophy of science.*

## Unexpressed cravings

Fishermen on the Coromandel coast, just outside Chennai city, knew the early morning swimmer rather well. For years they had watched C.V. Seshadri stride down the soft white sands as the sun emerged above the shimmering ripples of the ocean. He would plunge into the waves and head out for a long hard swim.

Then one morning he swam out, perhaps further or deeper, and never returned.

Some of those fishermen had known this man as a friend and scientist. Often he had lingered in their midst as they prepared their nets for a catch. 'CVS', as friends called him, was fascinated by the various simple devices the fishermen used to enhance their catch. An uprooted coconut tree, complete with branches, was sometimes suspended in shallow waters to serve as a mock-reef and attract fish.

Over the years CVS had worked with some of the

fishermen to design a Fish Aggregating Device. This was a large three-dimensional triangle made out of waste plastics and other discarded materials, like old tires. Submerged just below the ocean surface this device was a more effective mock-reef, with loads of fish gathering under its shade.

But CVS's bond with the land, the sea, the fishermen was deeper than mere sentiment or clever inventions. His sense of belonging, and that easy confidence, came with pride in a rich ancestry.

The Seshadri family could trace its lineage back to AD 1530. Orthodoxy, scholarship and good living were taken for granted in their household. Chetput Venkatasubban Seshadri was born in 1930 and grew up listening to his father recite entire passages from the Vedas, French and English poetry with equal ease. His mother never went to school but 'she soaked up knowledge like a blotter soaking up ink'.

Early in life CVS realized that this inherited package also included 'courage and idealism just this side of stupidity' and the faith that 'to be different is to lead, to create, to teach'. He liked to almost boast about a distant ancestor who was non-conformist enough to marry a widow and take hallucinogens to help him edit the Advaitic texts.

In CVS's life these traits triggered a particularly agonizing restlessness. His college years, as a science student, were filled with 'unexpressed cravings and unfulfilled ambitions'. He had a way with his hands and longed to invent things. After taking a B.Sc from the Mumbai University's Department of Chemical Technology, in 1958 CVS went to the United States. There he joined the Carnegie-Mellon University for a Ph.D in Chemical Engineering. Later, he was a research associate at the Massachusetts Institute of Technology (MIT) in Boston.

These experiences taught him that being an inventor

involves '... mostly guts and gore with very little glory'. The study of vapours and techniques for de-icing of aircraft wings fascinated the young would-be inventor, but not for long. Somehow, the invention of clever gadgets could not hold CVS's full attention. He began to feel that these devices were of no help to the mass of people in India, or the poor anywhere.

## Doubts about 'western' science

At the same time CVS became deeply preoccupied with some basic doubts about science as it had been taught to him. Is science a model of reality or is it reality? CVS asked himself. Over the years, he examined this question and decided that modern western science is only '*a*' model and there can be many viewpoints about our world. Thus, he began to explore whether the axioms of modern western science were indeed universal. At that time, in the early 1970s, these questions were neither respectable or popular. People laughed at the young CVS when he argued that science is not value-free.

But the questions refused to go away and rode in tandem, all life long, with his engineering research. Unlike most of his peers, CVS returned to work in India and teach at the Indian Institute of Technology (IIT), Chennai. In 1965 he shifted to IIT, Kanpur. Here he earned an enduring reputation as an outstanding teacher and for his research in fluid mechanics and biotechnology.

Among the students at IIT Kanpur he found many of his future fellow-workers. Sunil Sahasrabudhey, one of his many student-admirers, later wrote fondly about 'this handsome professor, always dressed in white cotton trousers and white cotton half-shirt tucked in, a sportsman and a democrat'. He would play a vigorous game of football with as much stamina as men twenty years younger than him. The Students' Senate insisted on CVS's appointment as the Dean of Students.

During the 1970s and 1980s, as the environmental crisis unleashed by modern industrialization came to be widely recognized, CVS was among the few Indian scientists who argued that these problems were not amenable to mere managerial solutions. Like several thinkers in the West, CVS traced the roots of the environmental crisis to the primacy of the Biblical notion of man's domination *over* nature. CVS realized that it made no sense to talk of ecology unless this foundational idea of western science was challenged.

Modern technological processes, CVS argued, create order in a controlled setting only by generating a greater disorder outside that sphere. The 'progress' of modernity created enormous prosperity in the West only at the cost of disintegration of resources and cultures in the colonies. And the Second Law of Thermodynamics, CVS found, actually sanctions this abuse.

Since the early-70s CVS was deeply preoccupied with the 'problem' of entropy. The dictionary explains entropy as 'a measure of the energy unavailable for useful work in a system, or the tendency of an energy system to run down.' This is actually the name for the energy that is irretrievably lost. This notion of eternal loss bothered CVS and so he started to critically re-examine the laws of thermodynamics. This search led him to discover that these laws are bound by a particular value system.

In a booklet titled *Development and Thermodynamics*, CVS argued that prevailing concepts of energy are not only human-centred, instead of nature-based, but are also inspired by the western, capitalist culture. 'Many concepts that are accepted as absolutely self-evident once stated or as arising out of a "scientific method" are really based on very deep-seated cultural roots that need not necessarily be universal,' CVS wrote. This observation was not unique to CVS. In 1954, Albert Einstein had urged that 'in the interests of science it is necessary over and over again to engage in the critique of these fundamental concepts, in order that we may not unconsciously be ruled by them.'

For example, the American Physical Society (APS) has defined energy quality from the perspective of the Second Law of Thermodynamics as follows: 'organized coherent motion is most precious, very high (and very low) temperature is next most precious, and heat at a temperature near ambient (lukewarm, cool) is degraded energy.' But, CVS pointed out:

> The monsoon over Asia and Africa carries billions of tonnes of water across the continents, performing countless gigajoules [sic] of work but the definition makes this work of low quality because it is done across small gradients at ambient temperatures . . .
> Thus, the APS has set strange standards of energy-quality, strictly related to economic exploitation. If one defined energy-quality as being inversely proportional to the amount of entropy produced per year per capita, then the Ivory Coast would have the highest energy-quality and the USA the lowest, since the USA creates the most disorder and degrades the most.
> . . . So it is an insult to nature to say that thermodynamics is an attempt to study nature and formulate laws of its governance; in fact, it seems to study only those processes which can be controlled and put in the service of the economic powers.

CVS went on to argue that such problems in science emanate from using the concept of an 'isolated system'. In reality, he insisted, there are no isolated systems and that isolability was a wrong kind of idealization to use for scientific formulations.

From the concept of entropy arises the assumption that the world is always running down like a wound-up clock. Why, CVS asked, should the world start with a big bang and decay ever after? These questions led him deeper into an examination of the religious values in science. Much of the problem, he found, lies in how the concept of linear time has entirely replaced the earlier concept of rhythms and cycles. 'The one-dimensional time of science is purely Biblical,' CVS wrote, 'and therefore not universal.'

Yet this veritable 'gospel' of linear time now rules all aspects of life. So CVS proposed a rhythmical notion of time, for ' . . . unless you change the concept of time you can't change the principles of science and then you can't change the dominant knowledge system. The axioms of science must be changed to change its values.'

These 'values' have in turn deeply influenced economic structures and defined 'efficiency' in particular ways. For example, centralized production of electricity at large power-plants made sense in Europe where the countries are small. In a country of India's size, centralized production is not the answer. Yet, as CVS lamented, that is the pattern we have followed using 'false arguments from thermodynamics and the incorrect "economy of scale" principle.' Thus, CVS pleaded for an *Indian* perspective on which such decisions could be based:

We in India have this very great advantage of possessing a value system that is completely different (from that of the Christian West) and we must make use of it in evolving our own knowledge system . . . Many scientists in the West, sensitized particularly by the damage done to the environment, have begun to question how and where the values are coming into science (and not just whether there is value in science). I could say no one except Indian scientists believes that science is value-free.

Eventually, CVS also proposed a new class of properties for energy which he called 'Shakti'. This, he argued, would enable us to define energy in ways which suit our specific geographic and cultural context.

Even while he worked on the philosophical problems of science, CVS was sharply attuned to the political shifts and currents of his time. He saw India as the location of two bloodless revolutions in the twentieth century: 'One when we eased out the British in 1947 and one when the western powers took us back through their economic theories in the 1970s.' He became a bitter critic of how we have been 'good passive receivers' of all things western.

'All this would be wonderful,' he wrote, 'if we could benefit our people more than we have or improve the resource base of the country to make it more sustainable.' But after nearly fifty years of attaining freedom, seventy per cent of the population suffers from one form or other of chronic malnutrition. This, he felt, is largely because in the so-called third world 'science and technology are not presented as a marketplace of ideas and models for the practitioner to choose and select from but as an absolute body of incontestable fact and a nostrum for all ills assailing the society.'

Therefore, the market forces and policy-makers deem it more 'efficient' to convert molasses into alcohol for industrial use, rather than into yeast that has food value for humans and animals. Similarly, farmers are urged to sell their sugarcane to centralized sugar mills instead of themselves converting it to *gur* (jaggery). This is in spite of the widely accepted fact that *gur* is nutritionally superior to white sugar and can be produced in small low-cost units at the village level.

As Claude Alvares once quoted Seshadri at his unabashed, radical best:

'I am all for abolishing sophisticated technology if for nothing else, so that we can learn for ourselves of ourselves. We have not even tried this alternative. They say, "but you are being a Gandhian." I tell them "You haven't tried being a Gandhian, what do you know about being a Gandhian?' . . . Seshadri objects if people call him an 'alternative' scientist. ' . . . I am really looking for problems from the field, and it is here that I have felt repeatedly that technology feeds science more often than the other way around. It is a complete fallacy among Indian scientists that science feeds technology.'

So CVS came to revere Gandhi for his sharp grasp on problems and his genius for devising appropriate solutions. Thus Gandhi's emphasis on khadi made sense to CVS because, as he explained:

. . . it was sustenance for the kisan during the off-season. It was a means of self-reliance, it was a means of barter, it was renewable in perpetuity.

Above all it was a teaching tool for mathematics, for the child who was being taught to spin. It was employment, crop and clothing all rolled into one. Invention is a social act. It is not science and technology bureaucratese. Nehru in his archaic Fabian zeal thought he could issue Papal bulls about scientific temper. The result is scientific distemper, our most widespread disease. Our people now have access neither to traditional knowledge nor new knowledge. They are illiterate in two epistemologies.

## The quest for an 'Indian' science

These problems came to trouble CVS to a point where he felt stifled in the formal science and technology establishment. In any case he had come to see the IITs as prize plantations at which teachers like himself were cultivating 'India's chief cash crop—our youth'. There seemed to be no point in training brains to be drained! So, in 1974, he decided to leave and follow his heart, 'to participate more actively in development issues'.

This urge to take science to the villages, to directly address problems of development at the level of daily life, flowered in many different forms in the 1970s. Even the Indian Science Congress held in January 1976, had rural development as its main theme. But the most creative and innovative initiatives were outside the formal science establishment.

The Kerala Sastra Sahitya Parishad (KSSP), a formation of the Marxist stream, was born in 1962 and worked with the slogan 'science for social revolution'. It aimed to bridge the gap between science in the abstract and people's everyday lives. In the 1970s the KSSP became famous for spearheading a successful movement to save Silent Valley, a stretch of tropical forest threatened by a hydro-electric project. It also played a key role in making Kerala a fully literate state. By 1996, the KSSP had about 2,000 units and 60,000 members all over Kerala. In the same year it won the Right Livelihood Award, also called the Alternate Nobel Prize.

The KSSP is the veritable flagship of the All India People's Science Network, which is made up of similar groups all over India. This network involves students and a wide variety of professionals—doctors, engineers, teachers, bureaucrats—in its endeavours. These include environmental protection, health, women's development, educational reforms and the spread of scientific agricultural methods.

In the Gandhi-Sarvodaya tradition, Devendra Kumar led the setting up of a Centre of Science for Villages at Wardha, in 1976. The Centre brought new life to Maganwadi where, four decades earlier, Gandhi and his colleagues had based the most intense phase of their endeavours for village industries. Devendra Kumar, a direct disciple of J.C. Kumarappa, worked to counter the false impression that Gandhi was anti-science.

At the Indian Institute of Science (IISc), Bangalore, A.K.N. Reddy led the formation of ASTRA, or Application of Science and Technology to Rural Areas. ASTRA was born out of the awareness that educational, scientific and technological institutions in India tend to be elitist, alienated and lacking in native roots. So the scientists who came together in ASTRA sought to initiate and catalyze work, at the IISc, which would generate technologies appropriate for rural development.

Over the last twenty-five years ASTRA has, through a sustained interaction with villagers in a part of Karnataka, designed and implemented many technologies geared towards people's empowerment. Some of its pathbreaking work is in the efficient use of bio-mass to produce energy in a decentralized manner. It has also perfected a wide variety of low-cost eco-friendly housing technologies.

In the Hoshangabad district of Madhya Pradesh, Kishore Bharati set about evolving a science teaching programme for teachers in government schools. The moving spirit of this effort was Anil Sadgopal, a graduate of the California Institute of Technology (CalTech), who quit his job at the Tata Institute of Fundamental Research, Mumbai, to live and work in the villages. Elsewhere, in Shahdol district, MP, a group of IIT graduates set up the Vidushak Karkhana and grappled with how to use their training to tap and enhance local skills.

Thus CVS's endeavour was not isolated. Yet the nature of his restlessness was, probably, unique. As Claude Alvares suggested in an article in the *Indian Express*, CVS may have been alone in thinking that working on the basic needs, like food and shelter, would transform science and technology itself. Alvares, himself a leading activist of the alternatives movement, saw CVS as a pioneer of *Indian* science. Such a science, Alvares wrote, would generate:

> . . . a scheme of intellectual thought with assumptions that reflect the priorities of the society in which it evolves, not the society in which it originated . . . If science must echo cultural values, these should be of relevance to life in our environment rather than to that of western society or its peculiar mode of production.

This is what CVS set out to do in a more intense manner

when he quit the formal science establishment and returned to his native South India. For the next three years CVS set up and ran India's largest yeast factory at Mysore. In 1977, he built his own working 'home', the AMM Murugappa Chettiar Research Centre. The MCRC devoted itself to one central concern: in a world of decreasing resources, how do we maintain a viable eco-system with a meaningful quality of life for all living beings?

As CVS already knew, there was no existing paradigm on which he could base his work. But he drew enormous inspiration from the experimental ways of Mahatma Gandhi and J.C. Kumarappa. For him Gandhi and Kumarappa were 'the archetypal Indian inventors. Holism at its best, holism incarnate.' He saw both of them building on the same cultural ethos which once created phenomenal temple architecture, evolved the concept of the 'zero' and over hundreds of years nurtured the neem tree for all its miraculous properties.

Like Gandhi and Kumarappa, CVS saw a profound absurdity in the endless race to 'catch up' with the western notion and model of *development*. He wrote:

What has this (western) paradigm amounted to in the twentieth century? Two world wars, one holocaust, countless millions of people displaced, ethnic cleansing, ethical wastelands, atomic weapons, environmental damage, the list is endless. To keep hearing that the good excuses the bad and be persuaded to believe in this, is again only possible with our colonial subservience. This then is also what western knowledge systems are all about. Ultimately they have not achieved eaglite [sic], their own Holy Grail.

**The Mahatma as a guide**
This affinity with the Mahatma and his disciple presented CVS with a tough yardstick for judging himself:

In working on problems of development of the country, and in particular on problems of rural people, one is often faced with the question: am I doing anything for them or am I doing it for myself? Most people in their professions probably face this question at one time or another. One can generalize this problem and say that there is a virus model of development and there is an organismic [sic] model. A virus attacks an organism and uses the organism to reproduce itself from the material it finds inside. Eventually the organism dies. Most development agencies are usually like the virus model. In our arrogance of knowledge, we know what the villager wants or can be given and instead of developing the village, usually end up only making copies of ourselves and destroying the village. For village you can read coastal littoral, jungle, wild life or any of the usual development areas. [As] Agencies spread, villages die.

On the other hand an organismic model of development will call for a symbiotic merger with the village and growth together with the local people; both developed and developer learn together. To the extent possible our work has involved close growth of both developer and developed and at the very least calls for living in the village. Only thus have we been able to bring about innovations in catamarans, energy devices, nutrition, etcetera. Many of our innovations have been done with local participation and suggestion.

Thus, the AMM Murugappa Chettiar Research Centre became a busy place where scientists and 'laypersons' worked side by side to promote holistic invention. The Centre soon became like an oasis, with its lush green, tree-rich compound in an otherwise dry and drab area on the edge of Chennai city. A few simple structures housed the offices and laboratories where scientists experimented with a wide variety of devices. In one corner of the Centre's small compound was a mini bio-gas plant, which could solve the problems of farmers who have only one cow. Much of the bio-gas technology is otherwise geared for big farmers or collectives and requires large volumes of cow-dung and other bio-mass.

Among other things, MCRC developed a technique for making paper out of silk cotton. This process uses *ceiba pentandra*, a plant which can be raised on wastelands. The silk cotton is treated with bacteria to form pulp and makes a good quality paper. Since the paper industry is responsible for much of the tree felling and land degradation, these substitutes for producing paper have a critical importance for the future. If put into large-scale use, this technique could lead to afforestation and provide a perennially self-renewing source of raw material for paper. Meanwhile the MCRC's screen-printing unit produces books on cloth. These sturdy books are put into wide circulation to impart simple techniques that could smoothen and improve daily life in villages. Some lessons are even printed on sarees, which may be worn or displayed and used much longer than posters on paper.

Biotechnology has been used at MCRC for diverse

applications like bio-gas enrichment, bio-fertilizer and heavy metal effluent treatment. Since 1977 there have also been successful experiments in bio-dynamic farming, a system where spacing of plants is very intensive, resulting in higher yields per acre. For these efforts the MCRC twice received the President of India Award for invention and the Jamnalal Bajaj Award for excellence in science and technology for rural development.

But these awards could neither sustain CVS nor quell the restlessness of dreams unfulfilled. For no matter how good his various inventions were, the larger picture was not changing for the better. Instead, it was worsening.

For example, CVS struggled in vain to have the Fish Aggregating Devices installed in shallow waters along the entire coastline. The design was simple and easily replicable using local materials. It would substantially enhance the catch of fishermen without having to make risky journeys into the open sea. It would also deter trawlers from fishing in shallow waters because these devices would entangle the trawler nets. The idea was taken to the Central government and the bureaucrats welcomed it into their filing system where it remained, pending foreign funding assistance!

Moreover, there was the ever-growing power of the 'market' as defined by modern economics. This market does not provide criteria for the optimum use of resources. For example, given a hectare of land the market may dictate cultivation of lucrative cash crops. What is needed instead is the best mix of fuel, fodder and food cultivation in which cash crops can be a supplement.

So over the years CVS became angry and disillusioned with 'us' , Indians. 'In 1945 I wondered how and why the German intelligentsia kept quiet about the concentration camps,' he moaned to friends, 'but now I ask the same question about our intelligentsia here, which quietly and easily allowed Gandhi to be rejected.' He felt oppressed by what he saw as our collective lack of commitment and faith in ourselves. He grew tired of having to constantly worry about mobilizing funds at every stage, and never being fully free to pursue the work itself.

What sustained him was the success of projects like the Spirulina diet supplement. By the time a child reaches the age of four, it has developed nearly eighty per cent of its adult brain. It is therefore imperative that pre-school children be fed well so that brain-development is not hampered. The team at MCRC then set about developing a rich nutritional supplement, Spirulina, out of algae that could be grown in villages. This supplement was introduced in a noon meal scheme for pre-school children in one district of Tamil Nadu. The National Institute of Nutrition observed its benefits over an extended period to prove its efficacy. However, lack of political will prevented it from being more widely replicated as a social programme. But it was successfully taken up by commercial producers, as a diet supplement for cancer patients.

Meanwhile, the growing caravan of fellow-travellers also sustained CVS to some extent. Seemingly different paths were converging with Mahatma Gandhi's. What excited CVS was that most of these fellow-travellers were young people who were groping their way towards answers. For most of these young friends and co-workers CVS was exciting because he thought differently and was eager to keep company with those who had the courage to experiment. They were not particularly concerned with trying to measure CVS's impact on the science establishment.

Some of these younger colleagues were his former

students from the IIT, Kanpur days. In the late-70s they had formed an organization called the Patriotic and People-Oriented Science and Technology Foundation (PPST) and later drew in CVS as its president.

### 'With a song on our lips and prayer in our hearts'.

The PPST became an umbrella under which a wide assortment of people began to explore how, and in what areas, the indigenous sciences and technologies of India may still provide viable and replicable answers for contemporary problems. Some of the work was archival and some was rooted in actual practices—like restoring old water systems, or local herb-based medicinal practices.

CVS's interest in traditional technologies was rooted in his conviction that the life processes of nature provide the only mechanism available to absorb the 'entropy' generated by human-engineered devices and processes. Years of work on development showed CVS that traditional wisdom was based on this truth and presented working models, both in terms of technology and related forms of social organization. Even more significantly, some of this traditional wisdom and its methods have survived to the present day. CVS was enthralled by the challenge of seeing how this wisdom could be suitably rejuvenated to serve contemporary needs.

This work was in sharp contrast with the mind-set of decision-makers in the mainstream. As CVS wrote:

> Consider the energy problem. For fifty years we have, by semantic labelling, called the bulk of the energy used in India 'non-commercial'. This refers to the fact that fifty per cent of the total energy used in India is consumed by the cook-stove. Just because village women gather their own fuel, this has

become 'non-commercial' and therefore of less intrinsic value, not in a purely literal sense, but because the investments in providing fuel-wood to our people are marginal. Most of the social forestry schemes end up supplying paper-mills or other market streams. This story, as said before, can be repeated in most areas of endeavour.

CVS was deeply agitated about the total absence of public debate on such issues and lack of information about decision-making processes in the government. This inspired him to contest the 1990 Lok Sabha elections as an independent candidate in Chennai.

... it was a total revelation that elections wage war on people . . . No independent candidate has any citizenship rights and you cannot sue the government for restoration of such rights . . . The election process is a travesty of all that the Mahatma died for. What saves the elections and perhaps the civilization is the essential goodness of the Indian people. This may be a cliché but the strains on the country are showing. With a song on our lips and prayer in our hearts, we hope that the civilization will survive and that the country remains intact.

Two years later this faith was severely tested following the demolition of the Babri Masjid in Ayodhya, on 6 December 1992. As president of the PPST Foundation, CVS found himself presiding over a divided house. To his dismay one section of the PPST supported the demolition. Over several days and endless hours of emotionally charged discussions the PPST group struggled with this issue.

Neither 'side' could persuade the other. In moments of despair CVS railed about the inability of some to *'see'* the horrible implications of a politics of demolition.

In the absence of a consensus, the PPST group chose to remain formally silent on the issue of Ayodhya. The anti-demolition segment got busy in trying to ensure that the PPST's forthcoming debut at the national level was free of communal overtones. CVS went along with this at the cost of being bitterly criticized by many friends and admirers who had hoped that he would persuade the body of PPST to condemn the demolition. A year later, in December 1993, CVS took centrestage at the Mumbai IIT in welcoming delegates to PPST's first-ever Congress on Traditional Sciences and Technologies of India.

The large common room of the IIT men's hostel was bursting at the seams. Having packed the chairs and floor space, students were perched on window sills and crowding the doorways. Several of the PPST workers were explaining the purpose and context of the Congress. Earlier in the day CVS, resplendent in a khadi silk Indian-style coat, had formally flagged off the Congress at the IIT Convocation Hall. But it was here, face to face with actual students, that he was in his element. He urged the students to reflect on the content of science and technology in a civilizational context:

> Science is about models of reality and technology is about these models of reality actualized in man-made processes of home, agriculture and industry. Conversely, civilizational realities can be perceived through arts, artifacts and manufacturers. The 6,000 years of (India's) civilizational continuum, representing an unbroken science and technology tradition stretching from

agriculture to architecture to animal husbandry, to water management, to industry to health care, to theoretical sciences—is real. That it remained an object of ecstatic admiration by other civilizations for over thousand years is also real. That till about 1750 (this tradition) produced twenty-five per cent of the manufactured and traded goods of the international market is also real. And all this cannot be written off either as an accident of history or as an aberration of human recording.

That she (India) ceased to matter in the global context during the last 200 years is perhaps the most unfortunate event which we all must learn to erase from our memory . . . That the social formations which produced these marvels of yesteryears are still alive and living and can be rejuvenated is true and beyond doubt. This is the sum total of the Congress debate.

CVS did not betray awareness of any poetic justice in returning to the realm of IITs in this manner. He was too busy juggling various aspects of the gigantic five-day event. As expenses mounted, there was that perennial, energy-sapping struggle for funds. Besides, over the years CVS had attempted to avoid the 'conflict' inherent in pushing ideas too aggressively. His inclination to 'plough a lonely furrow' allowed him to cultivate a disinterest in the reactions of the scientific community to his work. He preferred to think that ideas sometimes do seep in on their own.

So CVS found some satisfaction in encountering the smiling, bewildered faces of IIT professors who came up to him sharing their amazement and joy over the richness of indigenous Indian technologies displayed at the Congress. For CVS this was a small step towards recognition for the village inventors and innovators who inspired Gandhi and Kumarappa.

But he knew that the real struggle would take longer and be an inward process:

> We need to make a much larger effort to get the commonality of our mind from people. Compassion and love grow from use. Where did we lose the love and affection for people? In remote villages the first thing they give you is love. In return we exploit them. In India only the personal example will do. This is what Gandhi showed us. His every day was an experiment. To ask what can you do with small movements like ours, is basically lack of faith. Big things happen from small triggers. Who could imagine that from this small mud kuti you could overthrow an empire!

\*

*A year after that day-long brainstorming session near Bapu Kuti in January 1994, I visited CVS at the AMM Murugappa Chettiar Research Centre. The spontaneous warmth and affection with which he greeted me was like that of an old friend's. As he showed me the various on-going projects and experiments at the centre he also listened keenly to accounts of my travels visiting various activists. What he enjoyed most, he said with a happy sparkle in his eyes, was that most of these people are 'adventuring' their way to Gandhi.*

*He still, constantly, felt the need to keep Gandhi's talisman close at hand—to ask himself if an action would benefit the 'last person'. CVS spoke of still 'learning to analyse every problem in Gandhi's mind—that's all you need to do. That gives you a clear pathway on how to proceed.'*

The day was fading and soon it was time to leave. CVS pulled out his motorbike, from under a tree where it was parked, and gave me a ride to my next destination. Then he rode off, disappearing into the swirl of Chennai city traffic. That was the last time we met.

Less then two years later he was lost in the waves off the Coromandel coast.

Those of us who were at least two generations younger, and just beginning to get to know CVS, felt bereft and somehow cheated of a vital part of our future. Some felt that the mystery of this maverick Gandhian and his eccentricities, were now sealed for ever.

I was one of those who kept meaning to respond to CVS's open-house invitation to come spend time working, reading, reflecting at the MCRC. CVS's youthful zest and enormous energy made it easy to forget the linear dimension of this mortal frame. Yet this is all the sea snatched away. The man's bequest remains, awaiting the nurturing care of fellow-travellers in this and other times.

# Baba Amte's Vanprastha
## The Agony and Ecstasy of Late Youth

*Murlidhar Devidas Amte was busy cutting a leafy vegetable in the kitchen at Sewagram Ashram. The athletic young man was accustomed to and enjoyed doing many different kinds of physical work. But there was a special delight in even this mundane chore at Bapu's ashram.*

*Gandhi arrived in the kitchen just as Murlidhar completed the task and handed over the vessel of cut vegetables to the cook. His glance fell on a few stray leaves of the vegetable left lying on the stone floor. Picking up each leaf Gandhiji washed them in a pot of potassium permanganate lying close by, and then tossed them into the cooking pot. To Murlidhar the morsels had not seemed so important. Then Gandhiji turned to him and explained. We are living on public funds, he told the young volunteer, we cannot afford to waste even a single tiny fragment. Murlidhar never forgot that moment. Years later it helped him to manage vast amounts of donated funds when he became famous as Baba Amte of Anandwan.*

*At that time M.K. Gandhi was already known as 'Mahatma' and Murlidhar was a fresh law graduate. Bapu Kuti was then a live home—a place of work, struggle and worship. It was not only the heart of Sewagram Ashram but the veritable headquarters of the movement for Swaraj through Satyagraha.*

*There Gandhi replied to thousands of letters, wrote editorials for* Harijan *and* Young India, *met with other history makers like Jawaharlal Nehru, Sardar Patel, Khan Abdul Ghaffar Khan and still made time for the daily sacrificial spinning, a good massage, playing with children and talking with an eager young man like Murlidhar Amte.*

*Gandhi usually had a mission for most people in his orbit. He urged the energetic and extrovert Murlidhar to make palm jaggery his life's mission. At that time, this idea held little or no appeal for the restless young man. Eventually he would come to agree with Bapu. But, by then, Baba Amte was in the twilight of his life.*

## Sunrise over the Narmada

Even with the heavy doze of medicines Baba Amte has just a few hours of sleep. Halfway through the night he gets up, puts on the brace which supports his damaged spine, and heads for the river flowing a few yards away from his home.

At that hour even the tiny creatures of the soil are hardly stirring. There is just the soft murmur of the river flowing by and sometimes a shooting star zooming silently down to earth. Leaning lightly on a thick bamboo staff Baba stands alone, framed by the timeless grandeur of the river. The gentle fragrance of carefully-nurtured flowers follows him back into the house.

Later, lying in his bed, Baba can see the early morning colours skimming over the waters. Baba's *vanprastha ashram* is located on a high cliff on the south bank of the river that the world knows as the 'Narmada'. For people who live along the banks, *she*, the river, has always been Rewa Maiya—mother, virgin-goddess, friend, and provider. Her journey begins hundreds of miles to the east, in a pond on the Chota Nagpur plateau.

Flowing gently towards its union with the Arabian Sea,

the Narmada accepts homage at innumerable ghats and temples. A little before she turns that luxurious bend at Kasravad, Rewa Maiya caresses the magnificently crafted ghats of Maheshwar, built by Ahilyabai Holkar. Perhaps the same craftsmen built the tiny Shiva temple that has stood near the village of Kasravad for a couple of hundred years before Baba came to live there.

Long before recorded time, pilgrims have walked the full course of the river in a reverential *parikrama*. On the threshold of the twenty-first century too there are countless such pilgrims. Many of these *parikrama yatris* are naturally drawn to this unusual ashram at Kasravad where an aging couple lives with a small team of workers who help to care for the steady stream of visitors. The *yatris* stop by for rest, a meal and *satsang* with Baba and Tai. Baba enjoys observing these guests and quietly sifting the genuine pilgrims from the less earnest ones. But, even in Tai's absence, he never falters from the rule that all such visitors must be welcomed and fed—no questions asked.

But most visitors are *yatris* of a different kind. They are Baba's fellow-travellers who come to share notes or seek advice. Many of these are young friends who gleefully rush down to bathe in the river. Though he cannot join in their frolic, Baba ruefully watches from the high perch, enjoying the distant sounds of laughter and splashing water.

Baba had been at Kasravad for seven years when I wrote a profile about him, which appeared in the *Times of India* under the heading: 'The Old Man and the River'. The next time I went to Kasravad, Baba had not forgotten about this—'What do you mean the *old man* and the river,' he roared at me in mock anger, 'I am in my *late youth*!'

On the walls of the porch is ample evidence of this extended late youth. There is the photo of a handsome young man sitting affectionately with two baby tigers and a fully grown lion. This is Dr Prakash Amte, Baba and Tai's second son. The older son, Vikas, who is also a doctor, is in his late forties and manages a vast enterprise called Anandwan, or forest of bliss.

The passage of time is more evident in the memories which crowd Tai's conversations. Perhaps she has travelled a longer distance. Half a century earlier, long before she came to be known as 'Tai' to the world at large, Indu Ghuleshastri was the quiet dutiful daughter of an orthodox Brahmin family. When she married the somewhat eccentric young lawyer from a wealthy Brahmin family, she expected her life to change. And change it did indeed. The *vanprastha ashram* on that grand bend of the Narmada is a long, long way from small-town life of Warora where her journey with Murlidhar Devidas Amte began in the late-40s.

## A childhood encounter

The streets of Nagpur were aglow with the excitement of Diwali. An eight-year-old boy ran towards the market clutching a handful of coins his mother had given him. Stuffed full with sweets, feeling that life was just grand, he rushed along all set to buy whatever he pleased. But suddenly he came to a dead halt. Before him on the roadside was a blind beggar. The man sat crouched on the edge of the unpaved road as gusts of wind raised clouds of dust and rubbish over him. He was holding up a rusty cigarette tin as a begging bowl and waiting for someone to drop him a few coins.

The little boy's excitement evaporated at this sight. How could such misery and pain exist in his bright, happy world? Removing that handful of coins from his pocket he dropped them into the tin. With the sudden, unexpected weight of coins, the tin almost fell out of the man's hand.

Sensing childish mischief, the man appealed: 'I am only a beggar, young sir, don't put stones into my bowl.'

'These are not stones but coins. Count them if you wish,' the little boy urged.

Putting the tin down on the tattered rag before him the man began counting and recounting the coins—over and over again. He could not seem to believe that any one person could drop so many coins for him. As the man went on feeling the coins and counting them, the little boy was struck dumb by a sadness which he never otherwise felt. He ran back home in tears.

That boy, Murlidhar Devidas Amte was born the day after Christmas in 1914, the very year that the first 'world' war began in Europe. Life at Hinganghat, a little town in Maharashtra's Wardha district, went on undisturbed, as though in another time dimension. In any case, as the eldest son of a wealthy Brahmin landowner, Murlidhar was protected from any material deprivation. His enormous energy was happily absorbed in an idyllic childhood with long hours of play, pranks and wrestling with other boys. Murlidhar's father disapproved of his over-boisterous, uninhibited son's 'unbecoming behaviour'. Till the twilight of his life Baba would fondly recall how his mother had always shielded him from his father's wrath. It was his mother who affectionately called him 'Baba' and the name stuck for life.

But there was more to Baba than pure boyish mischief. He rebelled against restrictions that prevented him from playing with the 'low-caste' servants' children. Even when he was too young to question whether they were indeed 'lesser' people, he protested against how they were treated.

Baba would defiantly go off to eat with them and later willingly take the punishment.

At the same time, Baba enjoyed the privileges and carefree life of a wealthy young man. Since his father was an officer in the government's finance department, the family lived in Nagpur for many years before shifting to the nearby town of Warora. By the time he was fourteen, Baba owned his own gun and hunted boar and deer. He developed a special interest in cinema and could see several films in a day. When he was old enough to drive, Baba was given a Singer sportscar which had cushions covered with panther skin.

In the year that Murlidhar turned sixteen, Mahatma Gandhi was attracting world attention by walking to Dandi and challenging the British empire with a pinch of salt. While Gandhi went to jail for this defiance, Baba completed his school education and entered college. By the time the Sewagram Ashram took shape, in 1936, Baba had become a lawyer.

## Tagore, Gandhi and other influences

By now the playful energy of young Baba had transformed into a burning curiosity. During the college holidays he travelled all over India to fulfil his craving to see beautiful places and soak up the company of fascinating people. This naturally took him to Shantiniketan and the orbit of Rabindranath Tagore. He had been drawn initially by Tagore's music but once at Shantiniketan, young Baba imbibed the poetic faith of the Brahmo Samaj. He never forgot these words of Devendranath Tagore:

The Divine Spirit permeates every pore of matter and humanity, and yet is absolutely different from both. There is no flight of fowls to their evening home that is not directed by the unerring hand of Divine Love. There is no lily in the field nor rose in the valley whose blossom and fragrance do not come from the breath of infinite beauty. There is no beauty, no wisdom, no faithfulness, no purity, no piety and self-sacrifice that is not inspired by Him. The goodness of all the good is a ray of reflection from Him, the greatness of all the great points to His throne on high.

Rabindranath Tagore's poems were an exquisite expression of this love. Shantiniketan, located amid lush natural beauty, was a microcosm of Tagore's ideal world—here was a community united in joy, work and love. Baba came away deeply touched and somehow altered for life.

Closer to home, at Sewagram near Wardha town, Baba was equally fascinated with Gandhi's relationship with God. Through Gandhi Baba saw that:

God is that indefinable something which we all feel but which we do not know. To me, God is truth and love, God is ethics and morality, God is fearlessness. God is the source of light and life, and yet He is above and beyond all these. God is conscience.

Simultaneously, he was deeply impressed by what he saw as Gandhi's scientific attitude to life. For Bapu's ideals were never some personal fetish but the rational basis for finding solutions to the problems of life. The result was modes of life which were both verifiable and replicable.

Baba realized that it was no small privilege to be living

in the 'company of two universal souls that inhabited Shantiniketan and Sewagram'. Even more he felt honoured to be able to quarrel with both of them, yet to love them immensely and also earn their love.

While the ideas of Marx and Mao inspired him, the Marxist revolutions in Russia and China did not. He felt closer to the worldview of John Ruskin and Pyotr Alexeyevich Kropotkin which emphasized the empowerment of the community with greater freedom from the state. Thus the poetic simplicity of Maharashtra's fiery social reformer, Sane Guruji, drew him like a magnet.

Yet, for a while still, his life proceeded along the conventional track. He built up a lucrative practice as an advocate in Warora. On weekends he looked into affairs at the family's farm of 450 acres, at Goraja near Warora. Soon he was organizing farmers' cooperatives and was eventually elected vice-president of the Warora municipality. And he still had time for hunting and games of bridge or tennis at the local club. But the money, prestige and comfort were not making Baba happy. Instead, he became restless. This surely could not be the purpose of life, he thought. Besides now he was even more appalled by the callousness he saw within his own family. He rebelled against the 'strong barriers' families like his own used to block out the misery in the world outside:

> I, who never had planted a single seed in the estate, was expected to enjoy the comfort of a beautiful farm house, while those who had toiled there all their lives had only the meanest hovels . . . I was charging fifty rupees for arguing for fifteen minutes while a labourer was getting only three-quarters of

a rupee for twelve hours of toil. That was what was eating into me.

So Baba set about changing what he could. Harijans on his family's lands had always walked a long distance to collect water because the village well was forbidden to them. Baba defied the bitter opposition of the upper-caste villagers and opened up the well to all people. During the Quit India movement, in 1942, he organized lawyers to take up the defence of the jailed leaders and was himself thrown into prison.

It was at work that Baba faced the toughest challenges. He discovered that many clients expected him to lie for them:

A client would admit that he had committed rape and I was expected to obtain an acquittal. Worse still, when I succeeded, I was expected to attend the celebration party.

Soon Baba lost all interest in the law practice. More and more he admired the 'richness of heart of the poor people' and despised 'the poverty of heart of the rich'. It was the 'common man', he decided, who was really uncommon. Perhaps one way of ensuring a full life was to become one with the poor and oppressed. But how to go about this? Even while the answer eluded him, he was sure of one thing. This quest for a richer life would be aborted if he married any one of the girls whose hopeful mothers were ever in pursuit of the most eligible young Amte.

So Baba let his hair and fingernails grow and spread the word that he had taken a vow of celibacy. To complete the effect he even feigned sitting in meditation. All this changed when he spotted Indu Ghuleshastri at a wedding. Baba noticed that amid the wedding festivities of her elder sister, Indu had quietly slipped away to help an old servant woman who was washing clothes.

## Marriage and a *shram* ashram

Having successfully made himself seem ineligible, Baba now had to work hard to persuade Indu's parents that he was indeed a suitable groom. Eventually, Baba and Indu were married in December 1946, and together they launched on an arduous joint adventure. On their wedding day Baba renounced his property and gave up his legal practice. In doing this he left behind his family, virtually forfeiting all claims on their support.

The couple began by setting up a *shram ashram* near Warora. About the same time, Sane Guruji was leading a campaign for Harijans to gain entry into the temple of Vithobha at Pandharpur. Though the temple is the chief pilgrim centre of the Varkari sect which has challenged caste rules in many ways, only the higher castes could actually enter the temple. A few months after Murlidhar and Indu's wedding, in 1947, Sane Guruji began a fast-unto-death at Pandharpur and succeeded in gaining temple entry for the Harijans.

Sane Guruji's example gave a deeper meaning to compassion in Baba's life. It helped him to nurture the growing conviction that 'What is weak defeats what is strong, what is soft defeats things that are stiff.' For the rest of his life, Baba carried in his heart this verse of Sane Guruji:

> Through my tears I shall reach my ideal;
> In my tears rests the power to crush steel and stone.
> My tears are my God.
> Never deprive me of my tears

Let my eyelids never get dry.

It was with these sentiments that Baba and Indu set up the *shram ashram* as an open house which anyone was welcome to join. Soon there was a poor Brahmin family that knew something about agriculture, one shoemaker, one umbrella repairer and some Harijan families. Together this unusual community cultivated a small patch of land and shared a common kitchen.

Indu, now known as Sadhna, had been brought up on strict rules of caste-segregation She now worked hard to struggle against her conditioning. It was as if she had jumped straight into the ocean without first learning to swim. A tough price had to be paid for taking this road in life. Since she lived with 'low-castes', Indu was no longer welcome in her parents' home. Baba and his wife were now considered outcastes themselves. So Indu could not count on her mother's help, when she was due to deliver her first child. Nor could she expect her mother to come and share a house with 'low-castes'.

Meanwhile Baba's involvement in various organizations deepened. Now, he was vice-chairman of the Warora municipality and chairman of the scavengers union. For nine months he worked as a scavenger, carrying baskets filled with night soil on his head.

**Turning point**
The turning point in his life came one rainy evening, as Baba headed home. A huddled figure lay on the roadside. At first it seemed like a bundle of rags. But then he noticed some movement. Baba looked closer and recoiled instantly. Lying before him was a man in the last stages of leprosy. The dying

man had no fingers. Maggots crawled over his naked body. Horrified by this sight, terrified of infection, Baba ran home.

But he could not run away from the self-loathing which began to hound him. How could he have left a lonely forsaken man to lie there in the rain? So he forced himself to return and feed the man. He also put up a bamboo shed to protect him against the rain. That man, Tulshiram, died in Baba's care and irrevocably changed young Amte's life.

Baba had always thought of himself as being fearless and daring. The encounter with Tulshiram shattered this self-image. The very sight of Tulshiram filled him with an irrepressible dread. Even as he cared for the dying man this fear would not leave him:

> I have never been frightened of anything. Because I fought British tommies to save the honour of an Indian lady, Gandhiji called me *'abhay sadhak'*, a fearless seeker of truth. When the sweepers of Warora challenged me to clean gutters, I did so. But that same person who fought goondas and British bandits quivered in fright when he saw the living corpse of Tulshiram, no fingers, no clothes, with maggots all over.

And Baba was absolutely certain that:

'Where there is fear, there is no love. Where there is no love there is no God.'

So what should he do? For the next six months Baba lived with the unrelenting agony of this crisis. There seemed to be only one answer, one lone way of overcoming this problem. He must live and work with leprosy patients:

> That is why I took up leprosy work. Not to help

anyone, but to overcome that fear in my life. That it worked out good for others was a by-product. But the fact is I did it to overcome fear.

And what of 'Sadhna'? They had discussed the possibility many times. But eventually it was Baba's decision. Indu said to him: 'You must follow the dictate of your heart. I shall find my happiness in following you.' Decades later she would tell a large public gathering, called to felicitate her, that had there been a women's liberation movement in her time Anandwan might never have happened!

Thus Baba, and Sadhna, set out on the path that is now history. He began by reading intensively about leprosy and offering his services at the Warora leprosy clinic. Soon, he was running his own clinic. In 1949, he went to the Calcutta School of Tropical Medicine to learn more about leprosy. By the time Baba returned home the discovery of diamino-diphenyl-sulphone had made leprosy curable.

With this wonder drug in hand, Baba began treating leprosy patients in sixty villages around Warora. Soon there were eleven weekly clinics within a radius of about fifty kilometres from Warora, with a total of about 4,000 patients. But stemming the disease did not make the afflicted whole again. For, 'a man can live without fingers, but he cannot live without self-respect.' And receiving charity is not particularly conducive to enhancing self-respect.

### The forest of bliss
So the Warora Maharogi Seva Samiti was founded in 1951 to help the leprosy patients to help themselves. The government leased fifty acres of scrub land to the Samiti, where it set up a farm cum 'leprosarium'. The land was

rocky, covered with scrubs and infested with scorpions and snakes. The nearest well was two kilometres away. As Baba gazed at his new home it was like:

> . . . looking at a new volume of my life. Perhaps it was symptomatic that there was nothing but a tangle of boulders, roots and creepers. Outcast land for outcast men. This was our lot from now on, I thought.

Baba turned to his patients and asked if they were willing to turn this wasteland into green fields. But would willingness be enough? Here was a hard physical task that would have daunted perfectly able-bodied men. How were men and women with deformed limbs going to achieve the impossible? Yet not one of them could say no to Baba. And so they set about clearing the land and building 'Anandwan'—the forest of bliss.

At first they made two small shelters with thatched roofs on bamboo poles. The digging of a well took almost two months. Food was scarce and funds perpetually seemed to be at rock-bottom. Within three years, the Amte family and a community of sixty patients had dug six wells and cleared enough land to have a substantial harvest of grains and vegetables. But this produce could not find a market in Warora. People feared contamination from food grown by 'lepers'.

It took a contingent of fifty young volunteers of the Service Civil International to solve this problem. These young people, from thirty-six different countries, spent three months at Anandwan building a clinic and two spacious hospital wards. Their action broke the barriers with the Warora community. Seeing the foreigners toiling away among the leprosy patients even local people felt moved to make some contribution and many provided food for the volunteers. Once residents of Warora began to come inside Anandwan, and see the sparklingly clean environs, the fear of contamination also receded. Eventually, Anandwan became a busy place attracting hoards of visitors from near and far.

Gradually, the scale and facilities of Anandwan grew. Once the leprosy-affected persons were fit enough to leave the hospital they ceased to be 'patients'. They became working members of the community, busy in the fields or workshops where a variety of products were being manufactured. This made Anandwan a virtually self-sufficient 'village'. Eventually, it needed to buy only salt, sugar and petrol from the outside. Everything else was locally produced at Anandwan. Most of the erstwhile patients, having learnt a skill, returned to the world outside, self-reliant and capable of earning their own living.

In 1962, when China invaded India, the Anandwan community did a fund-raising stage show and contributed Rs 2,000 for the National Defence Fund. Some years later, they used the surplus generated by their agricultural production, to set up a college in Warora. Eventually they added at Anandwan a College of Agriculture, a primary school for blind children, a school for deaf and dumb children and an orphanage. These multi-dimensional efforts won Anandwan a string of national and international awards which brought it both fame and funds.

## The 'coffin' becomes a womb

Baba lay motionless on the cot staring hard at the ceiling, his jaw tightly clenched. He felt as though he were lying in a coffin, awaiting burial. On one end of the bed was a contraption that kept his spine in traction for twelve hours every day. The vigorously physical man, whose energies seemed to recognize few limits, was now told that he may have to spend most of his life lying in bed. Murlidhar Devidas 'Baba' Amte was only fifty. The doctors diagnosed the agonizing pain in his back as a case of severe cervical spondylosis which was causing a progressive degeneration of the spine.

But the man who had turned around and attacked his own fears was not going to be so easily done in. When his body was confined in a prison of inactivity, his mind went flying in search of new possibilities. In any case, his work had reached a plateau. His sons were on their way to becoming doctors. Anandwan was running well on its own and could no longer absorb all of Baba's energies. Soon the 'coffin' began to seem like a womb in which the rest of Baba Amte's life took shape.

He now became preoccupied with building the vision for a New India based on his experiences at Anandwan. By the late-60s it was evident that the government's development programmes were never likely to reach the last man. The answer, Baba felt, lay in transforming a society based on subsistence farming into a highly productive agro-industrial system.

While his mind got busy with this new dimension of his mission, the spondylosis continued to relentlessly batter his body. In 1971, friends collected money and sent Baba to London for a major operation on his spine. This kept him in bed for much of 1971 and 1972. His agony was compounded by the need for another operation, performed in Mumbai some years later. These operations allowed Baba to live but left him with a permanent handicap. He would never be able to sit again. He could either lie down or stand, but only for limited periods.

Despite this physical degeneration, Baba's spirit fought back with renewed vigour. There were dark days and perhaps he lost a few battles. But eventually 'my pain and sorrows became the witness to my happiness . . . I asked only to be used till I lie down in the company of mother earth.' Thus the 'war' of will turned decisively in favour of victory for Baba's enormous creative energy.

The reflections in that enforced 'womb' made him long for the actual realization of *purna swaraj*—'a resurgence in free India of a defiant and aggressive effort at self-development by the silenced majority.' As one of his biographers, Hans Staffner, later wrote in *Baba Amte's Vision of A New India*:

> Baba Amte's success in building Anandwan had a two-fold impact on his mind. It increased his desire to lead India's suffering millions to a resolute effort at self-development and it strengthened his conviction that this could be done by rousing the impoverished masses to a creative awareness.

Baba now asked himself: 'If we could build up a happy community under the most difficult circumstances, why cannot healthy people do the same under much more favourable circumstances? Why can the youth of India not do the same?'

## Vision of a new India

For all the vehemence with which he posed this question, Baba somehow remained free of bitterness. He never seemed to doubt that it could be done. For, 'there is a divine spark in the heart of the common people, a spark that can be kindled into a mighty flame'. But how?

Closely observing developments in Russia and China, Baba concluded that a true revolution would make people aware of their own capabilities. It would propel them to practical action:

> I believe that political awareness without constructive work is impotent, and that constructive work without political awareness is equally sterile. If you must put a label to what guides my action, it would be 'creative humanism'.

Thus, Baba nurtured Anandwan as a model of the India of his dreams. This ideal society rests on two pillars, mutual recognition of rights and mutual cooperation for the common good. This meant that the dignity of every living being must be respected. In order to do this every person would have to be self-supporting:

> I believe as a society we have to evolve, through experimentation, a system which combines the principles of individual freedom and common ownership. And this is what we have tried, basically with success, in all our projects, involving leprosy patients, tribal people and the so-called 'disabled' persons. Consider the honey-bee. Its treasure is nectar, obtained even from the chilly plant. It is not at the cost of the flower. In fact, its act of extracting honey contributes to the progress of the flowers. You need not learn from Kahlil Gibran, Marx or Gorbachev, not even from Gandhiji. Choose instead to learn your lesson from the honey bees as your

silent partners: they will show you how to develop without destroying.

Translating these lofty ideals into practice never seemed difficult to Baba. He began by focusing his attention on a plan for a Workers' University. He envisioned students studying for a degree and simultaneously undergoing training for learning some practical skill. Each student would be given two acres of land to cultivate and experiment with and would be entitled to the yield of this land after paying for his board. This productive work of the students would make the university self-supporting.

This plan gained support from the Planning Commission and thus 2,000 acres of barren land at Somnath, about a hundred kilometres south of Anandwan, was given to Baba for starting this work. In this case, however, there was vigorous opposition by the local people. Eventually, much of the land had to be relinquished and the plan for a Workers' University was abandoned. The remaining land at Somnath was developed as a centre for annual youth camps. The first of these camps was held in 1967, with about 1400 boys and girls from different parts of India. Since there were no buildings there at that time the participants slept out in the open. Barrels of drinking water were brought over a distance of about two kilometres on a bullock-cart.

These young people were required to spend much of the day in manual labour—working in the fields, digging percolation dams, making *bunds*, clearing wasteland for cultivation and so on. The evenings were devoted to group discussions which were led by well-known personalities. Secularism, national integration, socialism, democracy and students' problems were some of the issues taken up. And then there was time for songs, dances, plays, poems and games.

Over the years, the Somnath camps became a major social institution of Maharashtra, inspiring thousands of young people and imbuing them with a creative restlessness. It became the starting point for a wide range of social and political activists who went on to identify with different ideological streams from the Gandhian to the Marxist-Leninist. When Baba reached his 'late youth', many of these activists, then middle-aged themselves, would enliven his world by their endeavours in different fields.

The work at Somnath also led, in the mid-80s, to the Bharat Jodo Abhiyan. This campaign took Baba and teams of young people on a cross-country journey to appeal for communal harmony and peaceful solutions to regional disputes.

## No big dams

Hemalkasa was the place that truly shaped the politics of Baba's 'late youth'. It was also his most daring act of valour, defying his physical pain. In 1973, barely a year after he had undergone surgery for his back problem, Baba pitched a tent at Hemalkasa, a place deep in the forests about 350 kilometres south of Nagpur. This took him back to the carefree days, in his teens, when he had roamed these forests on his hunting expeditions. He liked being among the adivasis. Their innocence and cheer delighted him.

But, at the same time their material existence appalled Baba. For thirty years he had dreamt of ways to help the adivasis to benefit from modern civilization without becoming estranged from the beauty and strengths of their own culture. Now, he submerged the agony of his body to work vigorously to realize this dream. Travelling from village to village he began to work for improving health among the Madia Gonds.

In 1974, Baba and Tai's younger son, Prakash, graduated from medical college and came to work in Hemalkasa. Soon Prakash and his wife Mandakini, who had been a fellow-student, decided to settle there permanently. Like the senior Amtes, this couple faced many years of struggle with severe hardships, shortages of food, medicine and susceptibility to many diseases.

Gradually, the hardships decreased and a community of workers came together based on a shared bond with the local people, the wild animals and the abundant fauna and flora. This community includes Renuka, whom Baba and Tai had adopted as an infant, and her husband Vilas Manohar. Vilas later recorded the enriching explorations of the Hemalkasa family in a popular Marathi book entitled *Negal*, Tiger Cub. European friends who visited Hemalkasa saw Prakash and Mandakini as the Albert Schweitzers of India. In the late-80s some of these admirers convinced the principality of Monaco to issue a special stamp commemorating the young Amtes' work.

By now Baba had further fine-tuned his understanding of how 'development' was making the life of tribal communities more difficult. Two major hydel power projects were coming up in the area around Hemalkasa the Inchampalli dam on the Godavari River and the Bhopalpatnam dam on the Indravati River. These projects would submerge about two lakh acres of land, half of which was prime forest. As a member of the District Planning Board Baba sought relevant information on the projects and examined their impact on the tribal communities. On the basis of this study, he persuaded his colleagues on the Board that the projects would wreak havoc on the local communities with little benefit to society at large.

In July 1983, Baba wrote to Prime Minister Indira Gandhi, and urged the government to consider other ways of generating electricity. Why spend so much money on gigantic projects, Baba questioned? 'A series of smaller dams could, I submit, adequately meet the water and energy needs of the people, including electricity for industry, without degrading the environment. My discussions with government technocrats familiar with this region strengthen this view,' he wrote.

In a polite reply the prime minister promised to 'pursue the matter'. She directed the Planning Commission to carefully examine the case. Meanwhile, opposition to these projects was mounting from several different quarters. Environmental activists questioned the data on which the cost-benefit ratio of the project was based. For example, the Maharashtra Forest Department estimated the loss of 40,000 acres of standing forest at Rs 9 crore. But if the calculation was made on the basis of the recurring annual yield, enhanced by proper management, the estimated value was close to Rs 2,500 crore.

Baba joined the effort to mobilize a popular opposition to the projects and in 1984 thousands of tribals marched to the District Collector's office demanding that the projects be withdrawn. Eventually a combination of this local action and lobbying in the corridors of power led to the cancellation of these projects. This *sangharsh* drew Baba one step closer to his destined home on the banks of the Narmada.

## Narmada *bachao*

Rising partly from the bed, resting his weight on one elbow, Baba looked out of the window of the van in which he was travelling. The year was 1990. The van moved slowly across a bridge over the Narmada. A string of tractor trolleys preceded the van and several more were following behind it. Sky blue flags, carrying the emblem of the Narmada Bachao Andolan (NBA), fluttered all over the procession. The men, women and children crowded into the tractor trolleys were repeating the key slogan of the Andolan: '*Koi nahin hatega, bandh nahin banega* (No one will move, the dam will not be built)'.

The sun was setting in a bright orange splash over the river waters below, as Baba's van reached the centre of the bridge. Suddenly the tractors swerved sideways and came to a halt, blocking the road. The NBA now informed the accompanying policemen that they intended to block this bridge, and thus the Mumbai-Agra highway, till their demand for a review of the Sardar Sarovar Project was heard.

For the next thirty hours hundreds of people from different parts of the Narmada valley made the bridge their home. The specially-fitted van, which had earlier carried Baba to the corners of India on the Knit India March, now became the nerve centre of this protest action.

A few days earlier, Baba had taken yet another big leap into the future and bid farewell to his beloved Anandwan. Few people in that gathering on the bridge realized just where Baba was coming from, both literally and metaphorically. Some of the villagers were surprised to find that this 'baba' didn't look like any holy man or 'mahatma' they had ever seen. After the *rasta-roko* on the Khalghat bridge, a smaller procession led Baba's van with proper fanfare to the little village of Kasravad, some five kilometres from the town of Badwani in the western corner of Madhya Pradesh.

Soon the jubilant crowd melted away and Baba was left to quietly examine his new home. Before him, on the barren sandy slope, was a two-room cement and brick structure—which the local villagers had constructed for him. For a flash, time seemed to melt away. He seemed to be back at the beginning when he had first stood staring at the scrub land near Warora. Baba retreated into his van, away from the anguish of this inhospitable site. Already he missed Anandwan, his home for forty years. Then, slowly the river, *Rewa Maiya*, began to work her magic on him.

For all appearances the move to Kasravad was a political, strategic manoeuvre, a kind of public relations coup for the Narmada Bachao Andolan. But, like every other action in Baba's life this one was a response to a *pukar*, a calling. Once again, he was drawn not by an external *cause* but the inner pull of the eternal beauty of the Narmada 'so pure, so holy, that the mere sight of her absolves one of all sins'.

Baba's involvement with the issue of mega-dams had been growing through the 1980s. In the summer of 1988 the Anandwan community hosted a meeting of over a hundred environmental activists from all over India on this issue. The 'Assertion of Collective Will Against Big Dams', also called the 'Anandwan Declaration', became a landmark in the emerging movement against big dams.

With characteristic flair Baba had articulated the case against the Sardar Sarovar Project (SSP) in a booklet entitled *Cry O Beloved Narmada*, published from Warora in July 1989. Addressed 'To the People of India' the booklet, for all its poetic overtones, gave a concise account of why the SSP was a social, economic and ecological disaster-in-making. In 1987-88 the final cost of the project was estimated at over Rs 11,000 crore. The submergence caused by the reservoir of the dam would displace about one lakh people. In addition, thousands more would be displaced by the network of canals.

Baba used official data and tables to show that the benefits of the SSP had been greatly exaggerated and its costs grossly underestimated. He pointed out that the government had made a farce out of the statutorily mandatory environmental clearance. The booklet went on to argue that proper rehabilitation for all oustees was an impossibility. It also recounted the emerging protests against the mega-dam and government efforts to suppress the agitation through use of the Official Secrets Act and police force. Baba concluded with an appeal to 'My Beloved State of Gujarat'—pleading that the various alternatives to big dams on the Narmada be actively examined:

> When the frontiers of science are pushing relentlessly towards technologies as dispersed as the golden rays of the sun, I will not let my beloved state of Gujarat fulfil a death wish by adopting an antediluvian technology. The science of large dams now seems to belong to the age of superstition; the coming century belongs to the technology of mini and micro dams and watershed development ensembles. I want Gujarat to join in this bright future.

By the end of 1989 Baba had decided to move to the banks of the Narmada:

> The time has come to leave Anandwan, the place where I entered into the world of joy, the place that symbolizes the very meaning of my existence. I am

leaving to live along the Narmada . . . to attain a peace that all mankind desires. The struggle for a New India is taking place in the Narmada valley. Today the Narmada valley has become the arena for a new imagination and creativity, for a society in which there must be sufficiency for all before there is superfluity for some.

Now living on the banks of the Narmada, Baba heard the echoes of a pervasive violence against all forms of life, including the river herself. Can the mighty blessings of the mother goddess help us 'to yoke all our forces to shelter her?' Baba asked himself and his contemporaries:

> Will we be able to blaze a divine halo around her that no power on earth can defile? Or will her cries never be heard again? Will we bequeath to her only tombstones with a sad tale to tell?

While he pondered such unanswerable questions Baba got busy in, quite literally, sowing the seeds of a mini-Anandwan. Accompanied by Tai and helpers from his old home Baba planted carefully selected trees and bushes all around the two-room house. Soon a makeshift shed was added on the east side of the house, expanding the space to accommodate the inevitable stream of guests. But in the first year Baba was often on the road as activities of the NBA reached a peak.

### Facing the 'other'

Ferkuwa, a small *kasba* on the Gujarat—Madhya Pradesh border, was an unlikely place for a historical showdown and one of the most fretful moments of Baba's life. Yet here were

217

scores of people from the submergence zone of the SSP marching towards police barricades with their hands folded and tied. Leading them, his hands also tied, Baba appealed to the police that they be allowed to pass peacefully into Gujarat. But the reply was a menacing waving of lathis. Hundreds of people standing just behind the police shouted pro-dam slogans and with angry fervour told Baba to 'Go Back'.

In the last week of 1990, thousands of people affected by the project had set off from Badwani, M.P., on a march to the dam site. The 'Sangharsh Yatra' was halted at the Gujarat border. The *yatris* squatted by the roadside and refused to move. Medha Patkar and five others began a fast to draw attention to their cause. On the other side of the barricade, the wife of the Gujarat chief minister led a dharna of those in favour of the SSP.

For almost three weeks, both sides shouted slogans and allegations at each other across the police barriers. Baba, with his van stuck between the two camps, was caught in more ways than one. He knew that confrontation was not the solution. And he despaired at his own inability to convince, to persuade, the 'other side' about the folly of the dam. For almost thirty years the people of Gujarat had been told that the SSP would transform the state and become its 'life-line'. This dream was not easily challenged. On the anti-dam side, some of the younger activists doubted persuasion as a means and saw a tougher confrontation as the only way of resolving a conflict.

Baba persevered in persuading them that this was not a war between the people of Gujarat and M.P. Every sundown he became more anxious for the well-being of the activists who were fasting. As the fast crossed the three-week mark, supporters of the cause all over the country began to panic.

Medha's kidneys were rumoured to be in danger of collapsing. The Central government was deluged by national and international phone calls and telegrams, urging it to call for a comprehensive review of the SSP. There is no question of a review, insisted the Gujarat chief minister Chimanbhai Patel. Medha refused to break the fast unless a review was promised. And so the stalemate deepened.

Eventually, supporters of the NBA mobilized a team of eminent citizens to hold a review of the SSP. Thus, the fast was called off and the almost month-long road-side gathering of thousands at Ferkuwa was dismantled. The dharna had failed in its effort to get an official review of the SSP. But the month-long action, competing for media attention with nothing less than the Gulf War, put the struggle of the NBA firmly in public view. Medha now became a national public figure, featuring on the cover of several magazines. Baba returned to Kasravad convinced that the battle may have been only partly won but the tide of the war had turned in their favour.

## Homage to a fellow traveller

The first light had just broken over the river when a terrible blow struck. Someone came rushing from Badwani with the news that Shankar Guha Niyogi had been shot dead. Sorrow battled with anger as Baba began to pace restlessly in the fledgling garden of the Kasravad home. If he were younger, healthier, he could have rushed to Dalli Rajhara to be with the thousands who would be mourning their loved comrade. Baba had met Niyogi just once but had followed and admired the life and work of this unusual trade union leader. Now he felt even closer to Niyogi—for the man had known that his life was threatened but still refused to carry weapons or keep an armed guard.

Four days later, on Mahatma Gandhi's birthday, 1991, Baba wrote a message for the comrades of the Chattisgarh Mukti Morcha, whom Niyogi had led:

'It was a murder by proxy.
The palpably dazzling murder
Makes a mockery of our civilization
Which takes centuries to mature
And relapses into barbarity in no time.
He fell victim to the conspiracy
Of those who do not believe in
Sane, equitable and enlightened society
They mocked him, by their pious cruelty,
Those who craved his blood
Now call him martyr
A mighty fortress blasted by cowards.
SHANKAR GUHA NIYOGI

Call him the inspired mouthpiece of God.
He could bear great anguish,
Courage and conviction were his blood and bones.
I never saw a young man like him
With an astonishing sensitivity
Rich in compassion and bold wisdom.
He explained to his people who they are
And offered a road map for
Where and how they would chart out their struggle.
He gave the workers a taste of freedom and justice.
He gave full-blooded sincerity to his sublime task.
He made the toughest decisions
with amazing speed.
Here was a soldier's instinct, to deal from strength
And the shrewd touch of a gambler

Which kept the power-holders guessing.
He knew what trump cards they had,
He pre-empted them, showed the right direction
To his comrades and forged them into
One of the strongest trade unions.
He had an athlete's timing while in struggle
And a magician's ability to convince the people.
Above all—he had a gentleman's equilibrium.
Marxist by passion.
He left the politician Marx way behind
Who could be defused, defeated.
Marx, the human being, gripped him.
He withheld nothing, his sincerity was pristine.
SHANKAR GUHA NIYOGI

Niyogi delighted in crusade,
In a vision of the Future.
He revelled being surrounded by raging war.
All good citizens must act
For the common good
Becoming participants in the path
Marked by Niyogi
And proclaim courtesy to their opponents,
How much more effective is this, than
The obscene violence which killed Niyogi.
Oh Supreme Shame, comrades like him
Are dyed in their blood in this nation of Gandhi.
Bloodhounds—the mafia gangs, industrialists
And the petty politicians
Have started using their pet card
'Eliminate, exterminate Ye, those
Who oppose the regime'
In Chattisgarh—Or, here, in the Narmada valley.

The last sigh whispered
On the banks of Narmada,
'Civility invites civility; Justice invites justice'.
Niyogis do not die, they might succumb
A tribute to them—Reason and Resolve.
To sharpen the struggle, to widen the horizon
Tirelessly, as Luther said, 'Lest I rust'
The unshed tear in the eye of Narmada
Is a silent tribute to this comrade
Who now rests in the lap of Bliss.

The living example of Niyogi deepened Baba's
convictions about revolution. He began to see his own
existence with the quietude of Rewa Maiya as a
manifestation of what he calls a 'post-revolution
perspective'. At just about the time that Baba moved to
Kasravad the pulling down of the Berlin Wall had signalled
the collapse of communism. This event marked a turning
point in the history of ideas. Perhaps now, Baba thought, the
world would be ready to accept what he had learnt in his
youth from Gandhiji and Tagore—that every revolution
devours its children:

There is a danger that tomorrow's blade of the
guillotine may be smeared with your blood . . . A
true revolution is not destructive but creative. Its
face is not smeared with blood, but covered with
sweat. Negative slogans may appear at first more
powerful, but they are short-lived, constructive
movements, though they may appear weak, have a
touch of lastingness.

## Tomorrow's leaders

This was easier said than done. All around Baba a new generation of political workers were grappling with the apparent conflict between constructive work and bold struggle that actively threatens the status quo. For all the reverence and affection he won from some youngsters, Baba could sense scepticism from others. The sceptics doubted if the 'social-work' energies which allowed Baba to cure leprosy patients would help to stop the Sardar Sarovar Project (SSP) dam or transform economic relations all over India.

Unaffected by these doubts and criticism, Baba continued to exhort these new, young companions in his life's journey:

> Carry your ideals before you like banners; it is not enough to put them on pedestals. Ideals which grip the masses prove to be a mighty force. Their force is stronger than the hope of earthly gain and they are more productive of real wealth . . . Nationalized ownership that throttles all creative effort, will no more be the test of revolution. Participation in decision-making will stimulate workers to greater efforts and common ownership will be the aim.
>
> . . . The war-cry will no more be with Marx and Mao: the spirit of revenge cannot build a new world . . . Only a revolution which leads to a higher sense of human dignity can lead to a higher and nobler way of life. Revolutions based on hatred and violence do not really change the situation. They merely transform the people who had been exploited into a new class of exploiters but hatred and exploitation remain. Therefore, there is no substitute for

Gandhi's way of rousing the impoverished masses to creative awareness.

Two-and-half decades of youth camps at Somnath had given Baba the confidence that:

The new leadership in India is taking shape quietly, without any drum-beating through the newspapers. . . . Various centres, the centres of energy and strength in the life of society are gaining tremendous momentum. May be, the surging new generation of today appears to have lost its bearing, to have lost its soul. But it is absolutely certain that one day it will have its own leader and prophet. . . . I am absolutely confident that the phoenix of a new leadership is rising from the ashes of all its failure. Soon the world will witness the lightning hidden in its beak and the storm hidden in its wings.

### Christ's lute

These ideas and related work won Baba a vast fan following. But many of his most ardent supporters and admirers were dismayed by his shift from humanitarian work to political action which threatens to rock the boat. His opposition of the SSP and decision to move to Kasravad were even ridiculed as a misguided emotional gesture. But the toughest test of Baba's patience and equanimity came at the peak of the NBA's activities in 1992. That was when the Madhya Pradesh police practiced—what Baba Amte called— 'shout-at-sight tactics'. The police set up camp near his house and blasted various kinds of noise and abuse from loudspeakers round the clock.

And then, in December 1992, there was the agonizing

blow of the demolition of the Babri Masjid in Ayodhya and the communal violence which followed, all over the country. Baba and Tai immediately rushed to Surat, from where there were reports of the most barbaric violence. As he moved through different localities in his van, people warmly welcomed his soothing, loving presence. It was not a moment to dwell upon differences over the SSP.

Weeks later, when Mumbai suffered a prolonged period of communal violence, Baba and Tai went and parked themselves near Behrampada, one of the worst-affected areas. This allowed him to rush there in the middle of the night to oppose Shiv Sena workers who were preventing the fire brigade from reaching burning homes. He could not stop the riots but he could be with the suffering. Having witnessed all this, Baba returned to Kasravad a deeply saddened man.

Such experiences have brought Baba ever closer to Christ. Echoing in his consciousness is the sound of Christ's lute falling from his hand, as the Roman soldiers nailed him to the cross:

> The Cross on which you spent your last breath has become to me not a sign that your service has come to an end, I see in it the sum of all that gives value to our life. To me it is not a symbol of violence wrought on you. To me it has become the voice of compassion.
> The Cross . . . asks us to yield up the love of life for the life of love, to back our conscience with our blood. Where there is fear there is no love. Fear of leprosy, fear of loneliness in the tribal belt, this scarecrow of fear cannot be allowed to guide your conscience. Everyone should attempt to walk in the

shadow of that Cross. That means you are in the company of that life which scuttled itself to save others. I haven't the arrogance to say I can carry the mighty load of His Cross, but I do try to walk in its shadow. He wants to carve your life like a crucifix. Every calamity is a crucifixion, crucifying your ambition, your lust. Each is a tiny lesson, and then the imprint of the crucifixion is on your life. What is your plan of sacrifice today? You and I, petty souls, sacrifice for our children. Christ sacrificed for tomorrow's whole world. Whenever I see slum-dwellers, with their hunger and poverty, that obscene poverty, I feel He is crucified like that. When I come across a person suffering from leprosy, foul-smelling, ulcerous, I can see the imprint of His lips, His kiss. What did they not do to sufferers of leprosy in His time, yet the carpenter's son cared for them and touched them. That hand is an emblem for me, that hand which cared for the loneliest and the lost. The Christian is . . . he who not only lights the darkest corner in the world but also the darkest corner in his own heart.

This means living and working for a mission, not *seeking* death in its name. So though Baba sees himself as a ' . . . blood-hound sniffing out the sacrifices of martyrs in all times' he is ' . . . just living here by the river. I will not rush into the swirling waters, but if the water rises above my house I will not move.'

Several times over these years the waters did rise over sixty feet, from the regular sandy bank of the river, to touch the doorstep of Baba and Tai's home. In 1994, as the water crossed the danger mark, the local District Collector ordered

Baba and Tai to be moved to the Circuit House. Why did Baba allow this? 'What was I to do?' asks Baba with some exasperation, 'kick and scream, bite their hands?'

And so Baba Amte has arrived at an unexpected dilemma or crossroads. He expected to live by Rewa Maiya, for as long as fate decreed and then surrender to the flow of the river, if and when the time came. Both options are being denied to him. It is almost certain that every time the waters rise beyond the danger mark the authorities will remove him from his home. All the quibbling over whether this is an arrest or 'safe-custody' will not ease Baba's plight.

Cut off from the day to day hurly-burly of the movement, Baba is sometimes exasperated by the physical limitations on his mobility. He can no longer travel to the front-line of action as activists of the NBA set up various kinds of constructive work projects in the valley and simultaneously spread the struggle to the other dams to be constructed further upstream.

A Supreme Court stay order and shortage of funds has delayed completion of the SSP. But if the dam's wall rises any higher, at some point Baba Amte's *vanprastha ashram* at Kasravad will be submerged. 'Where will you go then?' his sons ask Baba. What next? He does not have a ready answer. This uncertainty troubles Baba Amte. Yet he rallies with the faith that God and nature will provide an answer.

### Life at Kasravad
The shade of a young banyan tree spreads over the hard, packed-mud surface on which a meeting of the Jansahayog Trust is in progress. The Trust was founded out of the approximately Rs 18 lakh Right Livelihood Award, or Alternate Noble Prize, conferred on the NBA in 1992. The NBA decided to use the interest on this money not for its

own work but to help the wide range of activists struggling against displacement and for an alternative model of development. The Trustees of Jansahayog, headed by Baba, meet twice a year at Kasravad.

Eight years after Baba arrived at this new home of his, the bald landscape has been transformed by a burgeoning 'anandwan' with tall trees and numerous flowering bushes. Tai is never short of flowers for her daily worship at the Shiva temple close by. All the vegetables served at meals are grown in the kitchen garden on the west side of the house.

After the meeting, the Jansahayog trustees enjoy the special care with which Tai serves them food. Most of them are staying the night but Medha Patkar is rushing away. Watching the flowering and maturing of Medha's enormous and unique energy lends a bright glow to the twilight of Baba's life. They have differed on many things and sometimes gently quarrelled. But each passing year at Kasravad has deepened a bond.

Tai looks forward to times when Medha can be persuaded to take a break from her non-stop travels and rest a while at Kasravad. There is a special joy in watching Medha doze peacefully in the shade of that banyan. She will be off soon enough, attending to loads of correspondence even as she travels to the next meeting in a crowded bus or second class train compartment. Baba frets about the effects of all this over-work on Medha's health but has learnt to let her *be*.

Baba and Tai are never alone for long. Children from the homes close by pass through, at all hours of the day, to greet the elderly couple and receive little pink sweets. Alok Agarwal drops in for consultations to report on recent events. Alok, an IIT-trained engineer, runs the NBA's Badwani office and has emerged as the leading activist of the agitation against the Maheshwar dam. Bureaucrats of varying grades of seniority come by to pay their respects. People from surrounding villages drop in sometimes out of good neighbourliness, just to chat—and at other times to discuss strategy as comrades.

At eighty-three, Baba's ailment-racked body still retains a touch of the muscular wrestler's physique. For all the aches and pains that are part of his daily life, Baba's spirit is effervescent. He reminisces about the past and reflects on the ambiguities of the future with an equally bubbling sense of joy. But there are times of exasperation, for life at Kasravad has not been easy.

For someone used to ceaseless activity and interaction, the quiet lull at Kasravad has sometimes been very difficult. He came in search of his own peace and Baba knows that the road to that peace is often troubled and turbulent. But eight years of intimate kinship with the Narmada has, Baba says, changed him completely: 'This is the place where I could build a dialogue with myself and detect the minutest vibrations of my mother, Narmada. We should decorate her with small dams that don't interfere with her flow.'

Baba scoffs at any description of his life at Kasravad as *sanyas*. He beams at Tai and says, 'This is Romance! We stand together breathless at the sight of the river.'

All over the world the struggle against the dams on the Narmada is seen as an intractable conflict between the forces of modern development and those who wish to transform it, to redefine progress itself. But for Baba this struggle signals the dawning of an age in which conciliation will replace confrontation. Those who live with this faith need the tenacity and stamina of long distance runners.

And a spirit which sees prayer as the 'sigh of a flower'.

*

*The sun has just set beyond that tiny temple of Shiva. The lilting notes of a flute float from the house to the darkening garden outside. Sanjay Sangvai, young friend and fellow-traveller, is sitting beside Baba's bed playing a bamboo flute.*

*Later Baba reminisces about Bapu's advice that he should make palm jaggery a life-long mission. Now, sixty years later that advice makes perfect sense. 'Bapu said, "Look at the palm tree, it is a tube-well of sugar"' recalls Baba. 'What a poetic expression for a tree whose leaves are used for making brooms!'*

*Gandhi had urged young Murlidhar to devote himself to a community-based promotion of palm trees. This would have meant a vast movement for the planting and nurturing of these trees, tapping their sap and processing it into jaggery. Destiny had other plans, but now, with hindsight, Baba sees Gandhi's idea as vital and brilliant. 'If I had taken up this mission and palm-jaggery had been established as a social and economic process, there would have been no sugar lobby and thus no ground-water crisis in Maharashtra today.' The prolific production and use of palm-jaggery would have created ample livelihood opportunities in rural areas and simultaneously added to the tree cover.*

*Perhaps, in comparison to that wider process, the green oasis and many enriched lives of Anandwan and the last stand at Kasravad, seem like a lesser achievement. Then again, these fleeting reflections and longings are carried away in the ceaseless flow of Rewa Maiya and the fearless* sadhak *renews his struggle to be of the moment.*

# Dastkar Andhra
## Weaving a Vision

*Half a century after Gandhiji left his home forever, the gentle whirring of box charkhas fills the afternoon quiet at Bapu Kuti every day of the year. Through blistering heat, torrential rain or bitter cold some residents of Sewagram Ashram religiously assemble on the porch of the Kuti for half an hour of spinning.*

*Sometimes there is a young learner struggling with the seemingly impossible task of turning a sliver of cotton into fine thread. Most such spinners are visitors who come to stay a while at the Ashram, in the spirit of pilgrims.*

*In the spring of 1987, I too was a fumbling trainee spinner who stared at the placid faces of the veterans in wonder. After the first two days I felt a tinge of dismay. Could it be that spinning on a charkha is a special god-gifted skill? Akhilbhai Pandya, an old Sarvodaya worker and my infinitely patient teacher, laughed merrily at this question and gently dissolved its absurdity. Never mind how often the thread breaks, he assured me, just start over again and keep going. Quite unbelievably at the end of five days I was actually converting most of the cotton into thread.*

*Luckily none of the ashram dwellers asked me why I was learning to spin. There was no clear answer, except that once I was at Sewagram it was natural to spend the afternoon learning to spin. The charkha seemed, instinctively, one of the paths by which one could travel into Gandhiji's world. Soon, as the spinning became more smooth, its meditative qualities began to unfold. I chose, deliberately, not to ponder upon numerous economic and technological questions about the charkha. For now it was sufficient that it somehow, mysteriously, held the key to a different world—a less mechanical, more creative world. But spinning did not become a regular habit and I let it rest at that.*

*Several years went by before the unasked questions about charkha were articulated through the work of friends who explored the possibility of reviving local markets for the goods of craftsmen. The charkha, I soon found, was just one element in their search. For as they delved deeper, an entire worldview began to emerge.*

*

### An odd scene

The wooden charkhas and pitlooms seemed incongruous on the grounds of the IIT at Powai, on the outskirts of Mumbai. Students of hi-tech disciplines, like lasers and robotics, stopped by to gape at these pre-modern instruments. Some watched in awe as a weaver arranged tie and dyed yarn, with mathematical precision, to produce an exquisitely patterned ikat fabric. This demonstration of weaving skills was a part of the first Congress of Traditional Sciences and Technologies of India, held at the Mumbai IIT, in December 1993.

Beside the clacking looms and whirring *sudarshan* charkhas sat an assorted group of people, deeply engrossed in discussion. There were research scholars, students, the odd economist, a faculty member of the prestigious National Institute of Design, experts in natural dyes, farmers experimenting with organic methods, and several activists working with craftsmen in rural areas.

Why were these people bothered about the old pitlooms and still more ancient charkha? What moved them to flock to that Congress?

The quest for these answers takes us back in time with two of the participants in that gathering on the lawns. Let us follow Uzramma Bilgrami, goldsmith and 'retired housewife', as she scours the villages of Andhra Pradesh, pulling disused charkhas out of dark, cobweb-covered storage lofts. And Shambu Prasad, erstwhile engineer, who ponders the real worth of the khadi he sometimes wears.

## A journey begins

Uzramma was born some years before India's midnight tryst with destiny. Her family held important administrative positions in the princely state of Hyderabad. A fine aesthetic in the small details of daily living was taken for granted in such a setting. But Uzramma was never particularly interested in the kind of exotic objects collected at the famous Salar Jung Museum. She was much more fascinated by the wares of the roadside potter and their many uses.

Marriage and life's journey took her to England for many, unbearably long, years. Even while she kept house, brought up two children and learned the craft of jewellery making, Uzramma longed to work with village craftsmen. Her interest in the aesthetic dimension was inextricably linked with a strong need to share the advantages of her privileged life. So every year when she returned to India for a month or two, Uzramma spent some of that time learning about the conditions and problems of artisans and craftsmen in two villages near Hyderabad.

Uzramma was always struck by the natural aesthetic harmony and beauty of village life.

But in most villages she found the craftsmen who

produced everyday necessities—like clay vessels and the more simple fabrics—on the verge of destitution. Many craftsmen, who were once skilled and independent producers, had now became mere wage-earners, employed at mechanical tasks in urban factories. Others, even less fortunate, went begging for work as casual labourers. The only artisans still thriving were the few who made decorative or exotic objects which would find buyers at a cottage emporium in some big city, or at Bloomingdale's in New York and Harrods in London.

Was there any way to help the local potter and the weaver of simple dhotis and ordinary cotton sarees? Such questions launched Uzramma on a journey of discovery. She pored over archival material and other literature which showed her how Indian industry and trade had functioned over the centuries. A wondrous picture of a vast pre-modern industrial base, sustained by an intensive network of trade across Asia and Europe, unfolded before her. This trade was partly facilitated by communities of Banjaras and other tradesmen who travelled cross-country in bullock-carts, leading to an exchange of a variety of goods.

Uzramma was particularly fascinated by details about entire villages of weavers who had fed this trade with an enormous variety of textiles, finding markets across two continents. It is well known that all this changed dramatically with the arrival of the British and the industrial revolution heralded by the invention of the steam engine. This modern industrialization severely undermined, and in some cases even destroyed, the business of craftsmen.

The industrial giants, India and China, were reduced to being merely sources of raw materials. As Paul Kennedy wrote, in *The Rise and Fall of Great Powers*, India was producing 24.5 per cent of the world's manufactured goods in 1750. By 1800 this share was down to 19.7 per cent and was 8.6 per cent in 1860. China suffered a similar decline from producing 32.8 per cent of the world's manufactured goods in 1750 to 19.7 per cent in 1860.

In Bengal, the first area to come under British dominance, the influx of imported mill-made yarn intensified the eclipse of domestic hand spinning which had been in decline since the eighteenth century because of the colonial policy. However, this decline was not uniform all over India.

Some home-based industries survived in remote areas like the north-east and tradition-bound regions of south India. Even in the early-90s, the domestic looms of Assam alone accounted for almost 35 per cent of the total handlooms in India. The weaving in these households is essentially not a commercial enterprise. Apart from fulfilling the fundamental need for cloth, the activity itself is an integral part of the family life, enriching its aesthetic content.

In most parts of India such domestic production ceased over a century ago. But Uzramma was amazed to find that in Adilabad district of Andhra Pradesh, about 30,000 independent weavers had survived till the 1950s. By the late-80s there were just about 1,000 independent weavers left in Adilabad district. Yet even then Uzramma met people who:

> . . . still remember having had links with particular weavers and getting household needs made to order. Weavers remember taking orders for a complete bridal trousseau, and the ceremonies and gifts with which they were received from them. There are local people who still take pride in the local traditions and continuities.

Such weavers made a livelihood by meeting the local demand and had direct relations with customers in nearby villages. In most other areas weavers had been drawn into the *karkhana* system run by cooperatives which made them mere labourers in the production process. The products of such weavers were also increasingly homogenized to fit some niche in the modern market.

Wherever she travelled in Andhra, Uzramma saw the tattered remnants of communities whose livelihood had once depended on some particular part of the cloth-making process from cotton cleaning to spinning the thread and dyeing the fabric. Many of these people, once displaced from their traditional occupations, had landed on the pavements of urban centres—eking out a wretched living as manual labourers.

Meanwhile, the few remaining weavers are handicapped by a dependence on mill-produced yarn, which is both expensive and often scarce. Spinning mills find it more profitable to export the yarn or sell it to powerlooms. Thus, weavers were starving not from lack of markets but from lack of the basic raw material of their craft—yarn. There was no locally available yarn because domestic spinning, as a part-time, supplementary income generating activity, had been wiped out long ago.

This, Uzramma found, was the price of modernization and post-independent India's desperation to catch up with the industrialized West. Why, she wondered, should a country whose cotton textile industry has a history of five thousand years talk of catching up? 'Catch up with *what*? Unbearable levels of pollution? An industrialization that invades every sphere of life so that communities are broken up and relationships vitiated?'

Perhaps this is why Mahatma Gandhi made the revival

of charkha his mission. Uzramma was not alone in thinking this. At about the same time, Nandini Joshi, a Harvard-educated economist based in Ahmedabad, was coming to the same conclusion. She realized that for Gandhi the charkha had been the sun in the solar system of village-based industries and thus the foundation for a prosperous society. In a book entitled *Development Without Destruction: The Economics of the Spinning Wheel*, Joshi argued that the revival of domestic spinning can help to solve the problem of unemployment in India today.

Even before she read this book, Uzramma had begun to think along the same lines herself. By the time Uzramma moved back to India and settled in Hyderabad in 1988, such questions had assumed a great urgency for her. Her children were grown up and independent. She was now free to devote herself full-time to a more active quest for practical solutions. And a part of the answer, Uzramma knew, lies in 'not waiting for a sweeping revolution or even the government to act . . . instead to take your own initiative at whatever level possible.'

The institutional vehicle for this onward journey was 'Dastkar', a Delhi-based organization founded in 1982 by people who shared a similar sense of mission towards craftsmen. Dastkar *haats* (bazaar) eliminated the middle-man and allowed artisans and craftsmen to sell goods directly in urban centres. Thus, Dastkar Andhra came into being in 1989 and the journeys of several kindred spirits converged to form a group.

Shambu Prasad was just about then graduating with an engineering degree from IIT, Chennai. For Shambu his degree was of little conventional use. Over five years at IIT he had found time for reflection beyond the routine course work. How, he wondered, 'can this training help us to solve the basic problems of India?' Several of his peers also shared this disillusionment with the methods and outcome of modern science and technology.

Thus going to USA for a doctorate, or even a technocrat's job in some corporation, held no appeal for him. As he explored various options, Shambu was attracted by the prospect of working among craftsmen. At just about the time of Shambu's graduation in 1990, there were frequent newspaper reports of suicides and starvation deaths among displaced weavers in Andhra Pradesh. How and why, he wondered, did the idea of khadi go so sadly awry? So when he heard about the emerging Dastkar Andhra group, joining them seemed like a good way of continuing his exploration.

Similarly, Annapurna had just received an engineering degree but was reluctant to follow a conventional career. An invitation to join the mission of Dastkar Andhra was far more alluring. Uzramma, the team leader, had an infectious enthusiasm that would continue to draw such fresh energies into the on-going journey. There was P.B. Srinivas, whom Uzramma met during her travels in Adilabad, who happily came aboard to join this emerging group.

Srinivas, a graduate of IIT, Chennai and IIM, Calcutta, was working among craftsmen at Adilabad with a fellowship for young professionals given by the Council for Advancement of People's Action and Rural Technology (CAPART). The meeting between Uzramma and Srinivas proved to be an important milestone for both of them. Together they developed an understanding of the problems facing people's industries and explored J.C. Kumarappa's *Economy of Permanence* and Gandhi's *Hind Swaraj* to enrich themselves and to point out possible solutions.

Both books struck a chord in these explorers. But Uzramma found the truth of Gandhi's ideas so self-evident that she wondered why *Hind Swaraj* is so highly exalted: 'Of course the welfare of *antodaya* [most disadvantaged] has to be our aim, how can we settle for anything less? I pay more attention to the practical details of how Gandhi worked out the ideal. *That* is the genius of the man.'

Thus, Dastkar Andhra's work was based on their faith in strong community life as the most sound basis for organizing healthy systems of production. In contrast, government policies have assumed that the traditional, community-based, textile industry is inferior, non-competitive and must be protected through cooperatives. The handloom sector was therefore pushed into a small niche, producing mostly fine fabrics. Over the years, weavers had come to echo the establishment's perception of them as helpless dependents needing government largesse. The Dastkar Andhra group wished to help the weavers to see themselves as textile technologists, the rightful decision-makers of the textile industry.

One of their first steps was to help six weavers in Chinnur, a small town of Adilabad district, to form the Chinnur Cheynetha Kala Sangam. This Sangam was a means of enabling the producers' community to recover control over their lives and initiate activities that could make them self-sufficient. The Sangam functioned as an institutional alternative through which new skills could be introduced on the basis of traditional strengths.

There was a stress on locating the production process within the home. This once again allowed women to play an active role in production, even as they looked after the children. The older family members worked on the pre-loom stages and neighbours took part in sizing the yarn. Gradually, many of the weaver families learnt natural dyeing, as an additional adjunct skill. Soon, the weavers were themselves wearing handloom cloth and inventing new colours on their own.

To learn more about natural dyes the Dastkar Andhra group got in touch with K.V. Chandramouli, whose expertise in this area was legendary. Chandramouli had spent almost four decades in studying and fine-tuning the art of natural dyeing. Much of his knowledge was acquired from the villages decades earlier, before natural dyes became nearly extinct. But it was not his technical wizardry that endeared Chandramouli to the Dastkar group. They were inspired by his commitment to ensuring that this skill was revived among the craftsmen.

Years later, Uzramma and her colleagues credited Chandramouli with teaching them the basics of 'how to share knowledge without self-importance, how to pass on the respect the knowledge deserves without making it seem difficult or obscure.' Working with Chandramouli strengthened the group's faith that knowledge need not be a source of personal gain. As they later wrote:

> There is an alternative view, one that gave stability to traditional societies all over the world and allowed them to perfect low energy technologies suited to their particular conditions, the climate, the soil, the water and their own abilities. According to this view, knowledge is the prerogative of the community, to be held in common for the general good.

But could this ideal be translated into reality? Dastkar Andhra's work among weavers in Chinnur and later with Kalamkari artisans in Srikalahasti and carpet weavers at Eluru was the testing ground. Six years later, Dastkar's members were confident that this collective quest is what swadeshi is all about. As Shambu wrote:

> The artisan is not only a repository of a knowledge system that was sustainable but is also an active participant in its re-creation today. The weaver was able to provide us details of the vibrant textile activity from his memories. This could have been an archive by itself but it was more important for it to be part of his life and ours, not an exhibit in a museum. Unless he is part of this quest, our vision for swadeshi would be limited . . . He [the artisan] often is able to extend the idea to frontiers one could not have envisioned.

But these creative possibilities had to contend with economic realities beyond the control of small collectives.

## The story of desi cotton

For centuries cotton has grown abundantly around Adilabad. The traditional cotton industry was closely integrated with village life. The cotton stalks provided fuel and the seeds were fed to cattle. The cattle, fed with unhulled seeds, provided creamier milk. The oil extracted from cotton seeds, in the village *ghanis*, lit the lamps after dark. There was virtually no wastage in this entire web of activities.

However, for several decades now, the cotton has been sold by farmers to traders who process it in large ginning factories, where machines remove the seeds from the cotton before packing it into tight bales. These are then sent off to distant spinning mills. The cotton grown virtually in the weaver's backyard returns to him as expensive yarn. Can this chain be reworked? This question became the next focus of the Dastkar group.

As a beginning, small wooden roller ginners were once again locally manufactured. Women were urged to dig out their old charkhas lying in some dark corner of the house. Soon, several charkhas were located and some women were ready to spin yarn. But the hand-operated roller gins proved ineffective. The soft cotton seeds kept getting crushed. At first it seemed that hand ginning was really not practical. Yet, hand ginning had been the norm for centuries. Could it be that the cotton was 'faulty'?

Most of the cotton grown today is from hybrid varieties of seeds developed in the USA. The indigenous, or desi, cotton varieties had stood up well to these manual ginners. So why is desi cotton virtually not grown today? To investigate this problem, the skills and enthusiasm of the larger Dastkar Andhra 'family' were tapped. Among these friends was L. Kannan, another erstwhile engineer who was working full time with the Patriotic and People-Oriented Science and Technology (PPST) Foundation in Chennai.

The PPST Foundation was formed in the late-70s by a group of young scientists who were disillusioned with the formal western political ideologies which seemed to be unrelated to the specificities of the Indian context. Over two decades the PPST attempted to evolve a vision of science and technology that emerged from our civilizational ethos and was wedded to the aspirations of the common Indian. Kannan's exploration of the politics and history of cotton cultivation was a part of this larger endeavour within PPST.

Just over a century ago India grew numerous varieties of cotton and from that produced the finest fabrics in the world. These desi varieties of cotton were superior in terms of absorbency, dye holding capability and durability.

However, the British-manufactured spinning machines were not designed for desi varieties but long staple cotton. Thus government policy, both under colonial rule and in independent India, promoted an American variety of long staple cotton and almost wiped out desi varieties.

These hybrid varieties of cotton require vast quantities of water and other expensive inputs of pesticides and fertilizers. Farmers who had once grown cotton mixed with food crops now opted for the rich profits that came from planting American cotton, provided the harvest was good. But this placed small and marginal farmers at great risk. For all its high returns, this mono-cropping left them vulnerable to severe losses in case of crop failure.

By 1998, the adverse effects of this cotton cultivation surfaced as a major social crisis when scores of deeply indebted farmers committed suicide in Andhra Pradesh, Karnataka and Maharashtra.

It is due to these hybrid varieties that cotton, which is cultivated over just 5 per cent of India's cropped area, hogs 50 per cent to 60 per cent of the nation's total consumption of pesticides. As Kannan wrote in 1996:

> Many of our cotton-monoculture areas resemble green-deserts, the entire region looking like a gas-chamber, with a heavy fog of toxins hanging in the air . . . These chemicals poison the land, contaminate the watertable, and enter the food-chain.

In contrast to this, desi varieties have many advantages. As the extended family of Dastkar Andhra wrote, in a jointly-drafted paper entitled 'Weaving a Vision':

Desi varieties need no irrigation and very little manure, and are hardy and pest-resistant. They're usually inter-cropped with food crops like tur, and can be planted in either kharif or rabi seasons. The crop ripens in five to ten months, depending on the variety and time of sowing. The cultivation is fine-tuned for regional variations of soil and climate. Irrigation is used at specific times to improve the quality rather than increase the yield. Pests are controlled by inter-cropping, and sometimes the same plant is a pest repellent, provider of green manure and also a source of dye.

As the investigation on cotton went wider they learnt that many naturally-coloured cottons had once grown abundantly in the Americas, especially Peru. As in India, the Peruvian 'desi' cotton trees were ruthlessly destroyed in order to protect the fragile hybrid varieties. In both countries there are still laws that restrict the cultivation of indigenous varieties.

Digging deeper into the problem of cotton, the Dastkar group located seeds for several varieties of indigenous cotton, including two which were long staple. This search took them both to research establishments and to farmers in villages. The most astounding lessons were provided by a small community of spinners and weavers in Ponduru, Srikakulam district, who were still making high quality khadi by the traditional means. There women were spinning yarn of hundred counts with the hand-processed desi short-staple cotton. This is inconceivable for any modern textile-making machine.

Such 'discoveries' made the Dastkar team feel more and more like explorers. Later, Shambu realized that Gandhi too had experienced similar feelings at several points in his khadi journey: 'Talking about the charkha, he (Gandhi) said, "I am an explorer, and having discovered a thing I must cling on to it. I can merely show the hidden possibilities of old and worn out things".'

Gradually, the Dastkar team became convinced that the search for swadeshi is partly an exploration of the hidden possibilities in traditions. This created an acute need for a more detailed and nuanced understanding of various traditions. Most archival material on economic history dealt only with the politics of trade and the workings of the East India Company. Formal 'history', they found, was not particularly interested in the details of how common people lived and managed their livelihood. Slowly another question emerged: can we write a different history from the traditional communities' point of view?

The contemporary reality has been shaped by decisions and choices made by individuals over perhaps the last two hundred years. The Dastkar team found that this has been a process by which the interests of the individual *as part of* a community had been supplanted by the interests of the individual *at the expense of* the community. There was need for a joint venture, by historians and communities, to understand the present and build a vision for the future. As Uzramma sees it:

The traditional communities have been separated from their history, like people [who have] no shadow ... Without a history there is no basis for a dream for the future. Those without shadows are condemned to live out others' dreams. Many weavers of Andhra don't remember what they used to weave a generation ago, or even five years ago.

245

The textiles in museums all over the world are not accessible to them, they don't know that their ancestral skills are the subject of learned doctoral dissertations or that their hereditary arts of vegetable dyeing are in demand in the most sophisticated of international markets.

Thus, Dastkar which started as an NGO for marketing artisanal produce, began to evolve the identity of a research organization. It looked at the history of innovation and attempted to understand why a particular path was chosen while another was not pursued. When it found a promising 'recipe' or direction for decentralized production *today*, this information was fed into creating fresh innovations. As Shambu later wrote:

We discovered that a particular path was pursued in history often by accident. We were keen to see why the others were left out and we believed that we could write a different history of innovations by looking at efforts that failed because in it there could be some whose time was not ripe and others which were deliberately crushed. This could lead to a different notion of research, one that is interested in failures. This is also an argument for people of 'defeated' cultures to look back. Such an approach worked in decentralized spinning as we realized that there are technical problems that have not been attempted for over a century, namely a set of machines that could gin, card and operate on short staple cotton. If we look at indigo we have the same story—we realized that [once] centralized production became the norm, research into decentralized production of indigo cake was ignored.

Throughout this journey, the Dastkar Andhra group's focus was on active application. This meant reorienting the entire production process to suit the nature of the indigenous raw materials. This would require not merely different machines but also changes in the chain of production. For example, the packing of cotton into tight bales robs it of vitality. If the cotton was locally processed there would be no need to bind it in bales. As in many other things, the Dastkar group learnt this on its own and later found that Gandhi had preceded it down that path and come to the same conclusions.

**Search for swadeshi**

Over the years the Dastkar Andhra group found itself stumbling over Gandhi at every step of the way. Eventually, Shambu felt irresistibly drawn to study Gandhi's khadi-journey. So he dropped out of the day-to-day work at Dastkar and devoted two years to researching the story of khadi in the first part of this century. It is common knowledge that khadi was not merely about cloth. But Shambu was amazed at the extent to which khadi held the key to understanding Gandhi's vision of community work and alternative institutions of creative dissent.

Shambu's journey into the history of khadi was propelled by the conviction that it is not enough to passionately denounce 'destructive development'. The 'how' and 'what' of an alternative model have to be articulated with as much energy and still greater rigour. Perhaps Gandhi's khadi experiments would offer clues for building viable alternatives.

Surprisingly, all the easily available 'Gandhi literature' had few details on Gandhi's concept of khadi. So Shambu plunged into an intensive reading of *Harijan* and *Young India*, the journals that Gandhi had edited. As Shambu delved deeper into these sources Gandhi appeared as a man with almost magical powers for bringing people together and creating a truly universal constructive agenda.

For khadi was not merely a campaign about cloth, it was a means of involving a diverse range of people. There was a vital role for everyone—from prince to peasant, missionary to mystic, women, poets, workers, mill-owners and even Englishmen. In the process, khadi helped to build connections between the otherwise separate streams of constructive work, mainstream power politics and radical dissent. Khadi became the testing ground for Gandhi's endeavour to dissolve the 'otherness' of any apparent opponent—whether it was the issue of swadeshi or Hindu-Muslim relations. This was done by softening the issue and creating a more congenial atmosphere for fundamental discussion about solutions.

To understand the actual process of khadi as cloth, Shambu examined the missing links between cotton growing, spinning and weaving. Now, quality and productivity began to take on new meanings. The fundamental axioms of workable institutions, he realized, would have to be changed:

I realized that the khadi movement rarely stuck to conventional yardsticks like the number of metres produced. One could always measure the growth of the movement by the number of villages covered or the success in getting the idea (across) to Congressmen. At its peak, the All India Spinners

Association was able to change its goals by shifting from the then routine one of sales to a spread of khadi that would not reflect in the balance sheet of sales depots. Khadi would, in this new disposition, continue to grow at people's homes in a self-sufficient manner. As Gandhi was once to remark, 'The greater the progress of khadi the more shall we find our methods have to be far different from those hitherto adopted by the commercial world.'

Today, khadi is narrowly defined as a few products made and sold by Khadi Village Industries Commission (KVIC). But originally khadi encompassed all industries outside the profit-oriented commercial sector. Khadi was a term for people's industries. It showed that greed and exploitation are not the inevitable basis of all economic activities. Instead, the entire chain of production, from the use of raw materials, to the management of the organization, the means of production, trade and marketing can be motivated by principles of sharing and non-violence.

From this perspective, Shambu began to see the work of most contemporary NGOs in a different light. Raising people's incomes is a major criterion for growth and success among funding agencies, NGOs and people alike. But, Shambu asked himself, is it really our job as community workers to raise incomes? Surely the essential objective is to strengthen communities? Strong communities can raise income levels but increased income levels do not necessarily strengthen communities.

Thus, for Gandhi, khadi was about food and promoting community values, and enhancing the organizational skills of the masses. Gandhi saw khadi not as cloth alone but as a means to create the greatest cooperative in the world, involving millions of people. Its essence was interdependence. A typical centre would have to interact with several spinners, ginners, carders, weavers and customers, irrespective of caste or creed. A community worker was to ensure this interdependence, the success of which would help prepare the villages for other programmes of sanitation, health, etc.

Khadi was not a social work programme of 'do-gooding'. Gandhi saw it as a 'sound economic proposition' and also 'a science and romance'. *This* was Gandhi the great inventor. Thus swadeshi today would have to redefine science. This would not be an east versus west debate but a collective quest for specific, practical answers. The corporate wisdom of the Charkha Sangh, from Gandhi's time, would be instructive.

The Charkha Sangh freely utilized the organizational skills of local merchants to spread khadi. The participation of the merchants in this venture never meant a dilution of the objectives of the Sangh. It had the confidence and the ability to counter the trends in the market by directing attention to marketing in rural areas. The Charkha Sangh redirected its profits, through the Kaamgar Seva Fund, towards research in spinning and weaving and setting up training schools. This 'corporate vision' of the Sangh and its keen business sense, Shambu decided, would have done most multinational companies proud. But unfortunately organizations like the KVIC have learnt nothing from the Charkha Sangh.

For Shambu, above all, the story of khadi proved that swadeshi is .about people, ordinary people, doing extraordinary work.

## Many miles to go

This conviction about swadeshi was the real fruit of Dastkar Andhra's labour. By most conventional criteria, the visible 'success' was limited. The endeavour to revive domestic spinning is yet to get off the ground. The natural dyed textiles of the six Chinnur weavers became popular and found markets all over India. But in 1995-96, Dastkar Andhra's total sales, through eleven exhibitions, were just over Rs 13 lakh—a bare speck on the larger economic scene. However, the group had *chosen* gradual learning over grand visible returns. So the Chinnur Cheynetha Kala Sangam remained at six weavers by choice.

The value of the work, for the group itself, rests on having demonstrated that it is possible in practice to make and sell good quality fabrics of natural materials to the benefit not only of the maker and user but of the community at large without causing damage to the natural environment or disruption to society.

This experience allowed the Dastkar Andhra group to articulate what it had once felt intuitively. Along with friends like Kannan and Vinoo Kaley, it prepared a paper entitled 'Weaving a Vision' for the first Congress of Traditional Sciences and Technologies of India, at Mumbai IIT in December 1993:

> The textile industry of the future has to be seen in a complete and dispassionate way, with its associated agricultural practices, its tool makers, its dyers and printers, its spinners, ginners and carders, a veritable dynamo for rural prosperity. There's no pollution and no waste. It will be a people's technology with access for all—to the skills, the materials and the markets.

The textile making activity makes it obvious that technology is not merely the aggregate of tools, techniques and skills. Technology comes into existence and derives sustenance from several supporting structures, complex social relationships and value systems. Traditional technologies were not created in cloisters by experts seeking to hand down goodies to the ignorant masses. They were evolved by the synergy of artisans, craftsmen, farmers and others, each one involved creatively, without blindly accepting any single person or group as being privy to expertise. Technological development was a collective pursuit rather than being one where a large section of the population is led by the nose, as it were, by a supercilious minority pretending omniscience.

Once this is clear then it follows that the existing order cannot be changed by merely managerial tinkering. There is need for a more radical transformation. Just how this will happen for society at large is not yet clear. But in some spheres the Dastkar Andhra group's journey is converging with larger trends. For instance, now all the leading cotton research institutions of India acknowledge the importance of organic farming and 'eco-friendly' cotton.

On the face of it, many global market trends appear to favour products which the Dastkar group has been working on. Pure cotton clothes are at a premium in the West and the demand for natural dyes in Europe is growing. But, as Chandramouli always took pains to point out, it would be tragic if the natural dyes business is cornered by large factories, leaving out the small artisans. Yet, by the mid-90s, the success of Dastkar Andhra's natural dye workshops all over India was overshadowed by the problem of raw materials being cornered by larger commercial interests.

The Dastkar group has struggled to convince policy-makers that natural dyeing is viable only in the hands of small producer communities who understand the need to be responsible to the resource base. Meanwhile, they tackled the scarcity of dye-bearing plant material by collecting seeds of such plants from all over India. The seeds are being multiplied by groups like Timbaktu Collective, near Dharmavaram, and Swadeshi Trust at Venkatrampuram, near Tirupathi. These 'modern *tirthas*', as Shambu likes to call them, are also trying to grow certain varieties of indigenous cotton which have a natural colour. Eventually, if this is done all over India, such actions could help to preserve the bio-diversity of dye-bearing and cotton plants, making them available to artisans at affordable rates.

The potential for such cross-country linkages has been explored partially through the Textiles Working Group formed at the PPST's first Congress on Traditional Sciences and Technologies of India. This network has made it possible for a wide variety of individuals and groups to exchange information and support each other. For example there is Ramakrishna, another IIT engineering graduate, who has devoted much of his time to investigating, in detail, the viability of decentralized home-based spinning. Ramakrishna advocates a concerted effort to redesign spinning technologies. These new designs could borrow elements from the modern process, machines developed by the khadi establishment and traditional techniques used over the centuries.

Sharing these findings in the newsletter of the Textiles Working Group, Ramakrishna wrote: 'There is nothing to suggest that the decentralized process is unfeasible—on technical or economic grounds. If anything, the new technology can operate under far more favourable terms than the present mills.' This is because baling and transportation of cotton would not be necessary. Apart from this, even the cost of machinery and other infrastructure would be much lower; operating in small volumes, and in local contexts, the working capital costs and inventory holding costs would be very low.

Such live inputs also enhanced Dastkar Andhra's confidence in its ability to work as a research organization devoted entirely to the interests of the artisan. As their 1995-96 annual report stated: 'This has been made possible by the creation of an atmosphere where the expert in the area, the field workers and the artisan community can work together as a team to look into the various aspects of the technology.'

There are of course tangible differences between the perceptions of urban activists and the artisans. As Uzramma has found:

> There is a gap between how the weavers see themselves and how we see them. They have a sense of being supplicants, and are not assertive as we want them to be . . . If they don't assert how will change come about!? We are saying that you [weavers] are the technologists, you should set the terms. They tell us to come down to earth and take stock of reality. This is the gap between them and us . . . We must continue to work together and dialogue. By working together a common thinking will evolve. If the work is thorough, the effect is tremendous, even if it's with six weavers. It is on the

basis of this solid experience that we can forge ahead.

There is no certainty that this would automatically revive the confidence of ordinary weavers at large. For too long now they have seen themselves as left-overs of a bygone era, the practitioners of an economically unviable craft. The success of a handful of local endeavours cannot convince them about the future viability of handlooms. In this context it may well be asked how far the Dastkar group has moved from its starting point. Is the group's conviction about the viability of charkha and handlooms just a stubborn optimism or faith?

Perhaps faith is an essential requisite for anyone who challenges the rigid complacency of any given 'order'. Such faith is not 'outside' of the material reality. The work among craftsmen provides an empirical basis for showing that though village self-sufficiency is no longer possible, there are enormous possibilities for prosperity through interdependence among villages.

For this to be widely accepted and implemented the concept of 'viability' will have to go beyond balance sheets. 'We do not abandon general elections on the grounds of affordability,' they argued in 'Weaving a Vision'. 'Similarly, but much more importantly, a technology choice has to be made that leads every one of us to a life of peace, dignity and harmony.' For this, Uzramma adds, policy planners will have to 'overcome their obsession with gross national product, balance-of-trade and export surplus, etc. Instead, policies should seek to involve communities and ensure that their skills are used to make common man's cloth, not for the fickle export market.'

This means redefining 'progress', which in itself is an

epochal and civilizational mission. Even while attending to the nitty-gritty of fabric textures and shades of dyes, the Dastkar group has been struggling with this challenge in the arena of 'ideas'. As they wrote in 'Weaving a Vision':

> What are the steps necessary to re-construct the paradigm of an industrial structure rooted in our traditions? How can we move away from the ivory-tower of technological advancement that robs people of a chance to fashion their world? Can we involve every practitioner in a profession creatively as an inheritor of a legacy, and an innovator in his own right, rather than as a mere replaceable factor of production? . . . What are the specific elements of a new structure that we need to evolve? What are the initiatives that can bring us closer to realizing it? It is time we put together insights from diverse sources into a comprehensive vision with a concrete agenda for the future.

So when the Dastkar Andhra group's 'Manifesto' talks about 'the vision of an ideal and a belief in its perfectibility' it is quick to add that this ideal does recognize existing reality. The past can inspire but the challenge is certainly one of creating new ways to meet new challenges. A whole new tradition has to be developed. And the Dastkar group firmly believes that 'there are no deadlines for its realization, and the vision takes into account the many stages and innumerable steps to be taken in the slow process towards attaining it.'

This apparent lack of urgency may seem at odds with the intensity of purpose. But, for all their missionary zeal, the Dastkar group is not made up of vehement proselytizers.

They live by a faith in the energy of the seed and try not to fret over the size of the sapling or its rate of growth. For them learning and strengthening the foundation is more important than dramatic, visible results.

Thus, they feel that there is a vital need for a more nuanced understanding of Gandhi in today's context. For Shambu this is a pre-requisite to 'reinventing' Gandhi's approach to suit contemporary needs. The journey is made joyous by an expanding community of friends who are also fellow-travellers. Together they are all groping for effective modes of action. This 'search' for answers is simultaneously personal and collective. Shambu feels that many of his peer group, highly educated men and women in their late twenties, need something more than what the mainstream culture offers. And what, Shambu asks himself, 'can be the new idiom for a confused youth who has to choose between "the choice of a new generation" and "the real thing" being thrust down their throat?'

Now, after almost eight years of this work, Shambu says:

> Today I can wear my khadi kurta with pride. We are perhaps at the beginning of a new swadeshi movement. We may not be in a position like Gandhi to take a pure swadeshi vow, but we need to in our own lives take the vow like many who took it in 1919 when the movement was yet to start. It is by several of us saying 'No' to globalization that we can create the atmosphere, and Gandhi was clear about that. The middle classes and the educated few have a big role to play to provide the atmosphere for the movement to spread. Gandhian politics was all about creating the right atmosphere and it had to start with the individual. Perhaps we could today

start with at least affirming our faith in the 'alternative' before one or several amongst us works out its details.

The stress on personal example and group action is one way of dealing with unresponsive power structures. As Uzramma sees it:

The internally consistent system of modern economics is impervious to critical scrutiny from outside. [An] assertion of personal choice can be the only dampner on its revolting hegemony. Can the individuality of·man and the life of communities, now seriously threatened by modernism, be the moral basis of all activity against massification and dehumanization?

For some this question carries a searing agony. Even if the individual and community form a *moral* basis for action, how will this be translated into a political movement which can transform state power? There are few workers today with even a fraction of Gandhi's genius for simultaneously working on the blue-print of an alternative model and engaging in a vigorous political struggle.

This quandary was painfully brought home by the suicides of cotton farmers in Andhra Pradesh. The Dastkar Andhra group had foreseen and cautioned against such a tragedy. Its work offered clues for long-term solutions to the farmers' woes. Yet its understanding and perspective was not able to grab the centrestage even at a time when public attention is focused on glaring symptoms of the problem. Most of the discussion on this issue, within the mainstream media, is restricted to seeking managerial solutions within the existing system.

Thus, there is an acute awareness that all their vigorous actions are merely tiny drops in a vast ocean. But, as Shambu says, 'true intent has its own sanctity which does not depend on its being big or small.' Besides, as they argued in 'Weaving a Vision':

> The functions of a society and its evolution depend on the strength of its social fabric. And the strength of its fabric depends not on its stronger strands here and there but on the strength of its weakest threads and the way they are interwoven.

There is sustenance in the strengthening of even a few of the weaker threads.

Thus 'Weaving a Vision' culminated with this poem by Kannan:

> By the ceaseless shuttle
> of our quest
> that throws the weft
> of shared insights
> across diverse strands,
> if we weave
> the tapestry of our dreams
> the dawn of tomorrow
> cannot but drench
> the fabric in colours bright.

*

*The trees around Bapu Kuti cast long eastward shadows as the sun slid towards the horizon. The birds were in full chorus as they fluttered into their resting places. Akhilbhai was showing a novice*

*how to maintain her small box charkha. It's quite simple, he smiled.*
'Jahan sangharsh hai, vahan sneha le jao.' *Observe the points of friction and shower them with affection.*

# Kumarappa's Legacy
## The Quest for an Economy of Permanence

*Sewagram Ashram wore a festive look in January 1993. A couple of hundred people were gathered under the grand old trees around Bapu Kuti. A low, make-shift stage opposite the Kuti was decked with bright yellow flowers and mango leaves. The guest of honour was a man whose ancestors were lovingly called Harijans by Gandhi. But, on that cool, bright January morning K.R. Narayanan did not represent any caste. He was there as the Vice-President of India, inaugurating a celebration of Joseph Cornellius Kumarappa's hundredth birthday.*

*A third generation of young men and women, driven by the same longing that moved Kumarappa, were in the audience. For them this was one of many gatherings at Bapu Kuti—occasions when they met to share ideas and plan strategies for action. The full range of this striving is impossible to convey here. But we can catch fleeting glimpses of it from the journeys of these post-midnight's children who are spontaneously finding Gandhi and Kumarappa as fellow-travellers.*

*Let us begin by travelling a short distance, about ten kilometres from Sewagram Ashram, to the Dattapur centre of the Centre of Science for Villages . . .*

\*

## Kumarappa's legacy

The small rectangular meeting room at the Centre of Science for Villages, was crowded to capacity. A few dozen men and women were seated on the *chattai*-covered floor, under an arching roof made of clay cones. Others filled the room's various doors and windows blocking out the cool greenery outside. All eyes were fixed on a slim young woman who stood and spoke with laughter in her voice. They listened with affectionate eagerness to the woman whom they knew through newspaper photos as the leader of the Narmada Bachao Andolan. Yet Medha Patkar spoke with the ease and familiarity of an old colleague, even a family member. This was no remote 'star'.

Medha was there with several fellow-workers. They were all attending a meeting at Sewagram Ashram and had come for a brief visit to the field office of the Centre of Science for Villages at Dattapur. The group had just seen several techniques for converting leaves, twigs and cow-dung into energy and fertilizer; a system of drip-irrigation through little clay-emitters; low-cost sanitation and house construction, among other things.

Medha's words transported the listeners, briefly, into the realm of hard-pitched struggles. The more imaginative could sense in her, the raw energy of a determined warrior. One could picture just how this energy translates into 'satyagraha' on the banks of the Narmada and dharnas against the multinational Enron. And this, Medha was telling them, was only a small part of the larger picture. All over India, she said, some people are eager to replace the destruction of what is today called 'development', with something that gives full scope for the creativity of all.

This aspiration lies at the very genesis of 'CSV', as the Centre is popularly known. It is the longing for an 'economy of permanence'. That is, those modes of production and social organization which creatively tap the inherent bounty of nature rather than being at war with it. It is the dream of ensuring plenitude for all through a healthy balance between the material *needs* and *wants* of human beings. In the 1990s this vision is often implied in the catch-phrases 'alternative development' or 'sustainable development'.

Once upon a time, when Wardha was a sleepy little town, Maganwadi bustled with activity and excitement. In those days it was home to Bapu. And, even more importantly, it was the nucleus of vigorous endeavours to rejuvenate India's village industries. In 1934, around the same time that Gandhi moved to Wardha, he set up the All India Village Industries Association (AIVIA). This body was backed by various wealthy industrialists and its advisory committee included the greatest scientists and luminaries of that time—the botanist Sir J.C. Bose, the physicist Sir C.V. Raman, the chemist P.C. Ray, the agiculturist Sam Higginbotham and Rabindranath Tagore among others. Gandhi was keen to know the latest scientific developments and find ways of using this knowledge for the benefit of rural India.

As the twentieth century draws to a close this work still goes on quietly at Maganwadi. But now Maganwadi seems peaceful in contrast with the frenetic hustle-bustle of modern, satellite-linked, auto-infested Wardha. The two long wings of the high-roofed structure of Magansangralaya, built almost half a century earlier, still house a museum for village industries and technologies. But the smaller rooms house the offices of the CSV where 'here and now' problems are tackled every day. Just behind this large cement-and-brick building is a small mud-and-thatch hut called Kumarappa Kuti. Its kinship with Bapu Kuti is self-evident.

Joseph Cornellius Kumarappa lived here in the 1940s and worked as secretary of the All India Village Industries Association (AIVIA). Even today, the working day at Magansangralaya begins with a small prayer meeting on the gravel patch in front of Kumarappa Kuti. The meeting is usually led by a tall thin man with an elderly stoop.

Devendra Kumar first came to Wardha as a young man, over fifty years ago. The struggle for independence was at its peak then and like many young people Devendra Kumar wished to devote himself to a cause greater than a personal career. In any case, the prospect of a routine technical or managerial job in some industry held no allure. The fresh-out-of-college science graduate was keen to find ways of employing his limited knowledge of science and technology for the enormous task of rural renewal. And so he came in search of Kumarappa.

Sure enough, Kumarappa could relate to this yen. In 1929, a similar urge had led Joseph Cornellius to M.K. Gandhi. At that time Kumarappa was a young man, dressed in fashionable western clothes, just back from the United States of America with a Master's degree from Columbia University. In 1946, the balding, grey bearded Kumarappa looked at Devendra, his would-be disciple, and told him that contemporary science was imprisoned to the service of mammon. Was Devendra prepared to alter this? 'If you want to remove social disparities and foster peaceful ways of living', Kumarappa told the young man, 'the doors of Magansangralaya are open.' Devendra accepted the invitation and came aboard for a lifetime.

So, in 1946, Devendra joined the AIVIA and engaged in a wide variety of experiments under Kumarappa's guidance. Long before the emergence of the environmental movement, the AIVIA team at Maganwadi lobbied for promotion of renewable energy. To back up this appeal it worked out various ways to reduce use of fossil fuels and minerals. Non-edible vegetable oils were used to replace kerosene in lanterns. Oil from tree-borne seeds was used to make soaps, thus saving crop area for food. Enhancing the productive, commercial value of standing trees was seen as one way of preventing deforestation. Improved mechanical devices helped to enhance the bullock-power used for carts, oil pressing, grain grinding and irrigation. These were all steps towards ecologically sound modes of production, though the word 'ecology' was not yet commonly used.

Even in the early-50s, long before big dams became controversial, the AIVIA understood the limits of modern irrigation. Excessive use of irrigation and chemical fertilizers, they warned, may give short range gains in production but it would eventually destroy the soil and create a host of other problems. A system of water conservation tanks and ponds would not only offer better means of irrigation but also help stem the loss of top soil.

Devendra Kumar was now convinced that the prosperity of India's villages required decentralized modes of industry. After six years of work at Maganwadi, Devendra felt that it was time to actually live in villages in order to understand and improve them. So, along with a small team of fellow-workers, including his wife Prabha, he settled in the village of Machala on the Vindhya hills in Madhya Pradesh. This team soon realized that they were learning much more from the village than they could give in return. Devendra later wrote: 'We learnt the language of the spirit of the soil, the seasons, the nature, the people of our land and were inspired by it as well as astounded by the great challenges rural India posed.'

The Machala team organized a collective farming cooperative on 300 acres of wasteland. About thirty landless families and members of the group worked on the land using many of the devices innovated at Maganwadi. They also started schools for children, dug wells, provided medical facilities, built compost pits and struggled against untouchability. But their local success was being overpowered by rapid changes around them.

Government policies pushed the use of hybrid seeds, chemical fertilizers, pesticides and tractors. Over the next ten years, even as this group continued its local experiments, the rural rich began to get richer fast, eco-systems were severely disrupted and the village became more and more dependent on cities. Devendra watched as the cooperative and community spirit of the village evaporated and was replaced by individual competition for dwindling resources.

This brought home the limitations of isolated local endeavours. So in 1960 Vinoba Bhave persuaded Devendra to move on to work at the national and international levels. This led to his assuming a leading role in various Sarvodaya institutions. Among other things, he worked with Vinoba Bhave and Jayaprakash Narayan to help negotiate the peaceful surrender of dacoits.

By the mid-70s Devendra noticed a visible shift in the global climate of ideas. The wisdom of Gandhi and Kumarappa was becoming more acceptable than it had been in their own lifetime. This was the cumulative effect of several landmark events. Rachel Carson's classic book *Silent Spring* had aroused world consciousness about the impending environmental crisis as early as 1962.

By the mid-60s an Englishman named E.F. Schumacher

was telling western intellectuals that the core of Gandhi's non-violence was to be found in his economic ideas. In 1973 Schumacher, a Rhodes Scholar in economics, made international waves with a book which powerfully re-articulated the Gandhi-Kumarappa critique of modern industrial culture and its economics. The book, *Small is Beautiful: Economics as if People Mattered*, became a global catch-phrase and the basic text for those who aspire to build a more peaceable world. The cover illustration of the book's paperback edition included images of trees, plants, a butterfly, a man atop a huge tricycle and Gandhi.

For twenty years before this, Schumacher had been the top economist of the British Coal Board. He was also president of the Soil Association, one of Britain's oldest organic farming organizations. Schumacher wrote with the confidence of an establishment 'insider' and yet challenged the very foundations of modern economics. He belonged to the tradition of organic, decentralist economics evolved by pioneers like Prince Kropotkin, Leo Tolstoy and Gandhi. Close on the heels of Schumacher's work came the report of the Club of Rome. This international group of intellectuals, warned of the dangers of unlimited consumption and called for an alternative approach to development.

Meanwhile, in India, the formal 'Gandhian' institutions now lacked the radical edge of Gandhi's economic vision and were mostly restricted to running khadi centres. Instead a new generation, born well after Independence, was launching new kinds of projects and experiments which actively challenged the status quo and demanded an equitable and just model of development.

Devendra Kumar was among the few professed 'Gandhians' who determined to seize the moment and build on the many international advances in the 'battle' of ideas.

Thus, in 1976, he threw himself into founding the Centre of Science for Villages. This endeavour was rooted in the faith that the world was now more ready for an economy of permanence, than it had been in the post-war euphoria of western economies. The CSV would develop and demonstrate appropriate rural technologies for a community-based decentralized economy.

The effort elicited the participation of some of the leading policy-makers at that time, like Professor Nayudamma, Professor D.S. Kothari and Dr M.S. Swaminathan. But more than that it attracted a host of younger people who, like Devendra Kumar a quarter century earlier, had the yen for an economy of permanence.

*Economy of Permanence: A Quest for a Social Order Based on Non-violence* is the title of the book, by J.C. Kumarappa, which distilled almost two decades of practical and theoretical work. Kumarappa was born in Kerala and started out in life as an Incorporated Accountant, running his own auditing firm in Mumbai. Later, he went to Columbia University as a graduate student in economics. It was here that Kumarappa began to evolve his critique of modern economics, quite independently of Gandhi.

Early in life Kumarappa was convinced that man is not merely a wealth-producing agent but essentially a member of society with political, social, moral and spiritual responsibilities. While at Columbia he had studied Indian public finance and written about the British exploitation of India through their taxation policy. When he returned to India in 1929, and set about trying to get his thesis published, a friend suggested that Gandhiji would be intensely interested in reading it. And so Kumarappa found himself at Sabarmati Ashram, before an old man seated under a tree on a neatly swept cow-dung floor, working on a spinning wheel.

Gandhiji was amazed to find a student of economics whose views were exactly the same as his own. He immediately asked Kumarappa if he would undertake a survey in rural Gujarat. The result was a detailed, and later historic, survey of Matar Taluka and a complete transformation of Kumarappa. He went from being the urbane auditor in silk-trousers to a constructive worker in khadi dhoti and kurta—and eventually the principle inheritor of Gandhi's economic vision and work on village industries.

Like his mentor, Kumarappa had nothing 'new' to say. He simply observed the complementary manner in which nature's various creatures coexist and drew from it lessons for human society. Each creature on earth, Kumarappa observed, fulfils its necessary role in the cycle of life by performing its own primary function:

> In this manner, nature enlists and ensures the cooperation of all its units, each working for itself and in the process helping other units to get along their own too—the mobile helping the immobile, and the sentient the insentient. Thus, all nature is dovetailed together in a common cause. Nothing exists for itself. When this works out harmoniously and violence does not break the chain, we have an economy of permanence.

Kumarappa contrasted the economy of permanence with the economy of transience. The latter is most dramatically manifest in the massive use of chemical fertilizers and pesticides which gives high crop yields in the short run and eventually destroy the soil. Similarly, he warned against the disastrous consequences of preferring cash crops over self-reliance in food production:

> An economy that is based purely on monetary or material standards of value, does not take in a realistic perspective in Time and Space. This shortcoming leads to a blind alley of violence and destruction from which there is no escape . . . To lead to any degree of permanence, the standard of value itself must be based on something apart from the person valuing, who is after all perishable. Such a basis, detached and independent of personal feelings, controlled by ideals which have their roots in the permanent order of things, are objective and so are true and reliable guides.

In writing *Economy of Permanence* Kumarappa was aiming to reconnect the spiritual and material life so that 'the daily routine of mundane existence may be regulated in accordance with the dictates of our better self . . .' The economy of permanence would be a partial, everyday manifestation of what men of religion term 'eternal life'. Kumarappa realized that, in the mid-twentieth century this novel approach seemed a utopian impossibility to many people. So he rested in the hope that his work may some day ' . . . set others thinking on the ways and means of achieving the end aimed at.'

The political mainstream of post-independence India proceeded to ignore Kumarappa, treating him as a footnote in history. But his hope to 'set others thinking' was to be fulfilled by people who were still children when Kumarappa passed away in 1961. Among them was a thin man with a salt and pepper beard that made him look older than his fifty-odd years. For Vinoo Kaley, Magansangralaya and the Bapu Kuti *parisar* were like a home.

## Vinoo Kaley: the bamboo man

The *godhuli*, literally cow-dust, hour at Khamana has a timeless quality. It is easy to imagine the cows ambling back into the narrow village lanes, kicking up that haze of fine dust, always in just the same way. The ringing of cowbells mingles with rumbling of bullock-carts and the excited chorus of birds settling down for the night.

These are moments that warm the heart of city-bred Vinoo Kaley. In his khadi dhoti and kurta, Vinoo merges easily into the aesthetic of this north Andhra village. And yet he is quite distinct. Wherever he goes in the village, even those who barely know him call out—'Ram, Ram Guruji'. Vinoo replies, 'Ram, Ram', with an infectious good cheer.

How did Vinoo Kaley, resident of Nagpur and architect by training, come to work in Khamana? The story goes back into Vinoo's youth when he wandered all over India in a restless quest. At that time some parts of India were charged with the revolutionary fervour of the Naxalities. In 1968, when Vinoo graduated as an architect from the J.J. School of Art, Mumbai, some of his peers were going off to join the armed revolt against the bourgeois state. This held no appeal for Vinoo. He was quite certain that violence could not bring about a creative transformation.

Yet the need for a drastic transformation was self-evident. Twenty years after Independence almost half of India's people were lacking in the basics of life—*roti-kapda-makan* (food, cloth, shelter). It distressed Vinoo that his education as an architect paid virtually no attention to the housing needs of millions. Most of his fellow students were eager to sell their skills to contractors in urban areas. But for Vinoo the prospect of spending a lifetime producing concrete matchboxes seemed like a living death.

So Vinoo decided to just roam across the country. He was confused about what he wanted to do and hoped that these travels would throw up some clues. For starters, he felt inadequate about his own lack of practical, hands-on, skills like brick-laying. So, for a while, he worked as a manual labourer for a building contractor in Bilaspur, Madhya Pradesh. During his travels Vinoo observed a vast variety of traditional housing, each suited to the climate and natural resources of that area. With fascination and humility Vinoo learnt about the various combinations of building materials common people used: stone and mud, bamboo and thatch, wood and mud, and so on.

Along the way, Vinoo met up with several kindred spirits and just before the Emergency was declared, in 1975, some of them came together as a group called 'Academy of Young Scientists'. For the next decade this group grappled with the problems of rural India in many different ways. They attempted to combine their skills with the traditional skills of villagers to solve a variety of problems. And they persistently barged into the corridors of power to struggle for macro policy changes. The Young Scientists lived by the faith that the mind-set of policy makers could be broadened, perhaps even altered, through persuasion. For over a decade and a half Vinoo shared many adventures and ventures with this group of friends.

By the early-80s the economic plight of craftsmen had become the focal point of Vinoo's work. (Even as the twentieth century draws to a close the artisan sector contributes Rs 65,000 crore to India's Gross National Product. This sector earns approximately Rs 15,000 crore in exports. The various Viswakarma communities—artisans who work on textiles, leather, metals, wood, bamboo, stone, mud—are estimated to be about 2.5 crore families all over India. This means approximately a hundred million people or a little more than ten per cent of India's population.) All over India Vinoo found these people struggling for two simple meals and for their place under the sun. The need to find ways of ensuring livelihood with dignity for the craftsmen became the core motivation of Vinoo's life. This meant, firstly, challenging the common perception of craftsmen as poor, illiterate, backward people in need of patronage from the wealthy and powerful. This attitude, inherent to most government and social work efforts, had severely undermined the confidence and self-respect of the craftsmen themselves. Consequently, most young people of these communities were keen to abandon the traditional craft. Vinoo saw this as the portent of a looming disaster. If the trend continued there would be a 'famine' of technical skills in society at large as erstwhile craftsmen became deskilled, casual labourers.

This realization brought Vinoo squarely to the doorstep of Gandhi and Kumarappa. Now it became clear to Vinoo why village industries had been the core of Gandhi's mission. So critical was this task that Gandhi did not permit its workers to join the satyagraha and go to jail. It was the thread of this legacy which Vinoo and his fellow-workers picked up, in order to save and secure the well-being of India as a whole. This meant taking initiatives to act positively and actually create the alternatives.

This urge to action was boosted by the fact that India is one of the few countries where the ordinary person still uses crafts products in daily life—whether it is a bamboo '*soop*' or a clay pot or clay lamp or a grass broom. Gradually, bamboo became the primary focus of Vinoo's work, the linking thread for his mission.

Vinoo had been interested in bamboo since childhood. There was a large community of bamboo workers in Wardha, where he grew up. Over the years he had watched their mounting problems as bamboo became more scarce and expensive. The search for cheap and easily regenerating natural materials also led him to bamboo, for even wood does not grow and multiply as easily or rapidly as bamboo. After an extensive tour of the north-eastern states, to study the uses of bamboo, Vinoo's conviction grew even stronger.

Even today there are about twenty lakh families of bamboo artisans in India, that is approximately ten million people. Vinoo found that though their products play a crucial role in the rural agro-industrial web, these groups do not enjoy any clout in the society. Instead most of the bamboo craftsmen belong to communities which fall in the scheduled caste category. Similarly bamboo itself is grossly undervalued.

In the nineteenth century the British treated India's richly abundant bamboo groves as a 'nuisance' which slowed down their tree-felling operations. The colonial rulers deemed bamboo as a 'forest weed' and accordingly wiped out large tracts of dense bamboo growth. As paper mills came up, the remaining bamboo forests were leased to them at ludicrously low rates. These mills got this raw material at the rate of about Re 1 per tonne, which is approximately 200 pieces of bamboo. Meanwhile crafts societies registered with the Department of Industry paid Rs 2.75 for a single piece of bamboo. Today, almost two-thirds of the bamboo cut annually in India goes into paper or rayon mills.

The relative paucity of bamboo available to the artisans,

coupled with the low price their products received, displaced many bamboo craftsmen from their traditional livelihood. Thus, Vinoo began lobbying at many different levels for dramatic policy changes. Bamboo, he argued, could give us big dividends as an artisanal and house-building resource while paper could be made equally well out of sugarcane bagasse and other materials. The strength, load-bearing capacity and flexibility of bamboo make it virtually a 'regenerable steel'. Bamboo grows more rapidly than wood and is one of nature's best solar energy converters. The Chinese have already copyrighted 2,000 bamboo products under the new Intellectual Property Rights regime.

Given India's climatic conditions, farm forestry can be made a highly profitable venture. Large-scale regeneration of bamboo forests would simultaneously help solve the problems of deforestation and unemployment. This would, of course, require appropriate investments and initiatives in science, technology and design.

But what use was this theoretical knowledge? 'I felt that if there is any strength in my idea I must learn it (bamboo craftsmanship) myself,' Vinoo says. So he put himself through an intensive nine-month training by living and working with bamboo craftsmen. Then, along with traditional bamboo craftsmen, Vinoo began to experiment with the designing and production of many household items to see if bamboo could replace steel, wood or plastic and other man-made materials. Soon there were bamboo dish-stands, soap stands, bookshelves, beds, tables and even a bamboo door bell!

Along with other friends Vinoo formed Aroop Nirman, an informal group of professionals working on bamboo-related issues. Later, this group tied up with the

Centre of Science for Villages to conceive Venu Putras—a scheme for recruiting young professionals to work on different aspects of bamboo: from theoretical science-technology issues to design, production and marketing.

These experiments led to more than material inventions. They taught Vinoo that: 'Frugality is a way of life that gives higher freedom to human beings.' He also learnt that it is wrong to project 'low cost' as a panacea. For example, a tin roof seems monetarily cheaper than earthen tiles (kaveloo). But if all the social and ecological factors are taken into account, it is the kaveloo which is truly low cost and high value.

This is clear enough at the individual or group level, but how do you get wider social recognition for these truths. Vinoo realized that in the transition phase technologies evolved on the 'fringe' need more than functionality and economic viability. They must also have an active appeal. Matching contemporary tastes and needs to traditional skills is an exercise undertaken by countless urban benefactors of craftsmen. But Vinoo was much more driven by the challenge of enhancing the craftsmen's confidence in their own design skills. This would free them from dependence on urban middle-men and help to make them self-reliant.

This search led Vinoo to several villages of Adilabad district, in Andhra just across the border from Maharashtra. There, in Khamana, he began working with a community of bamboo workers and together they designed and created a line of bamboo bags and suitcases which matched modern molded luggage in style and strength. Soon the suitcases found a ready market in urban centres. A key scene in the vastly popular Hindi film *Bombay* showed the heroine carrying one of these bamboo suitcases.

Of course, this did not rejuvenate the local market. But Vinoo treated the suitcase venture as a transitional phase in which priority was given to winning greater respect and acceptance for bamboo products. Whether the sales of the suitcases in big cities succeeding in fulfilling this objective is unclear. But the work in Khamana realized an important part of Vinoo's dream. Within a year of the project the craftsmen were making their own innovations to improve the look and technical detail of the suitcases.

Yet this project, like many other such ventures, left many questions unanswered. How would the problem of scarcity of bamboo for craftsmen be resolved? Could bamboo products really compete with plastics and other synthetic substances which have edged bamboo products out of the market? The challenge of finding solutions to these problems, at the macro level, remains. But some basic elements did become clear through experiences in Khamana. Like most of his peers, who often come to gatherings at Bapu Kuti, Vinoo was certain that the management of social assets and natural resources must be decentralized. The lack of a ready model is not a deterrent, Vinoo assured: 'Let the village decide how its drains will be built, what its agriculture will be, who should get loans.'

Vinoo's journey was always closely inter-linked with that of the Centre of Science for Villages (CSV). It was through the work in CSV and with colleagues of the Academy of Young Scientists that Vinoo learnt hard lessons about the limitations of working through the planning process. At one point the young scientists accepted an advisory role at several levels of the Planning Commission. But this 'action' came to seem more and more inadequate over the years. What little impact they had was woefully limited and often of a fleeting nature. In 1997, the government of Maharashtra did adopt a policy of annually making 1,500 bamboos available to each artisan household at concessional rates—but these steps were far from adequate.

For the most part, since the late-80s, Vinoo devoted his energies to work in the field and to preparing people who can continue this work in the coming years. Vinoo was richly rewarded in this endeavour, with the ever-expanding company of younger fellow-seekers who were inspired by the simplicity of Vinoo's own life and his unwavering dedication to a mission.

These men and women, at the threshold of the twenty-first century, are 'thinking on ways and means of achieving' an economy of permanence. Their lives are simultaneously blessed with the infinite joys of everyday life and plagued by apparently overwhelming challenges. At the CSV itself, a persistent disquiet underlies the satisfaction about specific successful projects.

Over twenty years the CSV has designed a variety of easily replicable bio-gas devices and done intensive research on refinement of these techniques. It has also trained hundreds of masons who in turn have constructed thousands of these units. In the last ten years CSV has installed about 10,000 smokeless *chulhas*, called *Magan-chulhas*, in villages of Wardha district and trained 1,900 rural women in the construction of these *chulhas*.

The research work includes a wide variety of organic composting methods which have then been successfully used at various locations. CSV researchers have also devised various herbal pesticides which can be locally, and cheaply, made in villages. They found that most leaves which goats do not eat have pesticidal properties, as does the urine of goats and cows. Goats themselves are deterred from nibbling at crops which have been sprayed with diluted goat urine. A common wild plant, called *Beshram* in the north (*Ipomoea fistulosa*), is being used as the basis of a popular herbal pesticide. Its success in fighting pests that attack the cotton plant is comparable with that of synthetic pesticides.

Housing has been another major area of work at CSV. Arched roofs made of clay cones have become a veritable trademark of the CSV's low-cost housing. They have also developed a variety of techniques for making sun-dried mud-blocks, along with Aroop Nirman a group set up by Vinoo in Nagpur. The CSV team has also worked on the harvesting, preservation and construction applications of bamboo. They have given special importance to designing methods for strengthening the joints in bamboo, with the use of natural fibres, resins, fibers glass, wood and even steel.

In 1997, the CSV and Aroop Nirman jointly fulfilled a long-standing dream by bringing together 250 artisans from twenty different states of India. The gathering, called a 'Manthan', was the prelude to setting up a Rashtriya Karigar Panchayat. This Panchayat is visualized as a coordinating body run by the artisans to build a better future for themselves. Such a forum will hopefully give the artisans a greater confidence in their skills and their potential in the contemporary context. The restoration of their self-respect will infuse fresh energies into their lives and work.

Yet, all such successes and other thriving projects are still a mere drop in the vastness of India—just a glimmer of the originally grand dream of what CSV ought to be. This was the hope that CSV would become a self-replicating process, a veritable *movement* linking scientists, policy-makers and villagers all over India.

Vibha Gupta, who was a core member of the Academy of Young Scientists, has been with the CSV since its inception. Two decades later, after countless projects and an illustrated book on technologies for rural women, Vibha still has a wistful nostalgia for the original vision. Even as she pays minute attention to on-going projects at CSV, some part of her still nurtures the promise of a wider people's movement which transforms the face of rural India, not merely some villages in a few blocks.

Reflecting on twenty years of work Vibha says: 'The significance of Gandhi is that he worked simultaneously with the poor and the rich, the positive and the negative energies. Our focus is only on the poor. We don't balance it by lobbying with the vested interests and communicating with them. For this the basic assumption is that we believe in the basic goodness of man.' The eagerness to communicate, in this spirit, with the 'other' is rare within the fraternity. But perhaps it is a happy sign for the future.

It is in the hope of still being part of that wider movement that CSV has always firmly refused to take foreign funds. It relies on funds from various government bodies and some agencies of the United Nations. This policy brings CSV closer to the 'andolans' and distinguishes it from the largely project-oriented social work of most non-governmental organizations.

This is partly why Medha and the other visitors from different 'battle-fronts' are special guests at CSV. As Vibha welcomes them, she also urges the activists to help find ways of linking CSV's work with struggles in the field. Underlying all such gatherings of activists is the hope that somehow, some day these varied efforts at different levels of society, will all link into a larger coherent, politically powerful process. But how?

This was the question that had brought together that meeting at Sewagram Ashram, from which Medha and others had taken a break to visit CSV. The meeting was being hosted by Jansahayog Trust, an offspring of the Narmada Bachao Andolan. In 1992, a body of European fellow-travellers bestowed the Right Livelihood Award on the NBA. The Andolan, in turn, chose to use the Rs 18 lakh award not for itself but to assist other efforts for an alternative model of development. Thus, the Jansahayog Trust was created to ensure judicious use of these funds and to further the internal debates on the nature and scope of an alternative, or creative, model of development.

The meeting was being held at Kala Bhavan, a small hall about 200 yards away from Bapu Kuti. Among those present was Sanjay Sangvai, a veteran front-line soldier of the Narmada Bachao Andolan. So let us leave this meeting of December 1997 and travel about four years back in time.

## By the banks of the Narmada

Even at the height of its success, when its agitation was national-news, getting to the Narmada Bachao Andolan's head-office in Baroda was a steep uphill climb! The wooden ladder, rising from the street level to a small room on the second floor was perched at an angle of almost eighty-five degrees. One had the option of either clinging to a rope hung beside the ladder or pulling oneself up by hanging on to the rungs of the ladder.

A panting visitor, who managed to reach the top, was usually greeted by a beaming Sanjay Sangvai or Sripad Dharmadikari, sitting on the floor before a low wooden *chowki* (desk). Directly behind them on the wall was a tattered print of the famous picture of Gandhi with his eyes shut as though in prayer. The faded black-and-white picture stood out beside a small poster carrying the photo of a fifteen-year-old boy who had been killed in a police firing on one of the Andolan's rallies.

The walls of the narrow, one-room office were crowded with posters and stickers that broadcast the messages of similar struggles all over the world. There was the International River Network pleading to save the world's rivers from big dams and pollution. Beside it were appeals to save the rain forests, jostling with Friends of the Earth and the voice of oustees from the Bargi Dam, and so on. This assortment was joined by several copies of a small rectangular sticker which had a line drawing of Gandhi's familiar profile with the motto of the Andolan: *'Koi nahin hatega—bandh nahin banega.* (No one will move—the dam will not be built).'

Since 1989, this slogan had echoed across India from different locations along the river Narmada and even on the streets of Mumbai and Delhi. This was the proclamation of thousands of families whose homes and lands are threatened with submergence by the reservoir of the Sardar Sarovar Project, a mega-dam on the Narmada. The companion slogan which expressed their 'demand' was: *'Vinash nahin, vikas chahiye* (We want development, not destruction).'

The precise term 'economy of permanence' may not have been familiar to many involved in the Narmada struggle. But from the outset, the villagers who stood up against the Sardar Sarovar Project (SSP), were not merely clinging to their native habitat and livelihood. They were questioning the sustainability and poor cost-benefit ratio of such a project. Most of the middle-class youth, who became full-time workers of the movement, had already been groping for means of ensuring sustainable modes of production and resource use.

Thus, the Andolan became internationally known as a struggle which was challenging not merely one mega-dam but the model of development which makes such projects seem essential. Why, many a villager asked, can the nation not progress without destroying my home and fertile lands? This question brought the beneficiaries of modern 'development' face to face with those asked to 'pay the price' for it.

But the Narmada struggle was not just about this dichotomy between the victims and beneficiaries. The Andolan tried to show that the dam is merely one manifestation of an inherently unsustainable and unjust system of economic organization. It pleaded for modes of production and resource use which are rooted in harmonious cooperation with nature—an economy of permanence.

Many voices rose to fill the no-man's land of this dispute. Among them was Bava Maharia, an old resident of Jalsindhi an adivasi village on the banks of Narmada, in Madhya Pradesh. Speaking through two urban activists, Bava Maharia told of growing up in the lap of the river and its rich forests where 'we know how to live by suckling at its breast'. In a letter to the chief minister of Madhya Pradesh, Bava and his activist friends said: 'You think we are poor. We are not poor. We have constructed our own houses where we live. We are farmers. Our agriculture prospers here.'

Moving to modern semi-urban settlements, the officials told Bava, would mean progress for him and his family. But over fifty years of Independence many of Bava's clansmen have already travelled down that road. They have wound up as labourers who build fancy structures in cities but themselves live is squalid roadside hovels.

Bava's mud-and-thatched home at Jalsindhi looks like a distant architectural cousin of Bapu Kuti. Of course, few in Bava's village know about Mahatma Gandhi. Till now history, as we know it through text books, has tended to bypass remote villages like Jalsindhi. All this changed in Bava's life time as Jalsindhi itself became the location of such history.

The twin-bank rally was unique even by the NBA's imaginative standards. Hundreds of people stood on the rocky ledges on the Jalsindhi side and a larger crowd stood on the sandy bank across the river, on the Maharashtra side. The rally was inaugurating the Jalsindhi Satyagraha which was the Andolan's front-line of action in the monsoon of 1995. Rough waters and a shortage of boats had made it difficult to carry all participants to any one side of the river.

As the sun dipped towards the river waters, Medha Patkar drew on every ounce of her enormous lung-power to be heard on both banks. But the strong evening breeze mischievously scattered her defiant voice across the rippling water. This did not seem to bother anyone. They knew that Medha was reaffirming the resolve to intensify the monsoon satyagraha that had been an annual feature since 1993. For the first two years the Andolan had made history at Manibelli, the first village upstream of the dam, on the Maharashtra side.

Medha emerged through all these events as a national figure. On the roads, in buses and trains, people recognized her and many stopped to quiz her. Some wanted to know why she was 'anti-progress'? Others admired her as the voice of idealism and principled action. A few even saw in her a potential Gandhi-like leader. This inevitably made Medha cringe. Her naturally open and gregarious personality allowed Medha to remain unfazed by public attention. But all comparisons or ideological labels made her wary—whether it was 'Gandhian' or 'Socialist'.

Medha grew up in a devoutly socialist family. Her father, Vasant Khanolkar, was a well-known trade-union leader and her mother, Indu, was an active worker of the Rashtra Seva Dal, a wing of the socialist movement. The Rashtra Seva Dal, founded in 1941, trained youths in organizational skills and thus became a recruiting base for socialist activists. Medha imbibed this tradition of social and political involvement and at first linked her budding academic career with social work projects in the slums of Mumbai.

She first went to the Narmada valley as an action-researcher who planned to help the people affected by the SSP to secure their entitlements. But within two years, Medha and her expanding group of colleagues concluded that: firstly, proper resettlement was not possible and secondly, the dam itself is neither socially nor economically cost-effective.

Medha shared much of her generation's mistrust of most formal ideologies and their labels. These post-midnight's children grew up with a sharp awareness that there is not much to choose between Wall Street capitalism and state communism of the Soviet or Chinese variety. The struggle for a just and equitable social order must go back to the drawing-board and evolve its own terms. Thus, common, well-worn ideological labels were shunned.

Yet there was no hesitation in adopting the term 'satyagraha'. It seemed perfectly natural. This, in turn, left the Andolan open to questions about whether its members were truly striving to be rigorous satyagrahis, that is, unwaveringly committed to truth, non-violence and self-examination. By now the term 'satyagraha' had acquired a life of its own, quite independent of the meaning its originator had intended. It was used for any effort, or cause, that attempts to remain *physically* non-violent.

The Andolan saw itself attempting to expand and intensify the scope of satyagraha. But some professed Gandhians did not share this view and were critical of the manner in which this sacred term was being loosely used. Most of the Sarvodaya workers in Gujarat were also vehement supporters of the SSP, which has been seen by three generations of Gujaratis as the future 'life-line' of their state. A claimed kinship with Gandhi did not automatically include accepting the agenda of *Hind Swaraj*.

And the Andolan, whose necessity had been implicitly anticipated by *Hind Swaraj*, laid no claims on the historic Gandhi. So *Hind Swaraj* or *Economy of Permanence*, were hardly ever mentioned. Yet the *presence* of the civilizational Gandhi was never far from the hurly-burly of the Andolan.

Sanjay Sangvai was perhaps the one full-timer of the Andolan who had an older and closer acquaintance with Gandhi. By the time of that meeting of the Jansahayog Trust, at Sewagram in 1997, his peers saw him as a young 'veteran' activist, with the most amazing range of interests and abilities.

Sanjay was born a decade after Independence and grew up in the Marathwada area, which was culturally a mixture of Maharashtra and the erstwhile Nizam's state of Hyderabad. His elders spoke four languages: Marathi, Telugu, Urdu-Hindi and English. Gandhi was simply part of the atmosphere through out the school years. So Sanjay was not particularly drawn towards Gandhian literature when he reached college in Pune. His voracious reading focused on—Bertrand Russell, Dayanand Saraswati, Veer Savarkar, Swami Vivekananda, Mahatma Phule, Babasaheb

Ambedkar, Ram Manohar Lohia, the Upanishads, the Bhakti poets of Maharashtra, Pauranic stories, and the Mahabharat. He also looked closely at the experiences of Marxism in communist China and the Soviet Union.

Now Sanjay realized that what Gandhi had said and lived was an intrinsic part of the Indian heritage. What seems like 'Gandhianism' or environmental-humanism is in fact a part of the tradition itself. Sanjay felt that Gandhi fell short of the philosophical and moral rigours of the traditional context.

Now, the sparsely-built but fiercely-energetic Sanjay had a yen to travel and see other parts of India. So, after completing his Masters in political science he took off to explore the north. A deep curiosity drew him to Punjab, where Sanjay spent many weeks in villages and cities reeling with the turmoil of the Khalistan movement. Sanjay was fascinated to see the coexistence of severe terror with the simple beauty of people's daily life. These experiences showed him the utter inadequacy of the language and mechanisms of the political analysis taught in college. The jargon of social science, he found, was quite divorced from real life.

Meanwhile, back in Maharashtra, a farmers' movement led by Sharad Joshi of the Shetkari Sangathan was gathering momentum. This was Sanjay's next interest and he spent a lot of time attending the Shetkari Sangathan's meetings and talking to its workers. It was at this stage, in 1984, that Sanjay felt drawn to Gandhi and Vinoba.

He still found Gandhi too simplistic and lacking in the sharp, penetrating qualities of other great thinkers. But, Sanjay decided, there was a unique power in Gandhi's life. He now realized why his uncle had always said: 'Gandhi did not do anything that you and I could not do. But we don't do it and he did.' This strength, Sanjay realized, was derived from Gandhi's Buddha-like persona. Now he began to see Gandhi as a figure on the vast canvas of indigenous impulses engaged in fundamental questions about human destiny. Like the Buddha, Gandhi was indifferent to the possibility of a life hereafter. Gandhi's only concern was how to be moral here and now. And this concern with the here and now, is *politics*.

A few years later, Sanjay joined the Narmada Bachao Andolan as a full-time worker. Soon he became the Andolan's *Sanjay*, his Pauranic namesake who was gifted with a special extra-sensory vision and related the events of Kurukshetra to the blind King Dhritrashtra. Sanjay defied the limitations of his frail body to work ceaselessly, sending out detailed reports on every turn of events in the Narmada valley to the national and international media.

Through these years other childhood memories acquired new significance. Sanjay remembered that his grandfather admired Gandhi for always seeking means of action which were possible for the most ordinary person. Everybody can *sit* so therefore 'sitting' peacefully became a means of protest:

> I understood this during the Andolan—people are naturally non-violent. They don't want to throw a stone. If truth is on our side, why should we throw stones? . . . Political activity had become the property of heroes and activists. You need extraordinary courage and skill to be a Bhagat Singh or Subhash Chandra Bose. Gandhi changed this and for that reason alone he surpasses everyone else. This is what we learnt in the Andolan also . . . There

is no better guide than Gandhi for how an activist engaged in a struggle should live and act.

Even while many facets of the Andolan echoed the philosophy of *Hind Swaraj*, Sanjay remained sceptical about it. His reservations partly related to the apparent lack of complexity in Gandhi's analysis. Can human society really abandon the materialist impulses which have moved people long before the engines of the industrial revolution? For instance, decentralization of power, non-consumerism and local self-rule *'hamara gaon, hamara raj'* are at the core of the Andolan's perspective. But is this what people really want, Sanjay wondered.

Even while he shared his fellow-activists' longing for these objectives Sanjay felt, 'impatient with the idolization and simplification of the "village". This is an escape from reality. And Gandhi also must not be idolized. He is the minimum common denominator for us, that is why his photo is up in our office.'

Sure enough, both the city-bred 'environmentalist' and the villager found common ground with Gandhi whose image, as Sanjay says, provides:

> ... the most appropriate forms of struggle in which my elderly aunt can join, little children can join, young women can join. This becomes crystal clear when we sit without fear in front of the police. It's simple: if we don't lift a stone, how can they fire at us?

Yet the police do sometimes fire on unarmed protesters and then people get very angry. This does raise doubts about the strategy of peaceful protest. In the Andolan there have been those who at some point favoured a violent offensive on the dam site. But the counter-violent consequences of all terrorist movements are also well-known. Thus there is no option but to continue with peaceful protest.

Satyagraha for the Andolan meant not merely the physical act of sitting in protest but a multiplicity of simultaneous activities which included lobbying, raising public awareness, building a political strategy and working with professionals to strengthen the case against the dam. This was how the Andolan succeeded in pressurizing the World Bank to appoint an independent review of the SSP. The Bank had never before put any of its projects through such external scrutiny. This review, known as the Morse Report, was one of the Andolan's greatest strategic victories.

In 1988, when Sanjay had joined the Andolan, everyone said it was a losing battle. But the joy, he found, lies in fighting just such a battle: 'Every one joins in a winning battle, the real challenge is to turn a losing battle into a winning one.'

Ten years later it was the 'other' side that was on the defensive with serious doubts about the eventual completion of the SSP.

Sripad Dharmadikari came to the Andolan with a restless search for purpose and an engineering degree from IIT, Mumbai. By then, the tall and gregarious Sripad, had already outgrown several ambitions. The one time plan to start his own manufacturing unit and make money had lost its allure. Working as a pollution control consultant seemed futile. He was already sure that technology itself could not solve the problems created by modern industry.

The quest for kindred spirits took Sripad to Vidushak Karkhana at Anupur, in Madhya Pradesh, where an earlier generation of 'IIT renegades' were running a workshop to design and produce devices appropriate for the rural areas. But the turning point for Sripad came in January 1988 when he met Medha Patkar at a workshop on water management organized by Parisar, an environmental group in Pune. Medha spoke of the emerging struggle in the Narmada valley and urged all to lend their support to the movement. By December that year Sripad moved to the valley *'boriya-bistara lekar'* (lock, stock and barrel).'

There followed many years of grinding hard work, reflection, discovery and growth. Amidst all this Sripad found many of his peers stumbling upon the presence of Gandhi in many different ways. But they were all clear that Gandhi held open a door which invited everyone to re-examine some basics. For this reason alone many who were drawn into the vortex of the Andolan began to wonder about Gandhi's ideas and some went looking for details.

What amazed Sripad was that Gandhi:

> ... thought at every level, from individual to family to institutions—with no separation between all these. And of course he lived it all. That is the strength and the reason for his inspiration, not some specific utterance. For example, the charkha may or may not be *the* solution *today*. But what did he mean by it, what value did he see behind it? The challenge today is how to build a lifestyle and economy consistent with those basic principles.

Gandhi was never a *'mantra'* within the Andolan. Yet all its activists saw themselves as fighting the battle against Nehru's version of 'development' and for something closer to 'Gandhi's' version which, fifty years ago, had been pushed aside by the forces of history.

So even while they worried whether they could actually stop the SSP, there was a sense of satisfaction and confidence derived from knowing that the NBA had, at least, opened up the space for alternatives. Implementing the alternatives into their own individual lives, was a much tougher challenge.

Given the breakneck pace of the Andolan most of the activists had little time to reflect on such questions. They were, as Sripad put it, 'captive' to the immediate situations that came their way from day to day. Yet the process of growth continued both for individuals and the Andolan. Even during hectic phases of protest activity there were intense discussions among the activists on the larger context of the struggle. Much of their own growth Sripad later recalled, resulted from a constant process of 'looking at our own contradictions'.

For example, the Andolan criticized the dependency on chemical pesticides and fertilizers. Yet much of the agriculture in the Nimad region, a stronghold of the Andolan, was based on chemical inputs. Farmers who were active in the Andolan saw this contradiction but had no ready answers. But as people groped their way to a critique of the existing policies and practices, they also began to find fragments of answers.

This did not mean that their own lives were immediately changed towards entirely organic and sustainable means. But a space for considering and seeking alternatives had come into being. Sripad's sense of fulfilment rested in knowing that:

The awareness of the people adversely affected by this model of development, has grown and this is an irreversible process. So far the system is moving on the line of least resistance i.e. cities want electricity and water, and these have to be provided by any means. When the people protest the system will be forced to go in another direction, it must seek alternatives. The beginning has been made and the momentum is growing.

The magnet which drew scores of young people, like Sanjay and Sripad, to the Narmada Valley also exerted its force on others. But not all of them physically came to the valley. Many became part of the larger andolan, by anchoring their search elsewhere.

## From Here to Timbaktu

Dinesh stood out in the crowd of the unreserved second class coach of a Mumbai-Bangalore train. Well, it was more his luggage than Dinesh himself that invited attention. In the year 1993 it was outlandish for anyone, and at that a young man, to be travelling with a large wooden charkha. The puzzle might have been solved for someone who watched him closely. For the quiet, and somewhat diffident-looking, Dinesh was engrossed in reading a Kannada translation of M.K. Gandhi's autobiography.

This dhoti-kurta clad youth was returning home after attending the first Congress on Traditional Sciences and Technologies of IIT, Mumbai. 'Home' in those days was Timbaktu where the days are always blazing hot. The nights are sometimes chilling and as they melt back into daylight tiny drops of dew collect gem-like along the edges of leaves and petals. This Timbaktu is not the historic trading post of the Saharan desert. It is a thirty-two acre spread of land at Chennekothapalli, near the famous silk weaving centre of Dharmavaram in Andhra Pradesh.

On most days Dinesh was up at sunrise and wandering about the land, nurturing an assortment of saplings and other plants. Watching Dinesh hunched over a compost pit, at perfect ease in his half-dhoti, few could have guessed that he had, till recently, been a jeans-clad engineering student. He had left that life behind in his native Mysore. The Bachelor's degree in Electronics and Communications was also left to languish on some shelf of his parents' home. Dinesh was learning to live with their disappointment in his refusal to seek a conventional 'job'. They had never expected Dinesh's interest in MAN to lead him so far off the maintrack.

The Mysore Amateur Naturalists, or MAN, began in 1983 as a group of young, enthusiastic bird-watchers and field naturalists. They collected data on birds and fauna-flora around Mysore and tried to raise environmental awareness among young people. Even as they explored careers in the 'mainstream' they realized that this would not be in tune with their 'humble passion for responding to the rhythm of nature'.

Just about then the Narmada Bachao Andolan was creating far-reaching ripples and Dinesh actively considered joining the struggle. Similarly he was drawn to the struggle against the Tehri Dam and against the nuclear power plant at Kaiga in Karnataka. But at the same time he had been deeply moved by the book *The One Straw Revolution* by Masanobu Fukuoka, a Japanese plant scientist turned farmer. Along with these various magnetic pulls came a realization:

> Just as I wanted to go to the Narmada, Tehri and Kaiga movements, I wanted to go to Japan. But only 'I' could go and wherever you are, you are a part of

the problem . . . I realized that petrol and electricity are the two major building blocks of modern life. Without these everything comes to a standstill. Remove these for fifteen days and the whole structure will collapse. So movements like NBA, which question this, are very important and have to be supported. But most of us are not in a position to effectively say that we don't need a dam. In 'creating awareness' we write and the more we print, the more we destroy. There is also the issue of our lifestyle . . . Once in a way going by train etc. is okay. But we're too footloose, people travel so much but if you had gone to just one place and delved deeper there, trying different ways of looking at it, you could have gained the same knowledge.

So Dinesh decided that he was not interested in working in a very wide area, either issue-wise or geographically. At just about this time, in 1992, Dinesh was attending a Better Living Retreat on alternative lifestyles organized by Ramanna, an elderly farmer and nature lover, at Udumalpet near Coimbatore. There Dinesh met Bablu, a budding young farmer who spoke with infectious enthusiasm about an endeavour called 'Timbatku Collective'. It seemed like the ideal place for Dinesh to work in, so he followed Bablu to Timbaktu.

Bablu Ganguly sat straight and tall, on the built-in bed made of sun-baked clay bricks like the rest of the house. Above, wooden poles held up an intricately assembled dried straw roof. Somewhere on the desk nearby were sheets of the

Timbaktu Collective's stationery with its proud motto: 'Life We Celebrate You'.

Bablu's enormous zest in daily life, ensures that this motto does not require frequent reiteration. He simply *lives* this conviction. To begin with, this was why he could not slip into the kind of corporate job that his father held. There had to be more to life than running a company and gathering for a drink at the Bangalore Club! So he took off for the villages of Anantpur District and worked at mobilizing landless peasants through a non-governmental organization called the Young India Project.

Over the years Bablu found that just organizing the rural poor was not enough. Along with Mary, a colleague at Young India Project and several other friends he reflected on the inadequacies of a purely class-based understanding of today's society. The real problem is not merely distribution of wealth but how that wealth is being created and how we have defined development itself. This led him and his group of friends to many further questions.

How do we build a genuine mass movement for social change? This change would have to deal with the fact that industrial society has brought the earth to the precipice of disaster. This is a consequence of a global market based on avarice which controls tastes—changing habits, habitats and rituals. By the 1980s this was no longer an urban phenomenon. For years Bablu had watched:

> ... the plight of small peasants, who despite seeing their lands degenerate, queue for exotic seeds, subsidy and chemicals, sending them into a vortex of debt, borrowing from our future generations. We have seen how people have lost faith in their own knowledge and cultures, gleaned and distilled from

centuries of interaction with nature. Their skills have been continuously undervalued and undermined by the onslaught of modern science and technology, which can only see through its experiments of a few years, and the effects of whose interventions are yet to be felt.

So, Bablu and Mary, who were now married, and a small group of friends conceived of Timbaktu Collective as a nucleus of change where they would actually try and live out various alternatives and share them with the local community. The collective itself aspired to be:

A community which while caring for nature and tending for its basic needs can demonstrate a sustainable, alternative, decentralized, self-respecting, non-alienating way of life for all sections of society . . . we see our tasks as revitalizing cosmologies, caring for the earth and leaving it in a better shape than what we inherited. To this end, the rural poor, who are the most immediately affected by environmental degeneration, must be organized to protect our fragile environment while at the same time build for themselves a sustainable, decentralized and people-oriented lifestyle, agriculture, health, education, shelter, food, rituals and other practices.

This urge drew the group towards the philosophy of permaculture. This meant seeking a way of life in tune with the rhythms of nature and its ever-renewing bounty. What better place to do this than on degraded land. They would simultaneously renew the land and their own lives.

The Timbaktu Collective set out to re-establish the links

between agriculture and forestry relying on nature's own healing capacities, letting it do most of the work. This was in 1990. By the time Dinesh arrived aboard, in 1992, the fledgling Timbaktu community was already grappling with the challenge of regenerating degraded, desperately dry land. They installed two hand pumps and initiated several simple soil and water conservation techniques based on the principles of permaculture.

This primarily meant that they created conducive conditions by preventing grazing, building stone *bunds* to hold the run-off from monsoon streams, planting grass seeds and hardy species of plants. They used only organic manure, chemical fertilizers were off-limits. The Timbaktu community's faith in Mother Nature's healing capabilities was richly rewarded. Soon the water table rose, the number of birds and animals increased. Seeing the burgeoning greenery, villagers in surrounding areas were now enthused to protect their shrub forests. Timbaktu offered living proof that their fodder and fuel requirements could easily be met by permaculture methods.

The collective put out a big 'Welcome' sign for all those with an affinity to such innovative journeys. This was done partly by conceiving an annual retreat for any and all who either did similar work, or just wanted to enjoy the *feel* of Timbaktu. There was only one rule: Do what you like so long as you do not bother or harm any life form. It was this that encouraged Dinesh to make his home there:

> The first condition is to fulfil your requirements without creating any major upheavals, or disturbance in the environment around you or in an environment out of your sight. This leads automatically to other conditions. Then you have to

reflect on what are your basic requirements. I'm very uncomfortable personally, when riding in a car or motorcycle. If you ask [yourself] all these questions then you automatically come to the mirror, to examine the self . . . Then you are at Swaraj. Finally you end up realizing, though maybe not in an intellectual sense, the similarities with Gandhi. Some may call it Gandhianism or the Gaya hypothesis but actually there is no '*ism*'.

We have a few people who are trained to swim against a major flood. That is, all those who are in this work, not necessarily in NBA or Tehri but at different places. These are the few people who are even questioning. But this questioning is an important change in itself.

Since his college years Dinesh had been meaning to read Gandhi. It was not until he was settled in at Timbaktu that Dinesh sought Gandhi in writing and found the common ground of their ideas. But where did the charkha fit into all this? Why spin yourself? What would it prove? Says Dinesh:

At the Traditional Science Congress we had a lot of discussion on the types of cotton that may be needed to be revived or encouraged. Only by spinning yourself can you know the difference between the types of cotton, that is, how easy or different it is to work with. There could also be a spiritual dimension to spinning . . . I don't know what spinning meant to Gandhi or why he did it. I do know that food and clothes are the two major basics. They reflect one's lifestyle.

Life at Timbaktu nurtured not only the soil and plants but also the details of many on-going journeys of discovery. Bablu grappled with the need to stay put and nurture the land at Timbaktu yet also feel part of the larger 'movement'. He began to feel that he was no longer an 'activist' in the way that the term is commonly used. He felt more like a healer. And this feeling came with a process that was taking him deeper inland:

> Some years ago I'd said to a very hard-core Marxist audience that its time we stop thinking of non-violence as a strategy. It's a way of life. We are non-violent as a people. Gandhi is a mouthpiece for this. It's also very important to communicate to a larger public that Gandhi is not dead. This Gandhi is an intrinsic part of us, (in India) we will always come to the same conclusion—from Buddha, Mahavira, Vivekananda to Gandhi. It is time to stop borrowing from the West.
>
> People like us are not 'Gandhians', we don't accept many of his thoughts on religion and yet somewhere we see a lot of similarities. And we have come to it without participating in Sarvodaya or Gandhian work. We have come to it on our own. So to me Gandhi is what it is to be truly Indian, this is our *energy*.
>
> Buddha and Mahavira came and drew on this basic energy. It irresistibly draws people. We are all tending towards that even today. So we're finding Gandhi's thoughts even without trying.

This feeling grew more intense as the years went by. As the local economy came to be more and more dominated by distant forces, the need for an economy of permanence became more urgent. The Timbaktu friends watched farmers around them smother their lands with synthetic chemicals to get bumper crops of groundnut. The nuts were sold in the open market which feeds mass production of oil and various by-products at distant centres. So the farmers had more cash in the short run and the purchase of consumer goods increased but the nutrition level of their families often did not rise.

How can we initiate a process that stems this tide? Bablu asks himself. What we need, Bablu sometimes wishes, is a young person who will do the kind of survey in Anantpur, that Kumarappa did in Matar Taluka. Such a survey, he hopes, could be the starting point of a local citizens' initiative to launch modes of production and resource use which actually enhance the quality of life and people's health. The Timbaktu Collective has already initiated a process, involving surrounding villages, in the afforestation of about 4000 acres. It now also runs an alternative school with thirty students.

But eventually, Bablu knows, Timbaktu must endeavour to free itself of dependence on grants and donations and make a profit. In this age, dominated by the idea of profit-making, this is vital for Timbaktu to become both an attractive and powerful example. Otherwise the Timbaktu family will be seen by local people just as a bunch of likable idealists or plain eccentrics.

Meanwhile, many fellow-travellers have come to feel a part of the extended Timbaktu family and derive sustenance from the endeavour at Chennekothapalli. Among them is Shambu Prasad, another erstwhile engineer who chose to work among the craftsmen of Andhra. Shambu sees Timbaktu Collective as:

. . . a modern day ashram of the type Gandhi envisioned in Ahmedabad. To him (Gandhi) the Satyagraha Ashram represented a 'prayerful and scientific experiment'. The ashrams were in a sense centres for research in remodelling Indian society. Just as he chose religion outside the shastras, he chose community life outside of the traditional power structures where he tried to give shape to the India of his dreams. A space where the ideas of community work got defined. One cannot imagine the khadi movement without the Satyagraha Ashram and the role played by people like Maganlal Gandhi. Today's search for swadeshi too needs its centres for research and Maganlals.

In Dinesh one could see a modern day Maganlal. If Bablu had the vision for Timbaktu, it was up to Dinesh to work out its details. He was in a sense following Albert Howard's definition (in the *Agricultural Testament*) of the new investigator/scientist who would 'write his message on the land'. I saw Dinesh tirelessly working collecting seeds, even weeds, from the nearby villages. He would learn the botanical names as well as the local ones, enthuse others to take it on, experiment and at the same time work out the practical details of how to make vermi-compost, to dig trenches, to run a unit for making lime mortar, etc. Swadeshi today needs community scientists like Dinesh.

Swadeshi today will try and reconnect the common man at the margins to his commons. Swadeshi today is all about creation of public spaces, spaces like Timbaktu where the problems faced by common people are articulated, the erosion in community values is checked and people's inventive and innovative spirit recovered. Swadeshi will fill this lack of public dreaming places for communities to take up the initiative for change and challenge the monoculture of dreams, hopes and aspirations. Swadeshi is also to provide space for those like us who seek refuge from the hegemony of mainstream culture, 'to retreat, reflect, revise and revisit', like the birds in Timbuktu that carry seeds.

## Swadeshi in Venkatrampuram

The dense mango grove, on the edge of Venkatrampuram, was playing host to a meeting on Swadeshi. An assortment of about two score people were seated in a circle on the rough undulating soil, in the generous shade of the freshly harvested mango trees. There were some young people, from big cities, in search of a more purposive life. There were a few activists of Dalit groups and workers from non-governmental organizations involved in a variety of development projects. Two sympathetic bureaucrats had driven down from Hyderabad. And of course there were Uma and Narendranath, part-owners of that mango grove and the instigators of this unusual gathering in the sleepy little hamlet of Venkatrampuram.

G. Narendranath's grandfather, Venkatrama Naidu, was an enterprising businessman who made money by exporting local mangos to Mumbai. He then acquired large tracts of rice-growing land and turned them into mango orchards. The village of Venkatrampuram is named after him and lies about seventy kilometres from the famous pilgrim centre of Tirupathi, in Chittoor district of Andhra

Pradesh. To get there one has to reach Damelcheru, the nearest *kasba*, and then walk down a narrow strip of tar road across a kilometre of rice and sugarcane fields. Further, beyond the little road are fields of mulberry, groundnut, paddy, mango and coconut groves.

Narendranath's father left the village in his youth and made a career in the state bureaucracy. Since both parents were touched by the philosophy of Sri Ramakrishna Parmahamsa and admired Swami Vivekananda, their middle son was given the Swami's pre-Sanyas name—Narendranath.

Narendranath grew up in Delhi and studied at the Delhi School of Economics. Uma Shankari, who came from an orthodox Tamil Brahmin family, was a fellow student. In spite of family opposition to this inter-caste match, Uma and Narendranath were married in 1977. At that time they hoped to combine conventional careers with social and political activity.

Narendranath became an officer in a nationalized bank and Uma proceeded to acquire a Ph.D in sociology. But somehow the future which this life offered held no appeal for either of them. So far their involvement in political work was mostly 'talk' about critiquing modern development. But unless they actually lived out the alternatives, this talk seemed meaningless.

Uma felt strongly that:

> We didn't want to become an 'NGO', that is, full-time social workers with an organization, paid staff, a jeep, computer and foreign funds. We felt that ordinary people are slowly getting out of the tradition of doing public work as part of *grahasti*, a householder's life. People have come to believe that

public work should be done by the government or full-time paid social workers and they themselves should only be beneficiaries. Foreign funds bring their own distortions, with too much hype in poverty-stricken areas, an alien language etc. So we felt we should do full-fledged *grahasti* with full-fledged social work. This definitely means a lot of strain on our energies and our pocket. But this was a conscious decision.

For Uma and Narendranath settling on the family lands at Venkatrampuram and becoming politically active *there* was the most natural step. With their two little daughters the family moved into the upper portion of the double storeyed ancestral home. The house is surrounded by a large compound that includes cowsheds and other small structures. The twice-a-day bus service halts at the doorstep of this village mansion. Across a short stretch of fields runs a narrow-gauge rail line.

How does one live in such inherited space and yet break free of the *landlord* culture? Uma and Narendranath geared up to this task with a mixture of trepidation, caution and excitement. To begin with, they decided to break the barrier of untouchability which is still alive in thousands of villages like Venkatrampuram. The supposedly untouchable workers on the land were brought into the house and even the kitchen. This, Narendranath's father felt, was going too far. After all, he said, the sentiments of other relatives who shared the same compound must be respected. Narendranath sympathized with his father's concern but still had to do what seemed right to him. So for several years Narendranath ate his meals, not on the family dinning-table, but on the verandah floor with the workers.

Alongside, Narendranath remained an active worker of the Andhra Pradesh Civil Liberties Committee and investigated several deaths in police custody and cases of atrocities against lower castes. Over the years, Narendranath made friends among the various Dalit organizations in Chittoor District. He took the lead in organizing a series of *padyatras* during the birth centenary year of B.R. Ambedkar in 1990. The Ambedkar Centenary Celebration Committee prepared a questionnaire through which data was collected from each village through which the padyatra passed.

Apart from information on land ownership patterns, employment and quality of housing, the questionnaire focused on the treatment of Scheduled Castes. The results of the survey, covering 249 villages, were astounding. They found that 122 tea shops had separate glasses for the scheduled castes. Entry to Harijans was prohibited in 80 temples, of which 23 were Sri Rama temples. In 16 hamlets Harijans could not walk through the upper-caste area with any footwear. The freedom to vote was also restricted in many villages.

However, some Harijan families have benefited from government employment programmes and their children are now attending school.

The appeal of the Ambedkar Centenary Pamphlet was: 'Treat everyone as a human being.' It also urged people to sign a pledge that they would no longer practice untouchability. At the end of the *padyatra*, the Committee handed over the survey data to the District Collector. Narendranath worked hard to ensure that in every village the *padyatra* would be given at least one meal by an upper-caste family. However, eventually Narendranath and Uma's home was the only non-Dalit home where the *padyatra* was welcomed for a meal.

Narendranath was undaunted by this:

Once you do something like this it becomes a point of discussion for some time and it forces people to think. If we keep doing this, gradually things will change. But we need to highlight that the problem is still there, because the intellectual argument is that with development it will go [away] automatically. So I always give the example of America, the most 'developed' country, which still has so much racial prejudice. You have to push these changes.

For Narendranath it was impossible to do this work without often referring to Gandhi. But he found that even those who respect the Mahatma, abuse him for his stand on the Harijans. Among Scheduled Caste communities Gandhi is resented and Ambedkar is worshipped: 'All the people involved in the *padyatra* were Ambedkarites, I was the only one perceived as a Gandhian, because I stressed non-violence and I insisted on *persuading* the tea-shop owners.'

Narendranath has taken his cue from Gandhi's conviction that the upper-caste Hindus must do penance for the crime of ill-treating the lower castes. Ambedkar had insisted that the lower castes must help themselves by getting a good education, becoming organized and fighting for their own liberation. For Narendranath the views of Ambedkar and Gandhi are necessarily complementary. But Dalit activists tend to be sceptical about the role of most upper-caste people and see Narendranath as an individual exception.

Narendranath is not one to fret over any of this. He

works on with, what some friends call, his placid Buddha-like countenance:

> If you want to transform society to a higher order then you're playing with people's lives. There are very many serious things wrong with this society but if you condemn them you must also take the responsibility for the consequences, e.g. if you condemn the Ayodhya incident then you must do something more, you must show the alternative. People who are talking about alternatives, a new society, are very unequal to the situation. We are not developing the strengths, the equanimity. This is true for myself, the change must come first within me. This realization has come recently, over the last few years.

Meanwhile Uma, along with participating in these various endeavours, has concentrated on exploring different methods of watershed management in this drought-prone area. This led her to a study of the slow death of traditional tank irrigation systems. So, when the first Congress on Traditional Sciences and Technologies of India was being planned by the PPST group in Chennai, Uma became active in its section on water. As the coordinator of this section of the first two congresses, Uma built links with people working on the issue of water, all over India.

Meanwhile, Narendranath grappled with the problems of switching to organic farming, learning mostly by trial and error. It took him almost five years to learn the basics of farming. Only then could he begin the long and arduous process of making the switch. By then the land had been smothered with chemical pesticides and fertilizers for several decades. He started by minimizing or eliminating the use of chemical pesticides for various crops. In the case of paddy, ragi, groundnut, and vegetables he succeeded in controlling pests and diseases using basically neem and the *Ipomoea fistulosa* extract developed by the CSV, Wardha.

The biggest obstacles were the lack of high-quality organic manure and all the additional labour involved in using such methods. There are neither enough trees nor cattle for sufficiently large quantities of organic fertilizer. Therefore, to most farmers, the tractor, electric pumpset, chemical fertilizers and pesticides seem the easy way out.

Thus, Narendranath finds himself pouring in more and more money but not getting sufficient returns to make a good enough profit. Of course he has several self-imposed constraints. Often jaggery can fetch a good price. But since he knows that this jaggery is used to brew arrack, he has cut down its production. The small quantity of jaggery he makes from organically-grown sugarcane has few takers. So Narendranath has concluded that perhaps gentlemen farmers can be successful only in hi-tech agriculture and in orchard farming.

The neighbouring farmers watch these efforts keenly but remain sceptical. They readily agree in principle on the soundness of organic farming but are not convinced about its practicality. In order to succeed in the long run, Narendranath has concluded that:

We have to grow more leaf-manure giving trees, raise enough cattle, find a comfortable local market for our produce and make everything financially viable. The eco-friendly farmers have to come out with a judicious combination of farming practices which are not very cumbersome, that is, they don't strain the financial, labour and time resources of the farmers.

Today's farmers are caught in a bind. Their need, and sometimes greed, for money pushes them into the net of high-yield variety seeds, chemicals, tractors, power-driven pumpsets, distant markets and horticulture. It's now a gamble with high stakes. If there is a big green market, with attractive prices, then within no time most farmers will switch over to organic or eco-friendly farming. At present this is only a highly elitist urban market.

If we are thinking of changing the ways of thinking, from the market economy to local self-sufficiency, then we are swimming against the tide. Human nature being what it is, we seem to have a tendency to please ourselves, to live with least effort. So I don't know if organic farming will ever become a predominant ideology or mode of thinking. Necessity is of course the mother of invention, so let us see . . .

The hankering for local self-sufficiency is born out of the direct experience of unfolding life. Like the friends at Timbaktu Collective, Narendranath has observed the decline in people's control over the basic necessities of life as production of simple things moves away to more and more distant places. This process also reduces the possibilities for self-employment through local trade and craft. But there is an underlying philosophical commitment to Swadeshi as a means of ensuring, as Dinesh of Timbaktu said 'least harm to nature and least harm to fellow human beings'.

This was the core of Gandhi's concept of Swadeshi—

namely that we must use only those goods which are manufactured with our approval and within our knowledge. Only then can we be fully sensitive to the social repercussions caused by every one of our transactions, and this alone can pave the way for true world peace. It was in this spirit that Uma and Narendranath, thought of naming their activities 'Swadeshi Trust'.

Let us now return to that mango grove meeting on Swadeshi—a congregation of kindred spirits drawn to Venkatrampuram by bonds of affection. Uma and Narendranath's life and work attracts an ever-expanding circle of friends and fellow-travellers to Venkatrampuram. The rich range of their friends finds reflection in the discussions themselves.

Swadeshi was not an unquestioned gospel for all the participants. The Dalit activists resisted the term 'Swadeshi' because of its contemporary associations with the Rashtriya Swayamsevak Sangh. Besides, for them the concept of Swadeshi was meaningless unless it included land reforms and a firm stand on the hierarchical and exploitative caste structure.

For them it was not enough that Dalit concerns and Swadeshi were combined in the work and strivings of individual activists like Uma and Narendranath. Their doubts need to be addressed and resolved at the larger societal level. Most Dalit activists at that meeting were deeply sceptical about the 'Gandhian' view of a village-based economy. To them this meant a perpetuation of old social relations whereas the anonymity of the big city offered a chance to break out of the old patterns.

For many of the other participants this was a rare, direct, encounter with the Dalit 'position' on these issues. One of them, Shambu Prasad, later reflected on how isolated today's 'ashrams' are from the communities around them and from mainstream life. Writing about this meeting later, Shambu wrote:

Gandhi never saw truth and non-violence as matters of individual practice, but for practice by groups, communities and nations . . . If it cannot be practised in all departments it has no value. Swadeshi has to be more innovative and inclusive. This became clear in a meeting of the Swadeshi Trust at Venkatrampuram, where Narendranath was keen to have the Swadeshi agenda include the issues and aspirations of the Dalits and one could see how Swadeshi today has alienated the Dalits. To the Dalit representatives in the meeting Swadeshi and self-sufficient communities meant maintenance of the status quo of traditional power structures and retrograde thinking. The khadi movement however had seen khadi as also addressing the issues of the Harijan. Such links need to be made today as well. Gandhi himself might have chosen the seed as the symbol in today's context. During his time agriculture and forests were not under threat as they are today. If khadi was a universalizing symbol then, Swadeshi today would give prime importance to bio-diversity. Similarly in industry the artisan will be given prime place. Swadeshi today will try and reconnect the common man at the margins to his commons.

Uma and Narendranath realize that the larger quest for Swadeshi is beyond their realm of influence. Looking back on their own life and work Uma insists that it is 'not the stuff

312

of books or even booklets. We are too ordinary, people struggling to do normal moral *grahasti*—the corruption and rot around us makes us perhaps seem extraordinary. But we ourselves are very ordinary people.'

So they concentrate on trying to practice the ideals in their daily life and make efforts to enliven the debate on various issues within their immediate circle of friends and fellow-travellers. On the Swadeshi front this has meant using home-made tooth powder or twigs instead of toothpaste. Similarly their bathroom has locally-made bath powders and soap instead of the usual brand-name products seen now even in most rural homes. Clothing is either khadi or handloom but never synthetic.

Narendranath's big regret is his inability to make time to learn spinning. But he is linked with efforts to revive indigenous cotton varieties by planting some on his land. He still dreams of someday spinning this home-grown cotton and getting it locally woven into cloth he can wear.

The Swadeshi successes in agriculture have been similarly mixed. The drip irrigation techniques and organic fertilizers evolved by the Centre of Science for Villages, have boosted the Swadeshi ventures at Venkatrampuram. But the struggle to generate enough compost from less manure continues. Narendranath has managed to eject chemical fertilizers from his paddy and vegetable fields, but he has not been able to persuade the tenant farmers and share-croppers to make the switch. Likewise most of their neighbours in Venkatrampuram tend to be more spectators than participants in the innovative adventures of this unusual family at the largest house in the hamlet.

Uma and Narendranath have no quarrel with those who remain aloof to their striving. Both of them are deeply preoccupied with the dangers of judging others. As Uma says:

> Truth is a constant seeking for everyone. Some may fall short, but everyone is experimenting. At every point you have to work to formulate the truth. Then you commit yourself to it and base action on it. So we shouldn't have a contempt for people who think differently from us.

But this is not easily done. As Narendranath realizes:

> The problem is that once you have a critique of what is wrong then you begin to hate the people who are part of it. Then egoism creeps in. This is a constant quest for realization. Ramana Maharishi says that the ego and self, Paramatma and Atma, are all part of one. I don't know if Atma and Paramatma exist but we should try to go beyond our 'I-ness', dissolve our ego in compassion where we see ourselves in everyone, every being. Then we can see things much clearer, explain ourselves to other people and take better action. Then specific action or collective social work is all based on harmony and positivity.

*

*These images are fleeting glimpses, or mere fragments, of the multi-varied forms of a timeless striving. This is the yearning for a society where, as Kumarappa wrote, there is 'fair play for the weak, justice to the common man, where might will not be right and where there will be no premium on deceit and exploitation'. Is this necessarily utopian idealism? There were many who thought* so when Kumarappa wrote these words over fifty years ago. The same verdict is now passed on a Medha Patkar or a Dinesh or a Narendranath.

Their strength lies in not depending on the written word of any mentor. Therefore, Kumarappa's Economy of Permanence is an inspiration to many but not a literal gospel. Most of the contemporary adventurers on this path are alive to the task of going beyond such works. Kumarappa concluded his work by acknowledging that his prescription for a better world will call for 'a considerable amount of self-discipline and self-control'. He hoped that both would be 'forthcoming in the required measure and thus enable us to see the advent of the economy of permanence'.

Half a century later we know that to merely hope for this is not enough. This striving must invent its own creative politics and contend with the reality of power structures in society. We live in a time, Schumacher said, when people are sceptical of everything except scepticism. The struggle to build a creative politics must challenge this cynicism with a defiant faith in the higher faculties of human beings.

This is the aspiration that brings together gatherings at Bapu Kuti.

# Gatherings at Bapu Kuti

'The darkness can never swallow a lamp. Even the tiniest lamp lights up the dark in however small a way.'

—Sunderlal Bahuguna

'A goods train won't move by my pushing it, or even by getting ten others to help in pushing it. But our action may inspire someone to get an engine!'

—Vinoo Kaley

'The activists are at war with certain destructive forces which have a dynamic of power and speed. Unless the activists also have a power and rapidity that is compatible with those of the opposite forces there is never going to be a victory. You can't catch a plane flying at 1,000 kmph by flying at 750 kmph.'

—T. Karunakaran

At the dawn of the nineteenth century, most European countries and the United States of America traded in slaves. It seemed socially impossible and economically absurd that slavery should be abolished. Yet by the 1860s Britain had already abolished slavery and the USA was moving decisively in that direction.

At the dawn of the twentieth century the idea of a unified Europe seemed like a wild fantasy. After a hundred years, two 'world' wars and one cold war, this is a reality.

When the British Emperor landed at the Gateway of India in Mumbai in 1911, few could foresee that India would soon be engaged in a multi-faceted and vigorous struggle for freedom. It was even more unthinkable that the mightiest modern empire could be shaken by peaceful non-cooperation—the simple defiance of walking to the seashore and breaking a salt law.

At the threshold of the tweny-first century the idea of challenging the Wall Street concept of 'market' and redefining progress may seem ridiculously ambitious. The idea of a different kind of 'globalization', a process of international cooperation that gives primacy to local self-reliance, appears like an outright fantasy.

Yet these are the aspirations which energize hundreds of activists who flock to gatherings at Bapu Kuti. Whether this is a hapless defiance of powerful trends or another impossibility in the process of becoming history—only the course of the twenty-first century will tell.

Like the few stories collected here, these gatherings at Bapu Kuti appear on a vast canvas which is coloured by the strivings of people scattered all over the world. Some are individuals who are building lifestyles radically different from the 'hurry and worry' patterns of the mainstream. Others are engaged in mass movements resisting projects and processes which displace thousands of people in the name of 'development'. Some are using their professional skills to seek solutions and lobby with the powers that be.

Only a few find their way to this Kuti in the heart of

central India. Some, like the famous philosopher and Gandhi fellow-traveller Ivan Illich, spend long silent hours sitting on its cool mud floor. The Kuti, Illich found, 'demonstrates to the world how the dignity of the common man can be brought up. It is also a symbol of happiness that we can derive from practising the principles of simplicity, service and truthfulness.'

The search for such happiness invisibly binds a wide variety of people and their diverse forms of action. This quest has no point of 'arrival'. It is a ceaseless *process* which each individual defines in his own unique way—each undergoing his or her own experiments with truth. But it also represents a collective dream to build a society based on these values.

This ongoing journey requires faith in the power of a single lamp to hold the darkness at bay. It demands confidence in the power of humble actions to act as an inspiration, or magnet, and draw in greater energies. There is also need for a certain agility and strategic planning that puts these positive energies a few steps ahead of the negative trends. And, above all, we need a constant awareness that the 'other' is not really different from the 'self'.

Faith can sometimes be shaken by anxieties about visible successes. Thus, many activists ask themselves whether their work 'adds up'? Or, are these well-meaning energies destined to be swallowed by the relentless flow of time?

This question haunts those who see themselves fighting a losing battle in a world hurtling towards a science fiction nightmare. In that case a segment of the world's population will continue to live in tightly-encased enclaves of affluence and comfort while the majority is condemned to a brutish existence in ecological and economic wastelands. This scenario is already a stark reality for millions—whether in mega-cities like Delhi or thousands of resource-starved villages.

Then there are others who see human civilization poised at a critical, perhaps inevitable, turning-point. They believe that the ecological and moral crisis created by two centuries of modern industrial 'development' has generated compulsions for fundamental change which must shape life in the twenty-first century. These are the people who have firm faith in the power of an idea whose time has come.

Today, a wide variety of people across the world, are keen to honour Mohandas Karamchand Gandhi as The Man of the twentieth century. But those who work with faith in that 'turning point' believe that it is probably the next hundred years which could be 'Gandhi's century'.

This conviction leaves little room for the question: 'Does is all add up?' For the bearers of this credo the vital question is 'Where do we go from here?' Over the last ten years, this has drawn a wide variety of forums for meetings at Sewagram Ashram.

Among these forums are: the Azadi Bachao Andolan, an amalgam of groups and individuals organizing campaigns to counter the incursions of multinational companies; the Jan Vikas Andolan, which is a forum for debate, among activist groups, on the practical and conceptual challenge of building an alternative model of development; and Samvardhan, a group of organic farmers and activists working for preservation of indigenous seeds.

It was at Sewagram that the National Alliance of People's Movements (NAPM) issued its definitive statement, in March 1996, calling for a politics based on *samata*, *sadgi* and *svavlambam*—equality, simple living and self-reliance. The NAPM is the most current attempt to build an effective political platform of groups working for alternative development.

Gandhi is not overtly at the forefront in most gatherings at Bapu Kuti. Yet the echo of *Hind Swaraj* can be heard loud and clear. There is a uniform condemnation of the present process of globalization as artificial and unsustainable but *not* irreversible. It is sought to be replaced by Gram Raj, through the strengthening of local democratic institutions and people's control over their natural resource base.

Opposing the profit-dominated economic policies of privatization and liberalization most of these forums favour India's quitting the World Trade Organization and working for an alternative institution to regulate world trade in democratic, pro-people, and environmentally-sustainable ways. This naturally includes establishment of close fraternal relations with all neighbouring countries and the resolution of disputes through peaceful means.

Those who live by these values have always regarded the present form of capitalism and state communism as equally flawed. While the communist model is now history, the daunting power of market capitalism is still to be effectively and coherently challenged. It is possible that the frequent crises in market economies all over the world, will now draw more and more people into seriously questioning the prevailing system and searching for humane, equitable and sustainable systems of economic and social organization.

The call for more power to local producers and for enhancing the entrepreneurial energies of the 'last man', is only one dimension of this quest. A wide variety of endeavours are grappling for answers in different ways. For instance, the PPST is attempting to demonstrate that India can significantly reduce its dependence on petrochemicals and other fossil fuels through a rejuvenation of traditional technologies. Those engaged in this effort realize that humanitarian considerations are not enough to restore power to the traditional producers. There will have to be a strong economic logic.

Similarly, it will have to be shown that the values of 'simplicity, self-reliance and equality' are not a prescription for asceticism. An 'alternative' model of development must be *seen* to be more creative and fulfilling for *all*, not just a better deal for the most obvious victims of the prevailing 'destructive development'.

Over the last two decades there has been a proliferation of protest movements against various 'development' projects all over India. At the same time a wide variety of scientists and engineers have produced a wealth of technical work on viable alternatives. Yet, the demand for alternative policies, let alone an entire 'model' of development, is still on the fringes of the mainstream. These voices are still a long way from the centrestage of power politics.

This is partly because most of those engaged in such efforts actively shun power politics. As they see it, too many well-meaning workers have, in the past, been corrupted by power. Many gatherings at Bapu Kuti have been devoted to agonizing soul-searching about both the dangers of power politics and the futility of shying away from its responsibilities. The triumph of a hero like Nelson Mandela, inspires many but this does not help to solve their day-to-day dilemmas.

But perhaps the ultimate test, for those who feel the spirit of Bapu Kuti, is how *far* the ripples of their actions extend in society. This means not only reaching more people but also involving some of the most privileged who control resources and mould trends. It means evolving ways to tap the creative energies of the millions of ordinary householders who are troubled by the present and wish to be part of shaping a better tomorrow. For this it will be vital to dissolve the dichotomy between 'victims' and 'beneficiaries' of development by showing that the prevailing modes of living and production are eventually detrimental to all.

Baba Amte suggests that this is an idea whose time has come. For this, he believes, is the age of conciliation not confrontation. So we must find ways to move society to a higher level where things can be sorted out through dialogue rather than friction that leads to either emotional or physical violence. This, in turn, demands a conviction in the power of example and persuasion.

Thus, even the historical Gandhi's life exerts a magnetic pull. Here was an ordinary man, in many ways no different from any of us, who through sheer honesty and tenacity was able to grow and 'go beyond'. And in the process he also inspired thousands of others to rise to higher levels of being. Gandhi's uniqueness, Fischer wrote, lay in working with common clay and finding the soul spark in it.

This is the Gandhi who stands as a signpost to the dawning millennium. And the spirit of Bapu Kuti empowers all beings of common clay to delve for the spark within.

\*

*Stepping through that imaginary revolving time door, one last time, let us land at the prayer-ground beside the Bapu Kuti. It is the twilight hour of 11 May 1998. A few hours earlier, over a thousand miles to the north, deep in the crust of the earth, three nuclear devices have been tested by the Indian government. The* birds at *Sewagram Ashram* are settling down for the night with no more than their usual excited twittering.

As the sun dips below the trees to the west, the Kuti is closed for the day. Members of the ashram community are seated on the gravel-covered prayer ground. The sound of a gong is the signal to begin. Vedic hymns are sung, followed by Buddhist chants, the Christian Lord's Prayer, and then Islamic and Sikh prayers. It is a routine that has been faithfully observed on that ground for almost sixty years.

Perhaps that evening's prayer carried a tinge of sadness. With the nuclear tests, Bapu's legacy is apparently left more dramatically bereft. But is it necessarily a decisive blow? The answer rests with everyone who, in even the tiniest way, shares the spirit of Bapu Kuti. From worshipful squirrels to movers of mountains, all are needed.

# Acknowledgements and Sources

First and foremost I thank the countless women and men who are nurturing these dreams and endeavours. Most of them are not visible in this book. Those who feature in these stories are a small segment of a fraternity, dispersed all over the world, and most of them are somewhat uncomfortable for being 'singled-out' here. Therefore I thank them doubly for helping me to tell the stories as a fellow-traveller.

All of us are collectively grateful to the Sewagram Ashram Trust, and its workers, for ensuring that the ashram remains an open and warm space, welcoming a wide range of people.

Most of the travel for this book was facilitated by the Prabha Dutt Fellowship in 1993. I thank the Prabha Dutt Memorial Foundation and my friend the late S.P. Singh who insisted that I apply for this Fellowship.

I thank Anil Dharkar for putting me in touch with Penguin and David Davidar for accepting the idea even though the book did not fit into any familiar slot. And most of all I am grateful to Raj Kamini Mahadevan, a dear editor, who helped to shape a raw manuscript with a deft hand and enormous gentleness.

I am specially indebted to Shirin Mehta, who has

affectionately seen me through numerous writing projects and who painstakingly read, corrected and improved this manuscript at several stages.

This book, like much else, is made possible by the presence and blessings of my parents who have given me freedom to work for the love of it. I also thank my neighborhood community of the Basu, Mehendale, Mathur, Shetty and Sanzgiri families whose support adds joy to life and enables me to combine office and home.

This book is dedicated to the memory of two fiercely honest and kind men: Bir Dutt, who worried about this book even as his life ebbed away; and Vinoo Kaley, whose life and work inspired this book.

*

## SOURCES

*The Spirit of Bapu Kuti*

This chapter, like the idea of this book, took shape over numerous visits to Sewagram Ashram from 1986 onwards. The initial inspiration came from Vibha Gupta, Anand Kumar, Vinoo Kaley, and their two booklets mentioned below. Sadly, Vinoo did not live to read this. I thank the various friends who checked different drafts of this chapter, including Vibha, Lata P.M., Ravi, R.P., Sunita Pungalia and several others. I referred to the following books:

Miraben. *The Spirit's Pilgrimage.* Longman, Green and Co., 1960.

Fischer, Louis. *The Life of Mahatma Gandhi.* Harper and Row, 1983.

Thomson, Mark. *Gandhi and His Ashrams.* Popular Prakashan, 1993.

Kaley, Vinoo. *A Hut: Revolution and After—Krantigandha*. Housing and Urban Developmen Corporation (HUDCO) and the Academy of Young Scientists, 1987. The figures about gainful employment, in this chapter, are taken from this booklet.

Academy of Young Scientists. *A Study in Sepia: Man of the People Conceives Architecture for the People—Mrudgandha*. HUDCO, 1987.

Gandhi, M.K. *Hind Swaraj or Indian Home Rule*. Navjivan Publishing House, 1938.

### *Devdoongri: Life Along the Black Tarred Road*

This chapter is based on numerous visits to Devdoongri from 1988 to 1995 and regular interaction with the activists of the Mazdoor Kisan Shakti Sangathan. I thank all the friends in and around Devdoongri who always welcomed me as a member of the family, in spite of long absences. Also a special thanks to Aruna and Nikhil for carefully going through the various drafts, helping to add details and make corrections.

Most of the long quotations in this chapter are drawn from an unpublished report:

Roy, Aruna, Nikhil Dey and Shanker Singh. *Living with Dignity and Social Justice: Rural Workers' Rights to Creative Development*, 1992. This report was written as part of the Times Fellowship given to Aruna that year.

I also drew on literature generated by the campaign for right to information, primarily various issues of *Transparency: Bulletin of the Right of Information Movement*, published by the Press Institute of India, New Delhi.

## *T. Karunakaran: From Worryland to Merriland*

I first met Dr Karunakaran at Sewagram in January 1993. Subsequently, in January 1994 I spent a few days at Gandhigram Rural University, Dindigul. This chapter is compiled on the basis of that visit and subsequent correspondence with Karunakaran, who replied in great detail to the long list of questions I kept sending him. I thank him and all his fellow-workers who helped me during the stay at Gandhigram. I also thank Shambu Prasad and L. Kannan for going through the draft and providing important insights and details.

Some of the quotes in this chapter are drawn from:

Karunakaran, T. *Rural Growth Networks*. Society for Total Employment Planning, 1987.

## *Ravindra Sharma: A Silent Dawn*

This chapter is based on meetings with Ravindra Sharma, first at Sewagram in January 1993, at Mumbai in December 1993 and then at Adilabad in Feburary 1994. Vital inputs were provided by Vibha Gupta, Uzramma and Vinoo Kaley. I also thank Rumanna Hussain and Parvez Davar for their comments on drafts of this chapter.

## *Kahelgaon: Daring to Seek Mukti for the Ganga*

Information about the Ganga Mukti Andolan was collected over several years, starting with the National Sampoorn Kranti Sammelan at Bodh Gaya in October 1986. Over the years I met Anil Prakash, Ram Saran and several other people associated with the Ganga Mukti Andolan on their visits to Delhi. This chapter is largely based on a trip to Muzaffarpur, Bhagalpur and Kahelgaon in February 1994 and another visit in September 1995.

Many details on the history of the andolan are drawn from *Ganga Ko Aviral Behne Do* by Yogendra and Safdar Imam Kadri, published by the Ganga Mukti Andolan in 1990. The October 1997 issue of *PIRG: Update*, published by the Public Interest Research Group helped with details on the issue of the Farakka Barrage.

I would like to thank Suresh Kairnar for his help on the first journey to Kahelgaon and the entire community of Ganga Mukti friends who welcomed me there, paricularly Ram Saran, Yogendra, Lalan and Praveer. I also thank Anil Sinha and Anil Prakash for their comments on earlier drafts of this chapter.

## *C.V. Seshadri: Seeing Gandhi as the Century's Greatest Inventor*

This chapter is based on a few meetings with CVS, first at Sewagram in January 1993 and then at Mumbai in December 1993 and at the MCRC, Chennai, in 1994. Most of the details are drawn from the sources listed below. I thank Shambu Prasad, L. Kannan and Dr H.S. Shankar for their help in adding details to this chapter. The following material was also referred to:

Seshadri, C.V. *Equity is Good Science*. AMM Murugappa Chettiar Research Centre, Chennai, 1993.

Seshadri, C.V. 'Towards Holism'. *Seminar* (Issue 409), September 1993.

C.V.S. Scientist as Innovator-Epistemologist. Interview in *PPST Bulletin*. (Nos 19-20), June 1990.

Alvares, Claude. 'C.V.S.: The Scientist as Social Transformer'. *Indian Express*, 27 March 1983.


*Baba Amte's Vanprastha Ashram: The Agony and Ecstasy of Late Youth*

This chapter is based on several meetings with Baba, starting with his first day at Kasravad in 1990 and subsequently frequent visits between 1995 and the present.

Most of the information on Baba and Tai's early life, including several long quotations of Baba, are drawn from *Baba Amte's Vision of a New India* by S.J. Hans Staffner, Mitra Prakashan, 1990.

The poem in memory of Shanker Guha Niyogi, originally written by Baba in Hindi, is taken from a collection of media reports compiled by the Maharogi Sewa Samiti and entitled *Anandwan*. The poem was translated into English by Hari Thakur, and appears here in a slightly modified form.

I thank Baba and Tai, as well as Lata P.M. and Ravi, R.P., for their comments on and corrections to the first draft. Other sources for this chapter were:

Amte, Baba. *Cry, the Beloved Narmada*. Anandwan, 1989.

Amte, Baba. *The Case against the Narmada Project and the Alternative Perspective*. Anandwan, 1990.


*Dastkar Andhra: Weaving a Vision*

This chapter is based on several meetings, since 1993, with Uzramma, Shambu, Annapurna and others involved in the work of Dastkar Andhra. I thank Uzramma and Shambu for their detailed comments and corrections to the earlier draft. Other sources for this chapter were:

'The Outsider and the Samaj: The Experience of Adilabad', a note by Uzramma, 1998.

'Weaving a Vision', a background paper for the textile section of the first Congress on Traditional Sciences and Technologies, 1993. L. Kannan, Vinoo Kaley, P.B. Srinivas, Shambu, Uzramma and others.

'Quality Aspects of Indian Cotton: Historical Neglect and Research Possibilities'. Shambu Prasad.

'Organic Cotton: Niche Market or Paradigm Shift'. L. Kannan. Paper presented at the national seminar on eco-friendly cotton, organized by the Indian Society for Cotton Improvement, at Mumbai in 1996.

'Requiem for a Master'. Note by Uzramma in tribute to the late K.V. Chandramouli.

'The Search for Swadeshi: The Story of Khadi'. Shambu Prasad. 1997

*Textiles Working Group Newsletter*. PPST Foundation, Chennai.

Kennedy, Paul. *The Rise and Fall of Great Powers: Economic Change and Military Conflict from 1500 to 2000*. Vintage Books, 1989.

Dastkar Andhra Annual reports.

*Kumarappa's Legacy: The Quest for an Economy of Permanence*

This chapter draws on images from various experiences over the years. It opens on a scene at the Centre of Science for Villages in December 1997, when several of the people mentioned here were participating in a meeting called by the Jansahayog Trust at Sewagram Ashram.

The biographical information on Devendra Kumar is drawn from his editorial in the November 1997 issue of *Science for Village*, a bulletin of the Centre of Science for Villages.

Details on Kumarappa's life are from Vinaik, M., *J.C. Kumarappa and his Quest for World Peace*. Navjivan Publishing House, 1956.

The quotations of Kumarappa are from Kumarappa, J.C. *Economy of Permanence: A Quest for a Social Order based on Non-Violence*, Sarva Seva Sangh Prakashan, Varanasi, 1984. The book was first published in 1945 with a foreword by Mahatma Gandhi.

The segment on Vinoo Kaley is based on an exchange of information and ideas over ten years. Vinoo passed away on 11 June 1998, a few weeks after reading and making comments on this draft. It remains as he read it.

The segments on the Narmada Bachao Andolan, Timbaktu Collective and the Venkatrampuram family are based on experiences spread out over the last ten to twelve years. Bava Maharia's words are from his letter published in Santhi, S. *Sardar Sarovar Project: The Issue of Developing River Narmada*; INTACH, 1995. The quotations from Shambu Prasad are from his paper 'The Search for Swadeshi' refered to above.

Apart from all these living inspirations this chapter is written with thanks to E.F. Schumacher not merely for *Small is Beautiful: Economics as if People Mattered* (Harper and Row, 1973) but more so for his masterpiece *A Guide for the Perplexed* (Harper and Row, 1977.)

For their help on various drafts I thank: Devendra Kumar, Vibha, Sripad Dharmadikari, Sanjay Sangvai, Babloo Ganguly, Dinesh, Uma Shankari and G. Narendranath.

*Gatherings at Bapu Kuti*

The following is a listing of some gatherings at Bapu Kuti:
— Bharat Jan Andolan, a political platform of various mass-based movements.
— Jan Vikas Andolan, a forum for a wide range of groups and individuals, from welfare-oriented NGOs to more radical formations.
— Azadi Bachao Andolan, an political platform of groups engaged in fighting multinational products and campaigning for the use of Indian, and preferablly rural, products.
— Himalaya Bachao Andolan, a group led by Sunderlal Bahuguna which is struggling to preserve the ecological and cultural integrity of the Himalayan ranges, rivers and people.
— National Alliance of People's Movements.
— Patriotic and People-oriented Science and Technology (PPST).
— Samvardhan, a forum of organic farmers.
— Oceanic Circles, a group of young people studying traditional systems of knowledge and social organization.
— Bharat Jan Vigyan Jatha, a network of groups working on education and popularization of science.
— Medico Friend's Circle, a forum of health activists engaged in analysing both ethical and clinical issues relating to society and health.
— Prakriti, a forum of organic farmers.
— Rashtriya Swayamsevak Sangh.

Apart from the various formal Gandhian bodies, like Sarva Seva Sangh, Gandhi Peace Foundation, Gandhi Smarak Nidhi and khadi institutions, Sewagram Ashram is often the venue for youth camps, permaculture camps, adult educations camps, Vipassana meditation camps and gatherings of various religous groups including Hindus, Christians and Muslims. This is not an exhaustive list.

The quotation of Ivan Illich is taken from a speech he made at a meeting on Techniques for the Third World Poor, at Sewagram Ashram in January 1978. The speech was published by the Ashram as a leaflet entitled *The Message of Bapu's Hut.*

The idea of a turning point has innumerable proponents all over the world, in various disciplines. Perhaps the most commonly known work on this theme is *The Turning Point* by Fritjof Capra, Flamingo, 1982.

There is a wealth of literature now available, in India and abroad, about work done on alternative technologies and perspectives.

Among a few more recent works are:

Modak, Prasad. *Waste Minimization: A Practical Guide to Cleaner Production and Enhanced Profitability*. Centre for Environment Education (CEE), Ahmedabad, 1995.

Datye, K.R. Suhas Paranjape and K.J. Joy. *Banking on Biomass: A New Strategy for Sustainbale Prosperity Based on Renewable Energy and Dispersed Industrialization*. CEE, Ahmebadabd, 1997.

Agarwal, Anil and Sunita Narain. *Dying Wisdom: Rise and Fall and Potential of India's Traditional Water Harvesting Systems*. Centre for Science and Environment (CSE), 1997.

Agarwal, Anil and Sunita Narain. *Towards Green Villages: A Strategy for Environmentally-sound and Participatory Rural Development*. CSE, 1989

There is also a series of publications in Hindi by the Gandhi Peace Foundation which carries the masterly documentation, by a team led by Anupam Misra, of traditional water-harvesting systems in northern India.